The Principles and Practice of Bar and Beverage Management

James Murphy

(G) Goodfellow Publishers Ltd

Published by Goodfellow Publishers Limited,
Woodeaton, Oxford, OX3 9TJ
http://www.goodfellowpublishers.com

British Library Cataloguing in Publication Data: a catalogue record for this title is available from the British Library.

Library of Congress Catalog Card Number: on file.

ISBN: 978-1-908999-37-5

 Design and typesetting by P.K. McBride, www.macbride.org.uk

Printed by Baker & Taylor, www.baker-taylor.com

Cover design by Cylinder, www.cylindermedia.com

Dedication

To my friends and colleagues of the International Bartenders Association (IBA) and the Dublin Institute of Technology (DIT) who have supported and believed in me throughout my industry and academic career to date. Please accept this dedication as a small token of my deep appreciation.

Contents

Acknowledgements   x

1   The Development of Bars   1
1.1   Introduction   1
1.2   A brief history of bars and alcoholic beverages   2
1.3   Development of bars   10
1.4   Modern Bar design, layout and location   13
1.5   Ownership types – pubs and bars   17
1.6   Legal aspects affecting beverage businesses   19
1.7   The modern pub experience   19

2   The Role of the Bartender   22
2.1   Introduction   22
2.2   Roles of the bartender   23
2.3   Best practice procedures   25
2.4   Job description   27
2.5   Other beverage service personnel   29
2.6   Cultural appreciation   32

3   Bar and Service Equipment   33
3.1   Introduction   33
3.2   Bar area – large equipment   33
3.3   Bar area – small equipment and utensils   39
3.4   Glassware   46
3.5   Food service equipment   49

4   Serving Alcoholic and Non-Alcoholic Beverages   54
4.1   Beverage service procedures   54
4.2   Responsible service of alcohol   62
4.3   Beverage service and the law   62
4.4   Alcohol's role in modern society   63

4.5	Recommended safe levels of consumption	63
4.6	The body and alcohol	65
4.7	Management responsibilities in beverage staff training	66
4.8	Preventing guest intoxication and identifying over-consumption	67
4.9	Delaying or suspending service	69
4.10	The hangover	71
5	**Serving Food**	**73**
5.1	Introduction	73
5.2	Food service in bars	74
5.3	Food menus	75
5.4	Standardized recipes for food	79
5.5	Customer satisfaction	80
5.6	Food service procedures	85
6	**Customer Care in Bar Operations**	**91**
6.1	Introduction	91
6.2	Customer care	91
6.3	Making the difference	92
6.4	Creating first impressions	93
6.5	Customer care encounters	94
6.6	Cultural diversity and intercultural awareness	96
6.7	Understanding culture	97
6.8	Intercultural communications	98
6.9	Implementing an action plan for bars	99
6.10	Cultural influences on food offerings	101
7	**Health, Safety and Security in the Bar**	**104**
7.1	Introduction	104
7.2	Rationale for food safety	105
7.3	The bar layout	106
7.4	Steps critical to food safety and hygiene	107
7.5	Personal hygiene	112

7.5	Labelling of foods	115
7.6	Health and Safety	116
7.7	Identifying the hazards to reduce risks	118
7.8	Conflict and violence in bars	122
7.9	Principle areas to protect	126
7.10	The role of hosts and private security in bars	127
7.11	Insurance cover	128
7.12	Cellar safety management	131
7.13	Waste management	136
7.14	Performing a waste audit	138
7.15	Reduce and reuse – techniques for bars and restaurants	139
7.16	Waste management programs (WMP) and energy saving innovations	142
8	**Handling Cash and Payments in Bars**	**146**
8.1	Introduction	146
8.2	Payment systems used in the bar	146
8.3	Procedures and controls for receiving payments in the bar	151
8.4	Cash counting, floats and cash drawers	155
8.5	Fraudulent and dishonest activities	158
9	**Sales and Marketing**	**163**
9.1	Introduction	163
9.2	The changing marketplace for bars	163
9.3	Marketing opportunities and strategies	164
9.4	Positioning for competitive advantage	166
9.5	The mix for your marketing strategy	167
9.6	Sales in the bar	175
9.7	Food costings	177
9.8	Control and calculation of costs to achieve profit margins	179
9.9	The mystery shopper	181
9.10	Loyalty schemes	182
9.11	Social media	186
9.12	QR codes for marketing	188

10   Beverage Control Systems   **190**

10.1   Introduction   190

10.2   Managing costs and revenue to make profits   190

10.3   Policies for pricing   198

10.4   Stock control   200

10.5   Receiving, checking, storing and issuing controls   203

10.6   System of bar books   207

10.7   Cellar management   210

10.8   Control of possible losses in the bar   212

10.9   Controls for beverage production   213

10.10 Point-of-sale systems for stock and beverage control   214

Appendices   **216**

Appendix I: I am your customer   216

Appendix II: Food safety training – supervision and instruction   217

Appendix III: The mystery shopper diagnostic auditing tool for bars   220

Appendix IV: Conversion tables for food and beverage control   222

Bibliography   **225**

Index   **237**

Preface

Principles and Practices of Bar & Beverage Management has been designed to explain the complexities of managing modern bars, for students and/or those working on a variety of educational programmes in bar and beverage management, and for practicing bar and beverage managers, industry practitioners, in-house trainers and staff members who may wish to formalize and update their knowledge and skills in this area. The purpose of this book is to examine the wide range of subjects that come within the orbit of operational bar and beverage management and to relate these to the wider bar industry, irrespective of the style or size of the bar.

The bar and beverage industry today

The bar and beverage sector worldwide has undergone considerable change in recent years as consumer expectations have changed. A pub visit can be now all about having that one special night out, once a week or twice a month, in which the bar owner and their staff members are required to provide an integrated social experience. This experience must contain the tangible elements of the products, for example food, drinks, entertainment, and the intangible elements such as the service, atmosphere, mood and value for money.

Consumers are more widely travelled now and are more aware of international foods, flavours and styles of preparation and service. Customers expect the latest hot and cold beverages to be offered and served in a professional and engaging fashion. Pubs are driving business through involvement activities which include cocktail making or cooking classes, where customers can prepare their own tasty cocktails and snacks under supervision, plus tutored wine, distilled sprits and beer tasting sessions, carried out by staff members or guest presenters who are knowledgeable, efficient and friendly.

The economic, social and technological environments in which bars function has also changed to meet these challenges. Bars are adopting marketing techniques and technology to understand the competition and to target consumers in promoting their products and services. Recent legislative changes at national and international levels, and the subsequent high costs of accidents (including costs relating to litigation and compensation) have placed serious legal implications on bar owners and on their staff members to be aware of their responsibilities in relation to food safety, the responsible service of alcohol and security. Poor standards in these areas place customers and staff at risk of serious injury if not death. Bar owners must ensure, if necessary by enforcement, that all their staff members follow proper safety and security standards.

The traditional image of the bar as an owner-managed pub premises is changing, the sector now also incorporates bars within hotels, restaurants, micro breweries, night clubs, leisure, theatre and transport complexes. Owners and managers must now operate more effectively with flexible work practices to manage their diverse workforces and operational systems for business success.

Overview of the book

The chapters are each structured with specific learning aims and objectives, comprehensive indicative content, tables, illustrations and models of the significant issues surrounding the topic areas. Chapter 1 provides an overview of the origins and development of beverages and bars. It also outlines the issues involved in the design, location, ownership types, legal aspects and innovative practices currently adopted by bar owners to create the modern pub experience.

The next five chapters cover practical aspects of work in the bar. Chapter 2 highlights the role and professional duties of the modern day bartender and the organization of other beverage service personal in the bar. Chapter 3 provides a foundation knowledge of the identity, description and appropriate use of bar and food service equipment. The service of all types of beverages and the knowledge regarding how to serve them professionally and responsibly are explored in Chapter 4. The key elements involved in serving food and creating good food experiences in the bar are covered in Chapter 5. Chapter 6 considers the application of customer care skills and techniques when serving food and drinks, and also identifies the importance of culture and its influence on food offerings in the bar.

The final four chapters provide a deeper focus on the supervisory and management aspects involved in running a bar. Health, safety and security issues in the bar are explored in Chapter 7; this chapter also details techniques used to manage waste and energy in bars before considering the handling of cash and payment systems in Chapter 8. The areas central to the marketing and sales of products and services offered in bars are examined in Chapter 9, where the influence of loyalty schemes, social media and the use of QR codes are also considered. The key management issues are covered in Chapter 10, which deals with beverage control, identifies the major planning areas used to manage costs and revenue for generating profits and establishes the documentation and standard operating procedures for beverage control in your bar. The chapter also outlines the importance of stock control, and looks at the management tools used for controlling stock and the technological (POS) systems which interface with the stock, and the purchasing and ordering systems used to track sales and revenue in your bar.

It is against the background of these challenges that this book has been designed, to support learners as part of their broader based requirements in the bar, restaurant, hospitality, food and beverage and culinary management fields of study. The book is also designed as a primary reference source in meeting the professional skills development needs of learners aspiring to a career in bar management. The chapters are each structured with an overview, specific learning aims and objectives, comprehensive indicative content, with contains relevant tables, illustrations and models of the significant issues surrounding the topic area, plus suggested Internet and visual resources to support the reader.

I hope that you enjoy reading, consulting and adopting the principles and best practices highlighted in this publication as we enter the 21st century. *Principles and Practices of Bar and Beverage Management* is dedicated to raising the standards and profile of the pub and bar industry worldwide and to remind consumers of the excellent service and quality that exists within this industry today.

James Murphy, MSc (Hosp Mgt), MA(H.Ed), Mgt Dip.

Acknowledgements

If I was to mention everyone who had assisted me in the compilation of this book then another publication would be required to include them all. So please accept a warm and affectionate thanks to all those special people, with my apologies to anyone I may have inadvertently omitted. I would however like to express my thanks in particular to:

- The incredibly hard working team at Goodfellows Publishing for their support in the development of this book especially Sally North and Tim Goodfellow.

- The trade, industry associations, government and public service bodies around the world whose collective work helps to consistently raise the standards, safety and sustainability of the bar industry.

- The international, national and local food and drinks companies for their research and innovation in bringing new products and services which enhance the bar industry and for their collective sponsorship of awards and scholarships which help to recognise excellence in the bar, its managers and the staff members worldwide.

- My academic colleagues whose support, advice and encouragement has helped me realise that I could develop this book for everyone interested in managing or owning bars and the wider drinks world.

- The authors listed in the reference, bibliography, web and visual resources sections of this publication whose help with research or in the areas of their individual specialist knowledge.

- Last but certainly not least the picture credits. The author and publishers would like to thank the following for permission to reproduce copyright illustrative material: Fig 1.1 Swampyyank: Creative Commons; Fig 1.3 Best of European Union; Fig 1.5, 1.6 Grant Sims Signs, pubsigns.co.uk; Fig 1.8 BeijingBoyce.com; Fig 3.12 2012 BarProducts.com; Fig 3.17 American Metalcraft Inc, www.amnow. com; Fig 3.19 Eric Hart: Creative Commons; Fig 3.21 www.madeinchina.com; Figs 3.22, 3.23 Agarwal Hotel Shop; Figs 5.3, 5.4 Kauf House Info, Helmut Schonwalder; Fig 7.14 urbansecuritysystems.co.uk; Figs 7.17 BOC Cellagard; Fig 7.20 Clare Casey, University of Liverpool; Fig 8.7 Alpharetta Georgia.gov; Figs 8.5, 8.8 Cashcountermachines.com; Fig 9.3 Creative commons; Fig 10.3 www.bar-stock.com, Geckofoot bar stock control systems.

- Figures 1.10, 3.1 - 3.8, 3.10, 3.11, 3.13 - 3.15, 3.18, 3.20, 4.1, 5.1, 7.10, 7.13, 7.15, 8.2, 9.2, 10.4 were photographed by James Murphy.

Every effort has been made to trace and acknowledge ownership of copyright and we will be glad to make suitable arrangements with any copyright holders whom it has not been possible to contact.

Also available to accompany this text, *The Principles and Practices of Bar and Beverage Management - The Drinks Handbook*. A comprehensive training guide and authoritative resource that is packed with facts, explanatory illustrations and practical guidance. It provides an in-depth knowledge of the products, plus the technical skills, practices and latest developments in the bar and beverage area.

The Drinks Handbook provides a complete guide to beers, wines, spirit, liqueurs, ciders, hot beverages and soft drinks - where they're from, how they're made, how to serve and how to achieve maximum profits – and a detailed coverage of the World's leading brands of beers, spirits and liqueurs, an in-depth look at wines of the World and an indispensible listing of over 90 cocktail recipes.

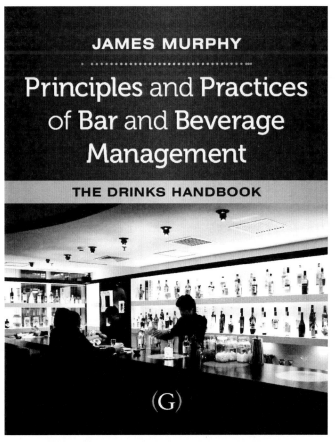

ISBN 978-1-908999-58-0 Hardback 360pp

See www.goodfellowpublishers.com for further details

1 The Development of Bars

Aims and learning outcomes

This chapter aims to provide the knowledge necessary to understand the origin and development of the bar and its alcoholic beverages, from the ancient times up to the 21st Century. It also explores the various types of ownership, designs, traditions and innovative practices which modern pubs and bars have adapted to sustain their business. On completion of this chapter the learner should be able to:

- Explain the origin of the pub/bar and its alcoholic beverages, from the ancient times to the 21st century
- Explain the development and identify the types, functions and traditions of modern bars
- Describe the modern innovative practices which bar owners are adopting to encourage business.

1.1 Introduction

Country bars, town bars, city bars and the 'local' pub are all social gathering places. They act as the primary focal points of most towns and cities, and they come in every size, shape and description. Although their opening times vary in different countries and cities, these establishments have existed for centuries, offering customers, travellers and tourists access to the food, drinks, music and the company of the local people. The sheer number of bars and public houses around the world and the fact that you can find one just about anywhere in some countries, may lead you to believe that certain nations are very fond of alcohol, but this is simply not true. You will find that these nations are usually very social people, and the pub is more often than not a gathering place. You will feel the pub's own particular atmosphere and personality as soon as you step through the door; some are quiet and reserved, some a little livelier, a lot like someone's home really. Most everyone's welcome, and the company constantly changes. The 'local' is the term used to indicate a customer's favourite bar – a home from home.

1.2   A brief history of bars and alcoholic drinks

Throughout history, there have been many names for establishments where people gather to drink alcoholic beverages. Bars or pubs, bierkellers, brewpubs, which were formally known as public houses or alehouses, are drinking establishments all of which have always been central to the national culture of a great number of countries around the world (Brandwood, Davison & Slaughter, 2004). In many areas globally and particularly in rural locations, the bar has always been the focal point and communications hub of the community (Cronin & O'Connor, 2003). The evolution of the bar is closely linked with the evolution of alcoholic drinks and the introduction of hospitality.

The consumption of alcohol lowers inhibitions, can facilitate relaxation and increase the enjoyment of dining, and has contributed towards a more sociable and convivial atmosphere between locals, invited guests and travellers for many centuries around the world (Babor, 1986). Bars have also helped change the political landscape in most countries; many individuals compare them to the coffee-houses of Asia and Eastern Europe or the restaurants of France (Austin, 1985). The uniquely different allure of bars has been that people of all classes could mix together. Early laws fixed the price that tavern-keepers could charge for drinks, so they couldn't cater just to wealthy patrons (Braudel, 1974). Bars have always been where people communicate, share their news and discuss the issues of the day. The only requirement was that you leave your rank or qualifications at the door because everyone has an equal say in the bar (Patrick, 1952).

Alcohol in the ancient times

Neolithic period

One of the earliest drinks known to have been produced is beer and dates back to the late Stone Age. The discovery of beer jugs has established the fact that intentionally fermented beverages existed at least as early as the Neolithic period around 10,000 BC (Patrick, 1952). Molloy (2002) supports this contention and adds that during this period wild barley was first domesticated and systematically harvested in the Fertile Crescent region of modern day Turkey, Iran and Iraq.

'Code of Hummurabi' – the oldest recorded hospitality laws

Hammurabi was one of the first dynasty kings of the city of Babylon (1810 – 1750 BC). The Louvre Museum in Paris contains a large diorite stela with the inscriptions commonly known as the Code of Hummurabi. O'Gorman (2010) contends that within the ancient inscriptions, there are laws governing commercial hospitality from at least 1800 BC. He adds that hostels and inns in Mesopotamia were in the business of supplying drinks, women and accommodation for strangers. Drinks included date palm wine and barley beer, and there were strict regulations against diluting them (p. 5). Driver and Miles (1952) in a further translation of the same stela show that the punishment for watering beer was death by drowning.

The Egyptians

Wine clearly appeared as a finished product in Egyptian pictographs around 4000 BC (Lucia, 1963a) and one of the oldest beer recipes can be directly dated to 1800 BC. Brewing dates from the beginning of civilization in ancient Egypt. Osiris, the god of wine, was worshiped throughout the entire country and the Egyptians believed that this important god also invented beer (Allen, 1936). Both beer and wine were offered to gods. Cellars and wine presses even had a god whose hieroglyph was a winepress (Wissler cited by Mok, 1932).

The ancient Egyptians made at least 17 varieties of beer and at least 24 varieties of wine which were used for pleasure, nutrition, medicine, ritual, remuneration and funerary purposes for use in the after-life.

Chinese drinking traditions in ancient times

A variety of alcoholic beverages have been used in China since prehistoric times (Granet, 1957). In ancient times people drank when holding a memorial ceremony, offering sacrifices to gods or their ancestors, pledging resolution before going into battle, celebrating victory, before feuding and official executions, for taking an oath of allegiance, while attending the ceremonies of birth, marriage, reunions, departures, death, and festival banquets in China. Around 1116 BC, alcohol was one of China's treasuries largest sources of income and was widely used in all segments of Chinese society as a source of inspiration, and hospitality and for combating fatigue.

Greece – from mead to wine

The first alcoholic beverage to obtain widespread popularity in what is now Greece was mead, a fermented beverage made from honey and water. However, by 1700 BC, wine making was commonplace, and during the next thousand years, wine drinking assumed the functions so commonly found around the world: it was incorporated into religious rituals, it became important in hospitality, it was used for medicinal purposes and it became an integral part of daily meals (Babor, 1986). As a beverage, it was drunk in many ways: warm and chilled, pure and mixed with water, plain and spiced (Raymond, 1927).

The Romans

A consequence of the massive expansion of the Roman Empire, following the fall of Greece, was the substantial and widespread development of viticulture and brewing throughout Europe. Beers were produced by the fermentation of different grains and the development of brewing was most rapid in countries where the soil and climate were not suited to viticulture. There were also beer-like drinks such as mead, made from honey and grain. The Romans also further developed the concept of the *taberna* (taverns).

The British tavern (alehouse)

The iconic British tavern can trace its origins back to this period when the invading Roman armies that first brought Roman roads, Roman towns and Roman pubs, known as tabernae, to the United Kingdom's shores in 43 AD (Mahon, 2006). Such tabernae were quickly built alongside Roman roads and in towns to help quench the thirst of the legionary troops. Ale, however, was the native British brew, and after the fall of the Romano-British kingdoms, the Anglo-Saxons established alehouses (usually out of domestic dwellings) to provide the locals with their favourite tipple, and the Roman word taberna eventually became corrupted to tavern. These taverns or alehouses not only survived but continued to adapt to an ever changing clientele, through invading Angles, Saxons, Jutes and both Danish and Scandinavian Vikings (Banks & Binns, 2002). The Anglo-Saxon alewife would put a green bush up on a pole to let people know her brew was ready. These alehouses formed meeting houses for the locals to gather and gossip and arrange mutual help within their communities. Here lie the beginnings of the modern pub. These alehouses became so popular that around 970 AD one Anglo-Saxon King, Edgar, even attempted to limit the number of alehouses in any one village. He is also said to have been responsible for introducing a drinking measure known as the peg as a means of controlling the amount of alcohol an individual could consume. This origin of the expression to take (someone) down a peg may be related to this (Hudson, 1920).

Drinking in the middle ages

Monastic influences

The period of approximately one thousand years between the fall of Rome and the beginning of the Renaissance era in the 1500s, brought many developments in drinks. In the early middle ages, mead, rustic beers, and wild fruit wines became increasingly popular, especially among Celts, Anglo-Saxons, Germans, and Scandinavians. The art of brewing essentially became the province of monks, who carefully guarded their knowledge. Monks brewed virtually all beer of good quality until the twelfth century. Around the 13th century, hops (which both flavour and preserve) became a common ingredient in some beers, especially in northern Europe (Cherrington, 1925). Ale, often a thick and nutritious soupy beverage, soured quickly and was made for local consumption. By the millennium, the most popular form of festivities in England was known as ales, and both ale and beer were at the top of lists of products to be given to lords for rent. As towns were established in twelfth-century Germany, they were granted the privilege of brewing and selling beer in their immediate localities. A flourishing artisan brewing industry developed in many towns, about which there was strong civic pride (Austin, 1985).

Middle Ages pubs

Some local inns and bars have a rich historical background and have been in existence or operational since the Middle Ages, for example the Jerusalem pub in Nottingham, England was built in the rock under the castle. It dates back to 1189 AD and is said to have acted as a recruitment centre for volunteers to accompany King Richard I (The Lionheart) on his crusade to the Holy Lands.

Other famous early inns include The Brazen Head in Dublin, Ireland since 1198 and the oldest pub in the USA, The White Horse Tavern in Newport, RI which has been serving patrons since 1673. Payment for drinks amongst early tavern owners in some 13th century taverns was made with 'beer or wine tokens' which were usually minted by the tavern owner because of the shortage of coinage in some countries. In the 13th century the Normans also introduced weights and measures for wine, ale and corn in the Magna Carta which was promulgated in England by King John in 1215 (Justice, 1707).

Figure 1.1: White Horse Tavern, USA.

Figure 1.2: Brazen Head, Ireland.

Figure 1.3: Jerusalem Pub, England.

Distillation, the wonder of the middle ages

Although the process of distillation was known in the East long before it was introduced into Europe, it was Albertus Magnus (aka Saint Albert the Great 1193-1280) who had first clearly described the process which made possible the manufacture of distilled spirits (Patrick, 1952). Knowledge of the process began to spread slowly among monks, physicians and alchemists, who were interested in distilled alcohol as a cure for ailments; they called it aqua vitae, 'water of life'.

Public houses and licenses

Alehouses, inns and taverns, which provide food and drink to their guests, became known collectively as public houses (pubs) around the reign of King Henry VII (the first Tudor king of England). These wine merchants (tavern owners) were more commonly known as vintners. In 1552, an Act was passed that required innkeepers to have a licence in order to run a pub, and by 1577 there were some 17000 alehouses, 2000 inns and 400 taverns in England and Wales. Taking into account the population of the period, that would equate to around one pub for every 200 persons.

Early modern period

16th Century

As the end of the middle ages approached, the popularity of beer spread to England, France and Scotland and beer brewers were recognized officially as a guild in England.

Interestingly the adulteration of beer or wine in this period became punishable by death in Scotland and the consumption of spirits as a beverage was on the rise for first time. Spirit drinking was still largely for medicinal purposes throughout most of the sixteenth century. It has been said of distilled alcohol that the sixteenth century created it; the seventeenth century consolidated it; the eighteenth popularized it (Braudel, 1974). It is claimed that the word 'bar' was also already in common use by 1592 at the latest, as the dramatist Robert Greene referred to one in his book *A Notable Discovery of Coosnage*.

17th Century

The rise of Champagne and distilled spirits in bars: coffee and tea were introduced around Europe and Britain around the mid-1600s but their prohibitive prices ensured that they remained the preserve of the rich, and their consumption did not take off amongst the general public until the 19th century. A beverage that clearly made its debut during the seventeenth century was Champagne. The credit for that development goes primarily to Dom Perignon, the wine-master in a French abbey. Franciscus Sylvius (or Franz de la Boe), a professor of medicine at the University of Leyden, distilled spirits from grain and flavoured them with juniper berries. The resulting beverage was known as junever, the Dutch word for juniper which the English changed to geneva and then modified to gin. Originally used for medicinal purposes, the use of gin as a social drink did not grow rapidly at first (Doxat, 1972). However, in 1690, England passed an Act for the encouraging of the distillation of brandy and spirits from corn and within four years the annual production of distilled spirits, most of which was gin, reached nearly one million gallons. During this century the first distillery was established in the USA on what is now Staten Island, cultivation of hops began in Massachusetts, and both brewing and distilling were legislatively encouraged in Maryland (Austin, 1985). By 1657, a rum distillery was operating in Boston; rum would become colonial New England's largest and most prosperous industry.

18th Century

In the Victorian era, things changed dramatically when cheap spirits, such as brandy from France and gin from Holland, hit the shelves of the pubs. The age of the stagecoach heralded yet another new era for the pubs of the time, as coaching inns were established on strategic routes around Europe. Such inns provided food, drink and accommodation for passengers and crew, as well as changes of fresh horses for their continued journey. Pubs of that time, even relatively small ones, would typically be split into several rooms and bars in order to cater for differing preferences of the differing type and class of customer. Entertainment in bars during this period revolved around freak shows with circus-like acts which travelled from bar to bar, also carrying animals preserved in formaldehyde. Bars also offered sports like wrestling, boxing or watching terriers kill rats, and these activities also included gambling. Labour in the 18th century was cheap and because life was short the working class used alcoholic drinks and the pub to escape their depressing situations. The upper class owning a lot of the taverns (or 'kabaks' as they were known in Russia) actually encouraged the practice of over-consumption and many young families starved. The work of temperance movements and legislation like the Gin Acts of 1736 and 1751, which reduced gin consumption alone to a quarter of its previous level, did return some semblance of order back to the pubs across the world especially in the USA and UK. The first recorded use of the word 'cocktail' is found in *The Morning Post and Gazetteer*, a London newspaper, on March 20, 1798, recalling debts owed to a bar (Brown & Miller, 2009). By the end of the 18th century a new room in the pub was established. The *saloon* was a room where, for an admission fee or a higher price at the bar, singing, dancing, drama or comedy was performed. From this development came the popular music hall form of entertainment - a show consisting of a variety of acts.

The 19th Century, industrialization and ice

Ice became commercially available in the 1830s, delivered by horse-drawn carts from insulated warehouses even in the hottest months of the year. Ordinary people started getting used to ice, expecting it and calling for it in their drinks (Wondrich, 2007). Ice was the marvel of the age, and combined with the drinks of the day it transformed the bartender's work. The nineteenth century also brought a change in attitudes as a result of increasing industrialization and the need for a reliable and punctual work force (Porter, 1990). In the middle of this century the American Jerry Thomas did something no other bartender or bar had ever done before – he authored the first bartender's guide ever published, entitled *The Bon Vivant's Guide or How to Mix Drinks*, in 1862 (Wondrich, 2007). Throughout the 1800s barkeepers had tended to regard their recipes as trade secrets not to be exposed. The increasing social division in this period also led to a new room being created in the late 19th century - the snug (or confessionals), a small, very private room that had a sliding frosted glass window, set above head height, accessing the bar. You paid a higher price for your beer in the snug, but nobody could see you. But it was not only the well off snobs who would use these rooms - prostitutes found them very useful as well. Ladies would often enjoy a private drink in the snug in a time when it was frowned upon for women to be in a pub or the main bar area. The local police officer would nip in for a quiet pint, the parish priest for his evening whisky, and lovers for a private cuddle.

Modern period

Early 20th Century, prohibition in USA

Prohibitionists advocated strong measures against those who did not comply with prohibition (1920-33). One suggested that the government distribute poisoned alcohol beverages through bootleggers (illegal alcohol sellers) and acknowledged that several hundred thousand Americans would die as a result, but thought the cost well worth the enforcement of Prohibition.

In Los Angeles, a jury that had heard a bootlegging case was itself put on trial after it drank the evidence, the defendant charged with bootlegging had to be acquitted (Times, 1928). Although prohibition's repeal occurred at 4:31 p.m. on December 5, 1933, there are still many dry counties across the USA today.

Figure 1.4: prohibition raids.

Late 20th Century, the rise of pub car parks and super pubs

The two most significant developments in this period were first the building of large pub car parks to serve the motorist in their new-fangled cars. Tied houses or pub chains started to offer restaurant style food and brand-driven beers all dressed up in a themed fashion (steak house, diner). This period also heralded the removal of the distinction between the saloon and the public bar. Modern pub chains bought up pubs or buildings in prime locations, for example old banks, libraries, and cinemas, and have them transformed into super pubs. These establishments were usually huge characterless places which changed their names and style regularly. Supermarkets around the world started selling large volumes of alcohol at cheap prices. This development changed the consumption trends of some nationalities with many individuals consuming more alcohol at home and attending bars only for occasional or special events.

21st century: the term 'gastro pub' was coined in 1991 when David Eyre and Mike Belben took over the Eagle pub in Clerkenwell, London. The concept of a restaurant in a pub reinvigorated both pub culture and British dining, though it has occasionally attracted criticism for potentially removing the character of traditional pubs (Norrington-Davies, 2005). The gastro pub phenomenon took off in the United States in the 2000s. In the late 1990s something also changed which carried into the 21st century in bars. Nostalgia was in and the widely travelled public starting looking back to a time when drinks were something a bit more special (Haigh, 2007), and liquor companies began producing greater varieties of premium spirits.

Bartenders began mixing with purpose, researching and defining obscure and defunct ingredients. Bars responded to this challenge with wider selection of freshly prepared cocktails, craft and speciality beers and spirits and specially selected wines for their customers.

1.3   Development of bars

The public bar

When the first pubs were built, the main room was the public room with a large serving bar copied from the gin houses, the idea being to serve the maximum number of people in the shortest possible time. It became known as the public bar.

Most pubs now comprise of one large room, although the modern importance of dining in pubs encourages some establishments to maintain distinct rooms. A few, mainly city centre, pubs, retain a public bar mainly for labourers or to allow their customers to dress down.

The bar counter

It was the pub that first introduced the concept of the bar counter being used to serve beverages. Until that time taverns used to bring the beer out to the table or benches (Brandwood et al, 2004). A bar might be provided for the manager to do his paperwork whilst keeping an eye on his customers, but the casks of ale were kept in a separate taproom. Private rooms had no serving bar. Customers there had the beer brought to them from the public bar. Isambard Kingdom Brunel, the British engineer and railway builder, introduced the idea of a circular bar into the Swindon station pub in order that customers were served quickly and did not delay his trains. These island bars became popular as they also allowed staff to serve customers in several different rooms surrounding the bar (Cole, 2007).

Pub signs

King Richard II of England in 1393 compelled landlords (bar owners) to erect signs outside their premises in order to make alehouses easily visible to inspectors, the borough ale tasters, who would decide the quality of the ale the houses provided. William Shakespeare's father, John was one such inspector.

Another important factor was that during the middle ages a large proportion of the population would have been illiterate and so pictures on a sign were more useful than words as a means of identifying a public house. For this reason there was often no reason to write the establishment's name on the sign, and inns opened without a formal written name – the name being derived later from the illustration on the pub's sign. The earliest signs were often not painted but consisted, for example, of paraphernalia connected with the brewing process (i.e. bunches of hops) suspended above the door of the pub or farming terms and local events. Other signs consisted of religious symbols (i.e. the cross) or heraldry (i.e. the coat of arms) of the local lords who owned the lands upon which the pub stood. Some pubs also had Latin inscriptions while others used name of battles (e.g. Trafalgar), explorers, sporting heroes and members of the royal family.

Figures 1.5 and 1.6: Pub signs.

Figure 1.7: Snug area.

Bar types

By the early part of the twentieth century, the bar had become without doubt one of the most important, popular and profitable adjuncts to many businesses. Bar owners can choose the bar's name, decor, drink menu, lighting, and other elements which they think will attract certain kinds of customers. However, they have only limited influence over who actually patronizes their bar.

- **Cocktail bar:** an upscale fixed bar, which can be located within a hotel, restaurant or airport, and has a good range of drinks, pricy, superior brands and table service.

Figure 1.8: Cocktail style bar in Beijing.

- **Dispense bar**: normally a fixed basic bar out of sight, with waiter service, a full range of products. Normally restaurant linked, using no cash, but a docket system.
- **Function bar:** a fixed or non-fixed (portable) bar type, varies for function type and size.
- **Wine bar**: an elegant fixed bar, focused on wine and wine related products, with some craft beers, restaurant snacks (small plates of food i.e. tapas).
- **Restaurant bar**: usually the same as a cocktail bar, but normally servicing the restaurant and waiting diners. A fixed bar, normally sited in the reception area.

Figure 1.9: Restaurant bar.

- **Public bar**: open to everyone, with a full range of products except de luxe brands, table service limited, fixed setting, full food range, no free snacks.
- **Cafe bar**: good food and coffees, with limited range of drinks, usually family run.
- **Pool bar**: situated by a swimming pool, usually using plastic glasses, serving a limited range of drinks, with opening hours dependent on the weather.
- **Beach bar**: similar to pool bars plus a simple restaurant or snack service.

Figure 1.10: A café style bar in Barcelona

- **Brew pub**: on-site brewing capacity, serving craft beers and traditional food.
- **Music bar**: specializes in live music (traditional, Jazz, Blues, etc)
- **Sports bar**: where sports fans can watch games on large-screen televisions (sometimes on 3D interactive screens)
- **Salsa/dance bars**: where patrons dance to Latin salsa or recorded music. A dance bar will have a large dance floor

Bars categorized by the kind of patrons who frequent them

- **Biker bars**: frequented by motorcycle club members and enthusiasts
- **Gay bars**: gay men or women dance and socialize in a relaxed and inviting atmosphere.
- **College bars**: usually located in or near universities, where most of the patrons are students, cheap drinks.

1.4 Modern bar design, layout and location

The design, layout and positioning of the service and leisure areas of the bar and restaurant are typically planned by the bar owner, architect, or interior designer, whose primary concern is layout and décor, while the working areas where the food and drinks are prepared and served are usually planned by a facilities design consultant or by an equipment dealer (Murphy, 2008). Going out today is about so much more than just the food and drink. People want a total experience, and the aesthetic appeal of a bar or restaurant is a big component of this (Hospitality,

2009). Experts say poorly thought-out designs can result in the failure of an operation. Modern bar designs are aimed at ensuring that customers will have a great experience and want to return. The individual spaces within the bar are now also designed to achieve certain business goals and create outstanding hospitality environments (Murphy, 2009; Mutton & Sampson, 2012). To achieve this they argue that the creation of an exceptional branded food and beverage experience in bars nowadays will encompass holistic hospitality design service, local market analysis, brand positioning, innovative concept creation, implementation and integrated graphics. Roberts (2008) suggests that the requirements of good bar design are highly specific. Functionality is as important as form, as is an eye to industry trends and the ability to create something that will survive the test of time (p. 80).

The variety of services, facilities and products that a bar offers will influence the type of customers it will attract, so the first consideration for new bar owners is to decide the type of bar they wish to run, young person's venue, trendy upmarket city centre venue, local community, gastro type or music bar (see Bar types section above).

Importance of good layout - ergonomics

In most circumstances these professionals work together from the beginning. Unfortunately, as many of my colleagues and friends in the licensed trade have told me, sometimes the facilities designer, equipment dealer and general management team are called in after the bar / restaurant has been positioned and its dimensions set, and must do the best job possible within the allotted space. This can be a very costly mistake to make for a number of reasons.

Good layout in the food and beverage preparation and service areas and their relationship to the overall productivity cannot be properly discussed without touching on the concept of ergonomics. Ergonomics is the science of work and is concerned the interaction of people and their working environment. It requires: (a) the study of the bartender, waiter, chef or the working teams involved, and (b) the provision of data for efficient and effective design of the bar. The task is to develop the most comfortable conditions for your customers and staff as regards:

- lighting, climate and noise level,
- reducing the physical workload (in particular in hot environments such as kitchens and busy bars),
- facilitating psycho-sensorial functions in reading instrument displays,
- making the handling of cooking and bar equipment /door levers and controls easier to use,
- making better use of spontaneous and stereotyped responses, (turning off equipment when you hear the alarm), to avoid unnecessary information recall efforts, and so on.

Murphy (2008)

1

The interaction between the bartender/food server and customer deserves particular attention, as this is an important aspect of licensed premises layouts. The so-called '*interface*' between the bartender or server and the customer depend on the quality of the layout and display elements selected by bars, so these must be designed for good communication links. Be careful of for example too high or too low working tables and bar stools.   The bar owner/ manager must decide how best to deliver the food and beverage experience through the three sensory channels: visual, auditory and kinaesthetic (movement perception); and between dynamic and static displays:

- in designing displays for maximum speed and minimum attention, use the kinaesthetic channel (counter displays).
- for maximum attention, use the auditory channel.
- for maximum precision and agreement between staff members, use the visual channel.

Murphy (2008)

The other major aspect of room layout concerns the way work and service stations are identified and controlled. Murphy (2008) contends that the goal for bar owners going forward will be to continue to create licensed premises that enhance functional effectiveness, improves employee welfare and attract the desired customers, giving them pleasure and encouraging them to become repeat customers.

The location of the bar

Davis et al (2012) contend that a bar in a local community area has a catchment for customers of no more than a five mile radius, and to extend this the bar must provide various forms of entertainment, themed nights and special attractions. Elliott (2006) contrasts in arguing that the radius for a traditional local pub may only be a quarter of a mile, but he maintains that a destination food pub can attract customers travelling by car and a catchment area of 15 miles is not uncommon.

When selecting a location for your bar, you should consider the following:

- type of clientele which the pub will attract (or currently attracts)
- kind of people (demographic profile, census statistics) in the catchment area
- the local population size in relation to the future business plans for the bar
- flexibility of the pub, can it be changed to attract more or new customers ?
- the local competition, what will it up against ?
- local and town planning, are there are significant plans in the area which might enhance or effect the intended business ?

Others considerations:

- visibility and positioning (prominence) of the bar – locations on the high street are the most desirable, with back street or less prominent bars you must work harder to get your message out

- foot traffic, how busy is the area and how many people pass by this location every day at different time periods

- proximity of the local facilities (schools, hospitals, public transport) and desirability of the area (i.e. good lifestyle, low levels of crime)

- condition of the pub (attractive, facilities already in place, in need of major repair, standard of the fixtures and fittings)

adapted from Elliott (2006)

For a further discussion of this topic (see Chapter 9 – Sales and Marketing).

The happy hour

Happy hour entered civilian use around 1960 and was typically used in bars in the late afternoon Monday through to Thursday, a promotion intended to boost business on what may otherwise be a slow day. In most cases the happy hour lasts longer than a single hour. Happy hour can differ from country to country. In most European countries the price of alcohol is strictly regulated and selling alcohol cheap or holding events entitled 'happy hour' is illegal because of its association with anti-social behaviour and drunkenness. In most countries during the period of happy hour a customer gets double the amount of drinks, but in some the customer will only receive free finger food, discounted drinks or entertainment.

The lock-in

An age old tradition, a lock-in is when the bar owner lets drinkers stay in the pub after the legal closing time: the theory is that once the doors are locked, it becomes a private party rather than a pub. Patrons may put money behind the bar before official closing time, and redeem their drinks during the lock-in so no drinks are technically sold after closing time. Although the tradition of the lock-in remains it's regular use is now rare due to strict Licensing laws and because most bars can apply to extend their opening hours beyond traditionally opening hours.

Social behaviour in bars

Much has been written in popular literature and fiction about pubs as quaint institutions, but pubs have contributed so much more. If anything, they hold importance as centres of social significance and cultural reproduction where the drinking practices and other aspects of a nation's culture merge, and where the questions of identity and identification continually matter (Wilson, 2005). In the majority of countries the bar owner is responsible for promoting this sociable and cultural atmosphere for their customers, but in some countries, like the US and the UK, patrons regulate the social behaviour and interaction between one another.

This dynamic of social behaviour and the subsequent variations in bar usage of patrons around the world over the centuries provides us with significant insights into the role of pubs internationally. For example in Cavan's (1966) study of American bar behaviour, patrons expressed a sense of ownership, describing the bar they drink in as 'our bar'. She proposed that 'the habitués of the home territory bar typically behave as though the premises were their own home, for which they themselves are responsible'. General duties are assumed by patrons such as: answering telephones, delivering drinks to tables, cleaning drink spills, collecting empty glasses, and running errands for supplies. This display of ownership is an accepted relationship between patron and staff, and regular patrons sanction certain moral standards and ritual behaviours.

Specific language is deemed appropriate as are sexual role-playing interactions between patrons. Cavan poses a most interesting question for bars internationally when she asks if patrons regulate their social behaviour and interaction amongst one another similar or on par to American and most European bars.

1.5   Ownership types – pubs and bars

Tied house

In the UK, a 'tied house' is a public house that is required to buy at least some of its beer from a particular brewery (Lillicrap & Cousins, 2010). Treavor (2012) adds that 'a tied house is also an establishment that has an association, financial or otherwise, with a liquor manufacturer or its agent that is likely to lead to its products being favoured'. He contends that this practice was quite common in Canada but new laws adopted in 2011 restrict or stop producers of alcohol from basically bribing licensed establishments by offering freebies to them in exchange for exclusive or preferred sales deals. Tied houses are illegal in the U.S. and prohibited under the Federal Alcohol Administration Act. In the U.S., tied house restrictions are mainly construed for prohibiting any form of arbitrary management control in the alcoholic beverage industry (US Legal, 2012). Alternatively, some breweries may appoint a salaried manager to run the pubs it owns, and this form of tie can sometimes be termed a managed house. Finally a publican may finance the purchase of a pub with soft loans (usually a mortgage) from a brewer and be required to buy his beer from it in return.

Tenancy house

The pub itself may be owned by the brewery in question, with the publican renting the pub from the brewery. This is termed a tenancy. (Robinson Pubs, 2012). Tenancy is one of the most established and traditional ways of running a pub. It offers the easiest way for a person to become the landlord of a pub and regional brewers tend to prefer this format because of the level of support it allows them to provide. They are normally short term agreement in the UK (initially 1-3 years), often with the tenant having the right to continue from year to year (sometimes referred to as a 'rolling' or 'evergreen' agreement) under the Landlord and Tenant Act 1954. The exact details of tenancies differ from pub chain to pub chain, but one thing that's likely to be included in all tenancies is a 'tie' which mean that the tenant is fully or partially tied to buying certain beers and other products from the owner or a designated supplier (similar to a tied house). This can even be as far reaching as to specify the wine or snacks that the bar are required to serve. A tenancy is valued on its fixtures and fittings, (trade inventory). Tenancies are not assignable. Tenants cannot sell on any business interest at a profit (good-will). When a tenant is ready to leave then he will have his fixtures and fittings re-valued and surrenders the tenancy to the Landlord. The tenant will be paid the new valuation, including stock and glassware. The tenant can also be held responsible for the general upkeep of the premises. Being tied to certain product ranges can be a good thing because the landlord may have already negotiated discounts with suppliers which could help the tenant make the most of his new venture. The tenant could also benefit from the experience of the landlord, who may have already tested the market to see which drinks work best in the pub's environment. One of the disadvantages of being part of a tied pub, is that the pub must rely on the popularity of the products it is contractually obliged to sell. So for instance, if the landlord is a regional brewery and the popularity of its brand diminishes over time, so will the bar's profits and the tenant may not be able to stock more popular brands because of limitations set out in the tenancy agreement. (Business4Sale.co.uk, 2012)

Free house (freehold/lock-up)

With these, the pub owner has outright (private) ownership of the property and business (Lillicrap & Cousins, 2010). A freehold is almost always 'free of tie' which means that the owner can buy beer and all other supplies from wherever he/she chooses. A freeholder can receive substantial discounts from his suppliers, making him competitive in the market place. Higher profits enables him to effectively service his mortgage interest repayments. A purchaser can normally borrow up to around two thirds to three quarters of the purchase price on mortgage as the freehold property offers a good security for a loan (Pubshop, 2012)

Franchise house (leasehold)

The publican has the right to occupy the property for a fixed term of years (sold a going concern). There are effectively two kinds of lease or franchise:

- Sale or assignment of a lease which has already been created - the lessee is committed to pay the rent throughout the term unless he can sell the interest by assignment to another purchaser.

- The grant of a new lease by a landlord - new leases are offered by brewers/ pub companies and private owners nowadays normally 'without premium'. This means the publican will only be required to purchase the trade furniture, fixtures, fittings and effects, plus stock and glassware. Sometimes a security deposit needs to be lodged. Be aware that new leases frequently contain a clause barring the sale or assignment of the lease within the first two years unless a penalty is paid, After that period the lessee can sell the business.

If the lease is assignable it means they can be sold in the open market almost like freehold, subject to the new purchaser being approved by the Landlord. If a publican is successful in their lease, they can sell on the 'goodwill' on the open market. However if the pub fails, the business may have to be sold at a substantial loss or, at worst, surrendered back to the Landlord for little or no payment.

The tenant has an obligation to comply with all the terms and conditions of the lease in order to stay in possession. Leases are usually subject to many conditions:

- Tie - free of tie, part tie or full tie and other supply or trading agreements
- Repairing obligation - internal repairing or full repairing
- Rent review pattern and how the rent review is calculated
- Service charge provisions
- Assignment clauses
- Insurance premium charges
- Decoration - internal, external or full

(Pubshop, 2012)

1.6   Legal aspects affecting beverage businesses

Businesses, organisations and individuals who want to sell or supply alcohol (especially bars and licensed premises) are governed and regulated by a wide variety of legal obligations. In most countries they must have a license or other authorisation from a licensing authority - usually a local council.. For example in the UK under the Licensing Act 2003 there is a statutory requirement for anyone selling alcohol, or authorising others to sell alcohol, to obtain a qualification that has the accreditation of the Secretary of State. The laws on selling and buying alcohol are clear, and violating those laws could result in arrest, prosecution and fines. It is the duty of every bar owner to make every staff member aware of the main legal aspects affecting their business. In a textbook of this nature it would not be possible to cover all the legal aspects which affect licensed premises and bars around the world. Government agencies normally provide guides which help bar businesses to understand their obligations in line with the local regulations for example in the UK these legal aspects are overseen by the UK Home Office: http://www.homeoffice.gov.uk/drugs/alcohol/. In the USA these legal aspects can change from state to state.

1.7   The modern pub experience

The challenge in the bar industry at present is not only to get customers to start visiting bars again, but also to ensure that they spend more money when they do visit the bar. The pub experience can be all about having that one special night out once or twice a month. The challenge is to provide cheap drinks and food for those on a budget and to provide a unique experience for customers. Some recent innovative practices include the following.

Engagement and involvement

Diageo developed a 'pour your own pint'. This system allows customers to sit at their own table with their own beer pouring tap and to pull their own pints which are counted and controlled by a computer, and this generates their bill at the end. Other engagement and involvement activities which bars are using to drive footfall include cocktail-making classes, where the customer prepares their own cocktails under supervision, and tutored wine, spirits, beer tastings and theme evenings, which also include guest presenters.

Game nights

Customers use electric consoles to challenge each other on the latest video games. The bar usually would provide some small prizes, (Playstation, WII challenges), Retro games which contain old school entertainment ping pong tables, playing pool, foosball, air hockey, darts also board games.

Use of technology

New systems will upload your pictures and videos from your phone onto the bar; allow you to choose music from a jukebox (1000s of music tracks for themed evenings) or to flick through different drinks and menus all with a touch of your finger. IBar is one example of an intelligent surface system which detects what a customer is drinking by the shape of the glass when it is placed on the bar top. The system also tracks how many drinks the customer has consumed, and will display the logo of the customer drink (a marketing tool).

Exotic or molecular cocktails with a twist

Serving cocktails in wacky or unusual vessels (i.e. Callooh Callay in East London, England serves a Rum Punch in a gramophone, Eden Freeman of Taylors Bar and Restaurant, New York offers his customers cocktails developed using scientific principles.

Speakeasy venues

Some bars are taking full advantage of the major interest in nostalgia, resurrecting classic cocktails and offering them in a secret or unusual environment in their bar. Bars are actually renaming themselves as speakeasies or Blind Pigs (this association is of course directly linked with the Prohibition period in America).

Themed music events

'Have it your way', customers encouraged to play their own vinyls, themed nights.

1

New glass and measure sizes in bars

2011 the UK relaxed the rules governing the serving of alcohol in half pint and pint size glasses (568ml) to now include a third size – 400ml. This new flexibility is in line with the demands of modern drinkers in relation to their waistlines and wallets. A 175ml new wine glass size was also introduced.

Price reduction ideas

Similar to the stock exchange, a series of electronic screens are strategically located around the bar with the major drinks available and drinks are reduced or increased depending on their popularity. Some bars also use afternoon and early evening deals titled, for example, Festive Fridays or Super Saturday.

Ladies' nights

Females are actively targeted with great food, discounted cocktails and drinks.

Conclusion

The tradition of going to the pub or bar can be traced way back to ancient times. Along with the church and provisions shop, the town or village pub has played a key role in most communities; even today, the pub is often the only place neighbours, friends and family get to meet in many towns and villages around the world. Pubs are constantly evolving with market demands and changing consumer tastes as they continue to strive to serve their communities and sustain their business.

The sheer camaraderie and companionship which pubs and bars offer forms an integral part of a nation's cultural core. Even though this core has come under major economic and regulatory pressure in the last few years it is crucial that we all support and nurture our pubs and continue to adapt and improve its offerings. Ray Oldenburg (an American sociologist) referred to the importance within modern societies of the 'third place', a location that is not work or home: rather a public place where people can easily meet, relax and interact. Although these third place locations (pubs and bars) have being vanishing in recent years, Oldenburg believes they are major contributors to the maintenance of social capital and of healthy community life.

2 The Role of the Bartender

Aims and learning outcomes

The aim of this chapter is to highlight the role of the bartender. On completion of this chapter the learner should be able to:

- Explain the attributes and qualifications necessary for the ideal bartender
- Apply the appropriate technical knowledge and procedures in the bar
- Know how to deal with enquiries in the bar
- Explain the importance of the bartender's job description and cultural appreciation.
- Explain the roles of beverage service personnel

2.1 Introduction

The general public has two very different perceptions of bartenders. On one hand, bartenders have always held an almost iconic role in folklore culture; they have the shoulder to cry on – the encyclopedia of drinks knowledge to draw on or the fatherly figure with the sympathetic ear for the love sick. Another image is that of the key master – the bartender holds the keys to a night of wild abandonment and sinful rites of passage. Bartenders must be always able to deliver excellence for their customers and guests. Their professional abilities and personality strongly influence the positive or indeed negative experience of the bar for the customer. The role of the bartender is never just about the preparation and service of the bar's products, for the bartender is crucial to creating that unique experience for their customers which hopefully makes them want to return by themselves or with family, friends and business colleagues on an regular basis.

2.2   Roles of the bartender

The bartender is responsible for maintaining superior levels of beverage service to all customers at all times. Their duties involve taking orders and handling cash and control procedures to ensure the highest levels of cleanliness, safety, accountability and storage of all beverages in the bar and throughout the licensed premises. In some bars, bartenders with special skills and knowledge of preparing mixed drinks can be referred to as a *mixologist*. All mixologists are bartenders, but not all bartenders are mixologists. Regan (2003) argues that as bartenders we understand that mixologists should really be called 'cocktailians'. Either way, bartender and mixologist are terms that have come to be used synonymously in most bars.

Successful bartenders will normally have gentle arms to guide the trouble-makers to the exits, gentle and strong elbows to raise a glass to toast a customer's birthday and to pour the contents (discretely) away after toasting. Strong wrists for shaking cocktails and gentle for stirring Martinis with precision. Acute hearing skills to take drink orders from multiple sources and to keep them in order, and strong hands able to be completely independent of one another, with the dexterity and motor skills required in modern busy food and beverage establishments to operate at various speeds. Regan (1993) states that 'a good bartender has as many faces as a clock'; while Murphy (2007) contends that good bartenders must be able to listen, to talk, to share and to deliver. Being able to listen to other people is an art and traditionally, if you respect the customer, the customer will respect you.

The bartender will play many roles in the bar, and management teams will seek to source and hire the very best bartenders to meet their new ever-changing hospitality environment. Bars are distinguished by their customers, their products, their marketplace and location, therefore the attributes and qualifications of the bartenders to be hired should differ per location. The majority of bar owners rank the following attributes and qualifications crucial during the recruitment, interview and trial periods:

- **Pleasing personality:** bartenders should be pleasant and good humored in their dealings with customers, superiors and colleagues.
- **Education**: bartenders must obtain or be given access to basic or advanced education commensurate with the bar and its marketplace. This might include additional courses in hospitality and customer care skills
- **Ability to work with other people**: bartenders should be able to work with their other colleagues and management and be capable of using their own initiative.
- **Honesty**: bartenders operate with large amounts of cash, tips, change and occasional requests from friends and the opposite sex for free drinks and food. It is therefore crucial that bartenders can be fully trusted at all times.
- **Punctuality**: to be on time for duty, as late arrivals cause a domino effect on service delivery for customers.

- **Personal appearance**: bartenders should present themselves well groomed, clean and neat, their clothes should be clean and pressed.
- **Personal control**: bartenders must control their emotions be considerate, quiet, courteous, tolerant and have respect for customers and colleagues.

The ways in which a bartender receives the customer and talks to them are of great fundamental importance. A bartender should always base their behavior on common sense and modesty.

Table 2.1: Bartender's personal appearance. (Murphy, 2005)

Male – professional image	Female – professional image
Posture: habitually upright, alert and interested	
Manner: alert, cheerful, ready smile, poised	
Neat, clean uniform free from stains, spots, perspiration and well pressed for example trousers, shirt, necktie, waistcoat, and apron.	
Black or dark socks	Black or dark stockings, tights, hose
Black non-slip, closed in shoes, conservative style, well shined and comfortable for standing hours at a time	
High standard of personal hygiene, frequent showers, use of deodorants and mouthwash.	
Clean shaven, no strong aftershaves	Some basic make-up, no strong perfumes
Hair close cut, styled neatly, well brushed or tied back	Hair styled neatly and tied back neatly
Hairnet worn over all hair (as appropriate)	
Name badge worn at all times, if appropriate	
Limited use of jewelry (wedding rings only)	
Nails trimmed and clean	
Body tattoos (discreetly covered)	
No alcohol, eating or smoking whilst on duty	

Personality

The single most important attribute which bars rank the highest is personality. Thurstone's research on personality, cited in Murphy (2009), highlighted the five major domains of openness, conscientiousness, extraversion, agreeableness, and emotional stability. The bartender's personality strongly influences the positive or negative experience of the bar for the customer. Bartenders are people, like everyone else and they take their personalities to work with them. The personality that comes into contact with the bar's customers will determine, to a great extent, the success of the bar. This unique experience is sometimes referred to as 'the moment of truth'. Most bar owners are well aware of how important it is to maintain this healthy relationship between their bartenders and their customers, regardless of their socio-economic backgrounds and position in the local community.

2

2.3   Best practice procedures

The bartender's duties and responsibilities will constantly change throughout the preparation, dispense and service and closing periods over a normal trading day in the bar. These changes will require the bartender to demonstrate their technical knowledge and skills.

Best practices for preparation duties

1 Apply relevant hygiene and safety practices when carrying out all preparatory tasks (i.e. wearing safety shoes and gloves were appropriate).

2 Check bar clocks for accuracy.

3 Clean draught lines and remedy faults in bar and cellar equipment (depends on your marketplace).

4 Clean floors, walls, furniture and toilets in the bar and lounge areas.

5 Collect the float and prepare the cash register.

6 Carry out a final overall checking of the bar prior to opening

7 Display and rotate stocks correctly (labels facing outwards, cleaning bottles and removing out of date items).

8 Dispose of empty bottles and cartons efficiently and clean the bottle skips.

9 Deal with linen, bar and tea towels.

10 Organize the cellar in a hygienic and safe manner.

11 Position tables, chairs, stools and drip mats at the bar counter, floor areas and beer garden.

12 Regulate heating, lighting and ventilation to ensure customer satisfaction, safety and economy.

13 Strategically display the relevant notices and menus for the bar.

14 Check and clean optics, hand held measures and spirit pourers.

Best practices for customer service and taking orders

1 Greet regular and potential customers in a professional and polite manner.

2 Acknowledge the presence of customers on arrival.

3 Maintain professional and courteous relations with your customer.

4 Communicate to the best of your ability linguistically in different European language(s).

5 Give continuous attention to your customers' tables and their overall comfort and safety (i.e. obstructions)

6 Keep a calendar of local, national and international activities.

7 Never be rude or argumentative.

8 Be always polite and helpful to telephone callers.

9 Try not to give false information or to make false promises.

10 Take orders, offering advice and checking customer satisfaction.

11 Know how to deal with queries concerning the services of the premises.

12 Know how to deal with an ill person (i.e. first aid).

13 Know local history and geography.

Best practice for dispense and service skills

1 Apply the local laws in all dispense and service operations (i.e. washing fruits before use, refrigerating dairy products, responsible service of alcohol, permitted ages, drunk or barred customers, illegal gambling).

2 Use fruit tongs for garnishes and scoops for fresh ice.

3 Carry a tray for service which is clean and dry.

4 Calculate correct prices on the register and present the bill in a timely fashion.

5 Clean all working stations and surfaces.

6 Change products during service – e.g. draught beer kegs and CO_2 cylinders – and apply the relevant safety regulations in the cellar area.

7 Prepare, portion and dispense all drinks and food while they are fresh, always making them look attractive.

8 Dispense a round of drinks in sequence and with speed.

9 Identify and avoid inappropriate topics of conversation.

10 Use the appropriate legal spirits measures and draught beer glassware.

11 Wash, polish and store glassware in their correct positions and in close proximity to required products

12 Work quietly and efficiently creating the minimum noise.

Best practices for closing the bar

1 Apply the procedures for dealing with cleaning duties at closing time.

2 Apply the closing procedure and safety precautions for ventilation, heating, lighting systems and open fires.

3 Assemble dirty linen and bar towels for exchange.

4 Attend to the cash register.

5 Call time diplomatically, encourage customers to leave, and bid them farewell.

6 Clean out the glass washing machine.

7 Carry out a final checking of bar and the surrounding areas before closing.

8 Lodge cash and receipts from the cash register and the house keys.

9 Sort empties into their own crates.

10 Store all perishable garnishes, milk, cream, and eggs.

2.4   Job description

A job description forms the basic requirements of a bartender's employment in the bar. The sample job description in Figure 2.2 is not an exhaustive list and there may be occasions when the bartender will be required to perform duties outside the scope of the job description, but this is a good starting point to help you understand the role. Bonuses, benefits and promotions are usually based on the success in meeting the requirements of the role.

Training and rewards

Traditionally, working in the bar was perceived as being low quality work requiring little intellect; therefore professionalism in the bar had been defined in terms of workplace competence and standards of performance. The nature and practice of this work drew little regard for the wider sociological, philosophical and ethical issues such as occupational health, responsible service of alcohol, food hygiene, honesty (in some circumstances), justice, and staff and client welfare (Murphy, 2006). In the past, the work was overall very physical and anti-social, which was mainly due to opening and closing times of licensed premises or bars.

These initial perceptions turned a lot of young people away from a career in the bar industry. Times have changed now, and if you chose to undertake bartender training, you would have the tools to do the job in the 21st century. Being a trained bartender means that you will be familiar with bar set up, pouring methods, liquors, basic cocktail-making skills, understand health and hygiene requirements, and have knowledge of the relevant licensing and local laws and their rigorous application. Bartender training provides an entry into the industry and the basics to keep a person there.

Figure 2.2: Bartender's job description

Job title:	Bartender
Place of work:	Behind the appointed bar
Responsible to:	Bar owner, manager or his deputy

Description of responsibilities and duties:

1   Maintain a pleasant personality and a smart clean appearance at all times

2   Implementation and sourcing of a balanced beverage and wine list that complements the bar's food menu.

3   Ensure that the beverages and wines for all functions and parties are in stock and are at the correct temperature for service.

4   Maintain superior levels of beverage service to all customers.

5   Monitor all beverage storage facilities to ensure that the proper storage techniques are being used.

6   Ensure that the highest standards of cleanliness and safety are being kept in the storage areas.

7   Produce cocktail, beer and occasionally wine menus to complement the food being served.

8   Ensure that all bar and waiting staff's beverage knowledge is at an acceptable level, and provide training where required.

9   Ensure that all cash handling procedures are maintained.

10   Ensure that all possible control measures are in place to deter cash or stock losses.

11   Take function bookings when required, during service hours.

Specific requirements

An excellent knowledge of beverages, wines and cocktails is essential for this role.

adapted from Lipinski & Lipinski (1996).

If you are interested in learning more about professional quality bartender training, contact your local training centres or institutes to obtain a prospectus of full or part-time programmes. These training colleges in recent years have merged vocational and liberal approaches to assist bartenders to become professional practitioners, capable decision makers, adaptable, reflective bartenders, able to accept personal and professional responsibility and to actively engage in improving the knowledge base of the licensed industry. Pay structures of the bar industry as a whole have been revolutionized in recent years, and in general, bartenders now enjoy hourly rates for all their work within and outside the actual service hours. Some bars will now offer incentives and promotion to bartenders who:

■   Achieve industry and academic qualifications which will indirectly and directly assist the business (licensed premises, pub groups, foodservices operations, events management)

■   Contribute to new business for the bar, restaurant or nightclub

■   Never take sick days (recognizing their lack of absenteeism)

■   Help to reduce business costs (no matter how small or large the savings)

■   Make themselves available to work the most anti-social hours (late nights) or busy sporting and festival weekends

(Murphy, 2006).

Some individuals will set out to bartend only for money. The cash tips and salary in some locations or countries are a great incentive and they can make a lot of money really fast. However, this is a defeatist attitude because if you chase the money it will lead you to bartend from one bar to the next. To be really successful, you have to bartend because you love the job, the social environment, the varied hours, the many characters you will meet and ultimately the enjoyment you can bring to people with your skills and experience.

2.5   Other beverage service personnel

Licensed premises are required to have enough staff to cover the full extent of activities in order to ensure efficient control and maintenance of order. In most countries a **staff plan** is required. This is a document which must be available for inspection in the licensed premises and which has to be kept up-to-date with regard to changes in staff. A **shift schedule** with full names of the members of staff and their tasks, which corresponds with the information on the staff plan, must also always be available in the licensed premises (Valvera, 2010). Persons under 18 cannot normally serve alcoholic beverages unless they have obtained an adequate vocational training in an educational establishment or through apprenticeship training which meets the requirements of the local or national legislation. The details of the duties of individual beverage service jobs can vary widely from one bar to the next, according to its size, the nature of its business and in some circumstances the traditions of the organization (Brown et al, 1994; Lillicrap & Cousins, 2010). In this section the various types of beverage service personnel and an explanation of their role is explained. Iit must be remembered that in medium to small sized licensed premises these roles may be combined.

Food and beverage manager

This person is usually responsible for the success of the bar's food and beverage operations. They will also be responsible for compiling food and beverage menus (in consultation with the relevant staff members) to ensure that the accepted profit margins and quality levels are achieved, staff recruitment, training, decisions on portion sizes, purchasing food and beverages products and finally holding regular meetings with section heads to ensure all areas are working effectively and efficiently (Lillicrap & Cousins, 2010) .

Restaurant (food service) manager

The restaurant manager is responsible for all day to day restaurant and food service operations of the bar. This includes staff development, training, staff duty roasters and the maintenance of all policies and procedures. In some large establishments each restaurant or food service area could have its own manager responsible to the food and beverage manager. Depending on the size, some establishments might also have an **assistant restaurant manager** who will fulfil the duties and responsibilities of the restaurant manager when they are absent.

Bar manager

The bar manager is ultimately responsible for the sourcing, ordering and serving of all beverages in the bar area, whilst maintaining the highest standards of service and keeping labour costs to a minimum, at all times. Depending on the size, some establishments might also have an **assistant bar manager or duty manager** who will fulfil the same duties and responsibilities of the bar manager when they are absent.

Responsibilities and duties

- Ensuring that persons appearing to be under the age of 18 provide adequate I.D. before being served.
- Ensuring that all stock levels are maintained (without overstocking) and there is enough stock present at all times.
- Ensuring function sheets are recorded and stock is ordered as required.
- Ensuring that all staff record wastage in Wastage Book.
- Providing proper induction process is provided for new staff.
- Ensuring that all staff provide the highest standards of customer care and providing training for the same as and when required.
- Completing a weekly staff rota ensuring fair distribution of hours to all staff.
- Ensuring all bar staff are aware of company policies including after hours drinking. A full list to be provided.
- Supervision of bar staff at all times.
- Ensuring all cashiering policies and procedures are followed at all times, and ensuring that staff are aware that cash discrepancies are neither accepted nor tolerated.
- Ensuring all bar food and drinks are served within the designated time frame.
- Ensuring that keys for the till and stores remain with bar manager at all times.
- Compiling and maintaining all cocktail lists, speciality coffee and wine by the glass lists.
- Having a full knowledge of (or seek training for) occupational health & safety guidelines.
- Ensuring each till has sufficient cash for change, and providing cash as and when required.
- Completing end of shift cash up sheets and making sure any variances are explained.
- Ensuring all possible controls are in place to deter and cash or stock losses.
- Ensuring the cleanliness and maintenance of all equipment and work areas.
- Ensuring that all bar staff attend responsible service of alcohol course
- Ensuring all staff are happy in their work, and making sure any problems are dealt with in a compassionate and professional manner.

(www.barkeeper.ie)

Barback

This individual (who could be a trainee or apprentice) assists the bartender and helps to keep up the stock levels (ice, beers, spirits, soft drinks, etc.) during service. They also support the pouring of some drinks, collect glasses and fulfil general duties around the bar area.

Sommelier (wine waiter, beer sommelier)

The sommelier is responsible for the ordering, storing and serving of all special beverages in the restaurant and throughout a licensed premises, and will be found in establishments which place a special emphasis on their wine, waters and speciality beer offerings (wine bars). An excellent knowledge of wine, beer and waters and their food pairings is essential for this role.

2

Head waiter (floor supervisor)

This role is dependent on the size of the establishment. The Head Waiter is normally responsible for all the service staff in the restaurant (or food service areas) and to ensure that the preparation, service and clearing tasks are carried out efficiently. **The floor supervisor – receiving** would be responsible for the same tasks in the bar (which can include food service areas).

Waiter (floor service staff, floor waiter)

Waiting staff are primarily responsible for maintaining a high level of service to all our guests at all times. Their duties involve taking food orders, ensuring company standards are followed, the timely delivery of all food and beverage items to customers in the restaurant, clearing tables and maintaining a clean and safe working environment.

Barista

'Barista' is Italian for 'bartender', and the role is essentially to prepare and serve espresso based coffee drinks. The quality of the skilled training of the barista is crucial. This includes the correct operation, maintenance and programming of the machine, grinding and tamping methods, extraction times, water temperature and quality, micro milk frothing, free pouring, latte art, roasting, coffee plant cultivation, drying methods and correct storage. All these elements play a key role in keeping customers coming back for their favourite coffee. Baristas will also serve other non-alcoholic drinks including milk shakes, smoothies and chocolate using specialist equipment (Bamunuge et al (2010). For a further explanation of their duties (please refer to the Drinks Companion).

Education for the bar and beverage industry

Training colleges around the world in recent years have merged vocational and liberal approaches to assist bartenders, bar management and all food and beverage service personnel to improve their skills and the knowledge base of the licensed industry. In a textbook of this nature it would not be possible to cover all the private and public educational providers and their subsequent educational programmes. If you wish to formalize and update your knowledge in the bar and food and beverage management areas contact your local or national training colleges for your region or area (the *Web resources* section below offers some options).

2.6 Cultural appreciation

Working in a bar, you get in touch with people with different backgrounds and different cultures, and it's of great importance that you have some knowledge about their different countries. When receiving foreign customers you might pick up even more information by talking with them. Everybody can enrich their cultural appreciation by reading papers, watching television and having discussions with their customers and colleagues. Although most bars will have cultural appreciation training for staff, bartenders can occasionally do something that offends each other or customers, when this happens, do the commonsense thing, and apologize sincerely (see also Sections 6.6 - 6.10 on cultural diversity)).

Conclusion

The bartender's professional abilities and personality strongly influence the positive or indeed negative experience of the bar for the customer. The role of the bartender is never about just preparation and service of the bar's products for the customer.

Moreover, the bartender is crucial to creating that unique experience for the customer which makes them want to return by themselves, or with family, friends or business colleagues on a regular basis. In this chapter we highlighted the many roles bartenders play in food and beverage service. Friendliness, professionalism and contribution to life-long learning combined with honesty, punctuality, pleasing personality, good personal appearance, good standard of education, the ability to work with other people, personal control and a commitment to personal development are amongst the crucial attributes and qualifications necessary for the ideal bartender. The provision of detailed job descriptions and best practice procedures can assist the bartender to recognize their duties and responsibilities in the workplace. Finally during all contact with a customer, the ways in which a bartender receives the customer and talks to them are of great fundamental importance for a bartender's job. A bartender should therefore base their behavior on common sense and modesty. The hospitality industry is a people-centered business and the choice of becoming a bartender is not just a career decision but also a lifestyle choice.

3 Bar and Service Equipment

Aims and learning outcomes

The aim of this chapter is to provide the knowledge and skills to operate food and beverage equipment. On completion of this chapter the learner should be able to:

- Describe the various types of large and small equipment within the bar area
- Explain the use and maintenance of bar equipment
- Identify the major glassware types available within the bar area
- Identify food service equipment and broadly explain their relevant use in the food service area.

3.1 Introduction

The storage, preparation and service of food and beverages in the bar and food service areas involves understanding how to source and operate various small and large pieces of equipment. This is crucial to the practice of good service and to delivering food and drink products to the highest standards in the bar. This equipment can differ depending on the food and drinks to be prepared and served, and the particular type of bar and dining areas, for example if the bar and food service areas are located within a hotel, restaurant, cruise liner or night club.

3.2 Bar area – large equipment

Glass washing machines

The primary objective of any good glass washing machine is to produce glasses that are hygienic and sparkling clean. The machine cycle must be rapid because turnover of glasses at busy times is important in the licensed industry (a good glass washing machine will wash about 1,152 glasses or 48 racks per hour at a setting of 75 seconds cycle, whereas a longer wash cycle of 150 seconds should produce 576 glasses per hour).

Glass washing machine, best practices:

- Never leave glasses to dry in the glass washing machine
- Maintain correct water temperature and sufficient detergent levels dispensed in the correct amounts
- Glass washing machines can be adjusted to suit your bar, for example water hardness, water pressure, chemical dosage
- Clean the machine and clear any blockages at the water jets, filter and rinse bars
- Wash glasses that have been used for dairy products, including specialist coffees, separately
- Do not wash trays, food containers or cutlery in the glass washing machine
- Never remove glasses from the machine before it has finished its full wash and rinse programme.

Ice making machines and ice purity

Ice is one of the most important ingredients in the bar industry. Ice must be clean and fresh and free of any flavour save water.

Modern ice making machines are self-cleaning and you can program the machine electronically to change its output based on daily and seasonal demands. These refrigerated machines are usually made of rustproof materials (stainless steel or heavy duty plastic) they contain a pump inside which circulates the water from a tank. Premium icemakers always contain a good filtration system, to ensure pure water and minimal build-up of chlorine and minerals found in most drinking water. The water runs through tubing to a freezer assembly, which freezes it into a single sheet of ice. The frozen sheet is then forced through a screen to produce ice cubes, or crushed to produce crushed ice. Different types of screens produce different sizes and shapes of ice cubes. Each machine however makes only one type and size of ice, but in some modern machines you can adjust cube size. When the ice is made, it is dumped into a storage bin where it is cool and fresh. This minimizes broad surface to surface contact with adjacent cubes in the bin, such as with square cubes, which can result in cubes freezing together in clusters. When the bin fills to capacity, a sensor inside the bin stops the ice making process until there is room to make and store more fresh ice. The main decisions affecting the icemaker's production are: available space - the warmer the air around it and the warmer the water it is fed, the less ice it will produce; heat generation in the bar; how many areas it will serve; ventilation; sanitation standards of the located area.

Types of ice

Ice can be crushed, shaved, cracked, or cubed, depending on the food or drinks it is intended to assist. The more ice you use in a drink, the cooler the drink will be, but remember that too much ice will also dilute a drink. This is particularly true of crushed ice. Other factors to consider are:

- **Clarity**: ice should be completely clear, made with pure, sanitary drinking water that produces no 'off' taste, color, or odour.

- **Displacement**: cubes should 'pack' well into the glass; you never want a customer to think they are paying for a drink that's mostly ice. The shape of the cube also determines how much of its surface touches the liquid and, therefore, how quickly it works to chill the drink.

- **Density**: how 'hard' or 'soft' the ice is frozen determines how quickly it interacts with the drink. The cubes also should not be so soft that they stick together in the ice machine or bucket. Local temperature and humidity impact density, as does where the icemaker is located in the bar, and its temperature setting.

Food safety and ice

Regular surveillance of ice for contaminants is vital for the protection of public health and consumer confidence. In most countries we use more ice than bread, and like any other type of food or drink we ingest, it can become contaminated and retain bacteria, causing illness.

The sampling and testing of ice from food premises is supervised by the health boards in each country, with ice samples taken for microbiological assessment. You should never: refreeze ice, scoop or transfer ice by hand, use glasses or ice buckets as ice scoops or store bottles or other foods in the ice machine. Contamination can also occur from other internal and external factors – two-thirds of the service calls for icemakers can be traced to dirty compressor and condenser coils. These coils hold refrigerant, which is pressurized and turns from liquid to vapour and back again during the cooling process. Bacteria can build up if ice machines and equipment are not sufficiently serviced and maintained, but contamination is most likely caused through the handling of ice by serving staff, customers or the following:

- Road works near the premises can effect the quality of your water supply from the rising mains.

- Ices cubes made in trays in the deep freeze section of domestic type fridges, as this involves more handling.

- The ice bucket – Health Board samples of ice taken from ice buckets in bar premises indicated high levels of contamination.

- The ice location – the machine is located in the cellar in most premises, and it is important that this area be rodent proof, clean and tidy, and that the materials used on surfaces, floors, walls and ceilings are within the hygiene regulations.

- Ice cube machines should be thoroughly emptied out and cleaned regularly at frequent intervals, so that they can continue to produce E.coli free ice cubes, which is the primary objective. This cleaning should include the water jets and all internal ice contact areas within the machine. Water and air filters used in conjunction with the ice machine should be changed at least once annually; sometimes in poor water quality areas this filter should be changed 2-3 times per year to ensure water purity. The warmer or dirtier the environment in which the icemaker must work, the more frequent its maintenance check should be.

■ There will be times when you notice that the ice cubes produced in your machine are incomplete and slightly discolored, even in sterilised ice machines with clean water filters. This can be the result of low gas levels in the condenser at the back of the ice machine. Don't despair – just call in your ice machine maintenance people and they will top up the gas levels which will result in clearer, fuller formed ice cubes.

■ Ice machine scoops and tongs should be thoroughly washed each day. The legislation states that these items should not be placed in the ice, but stored in a separate container containing some antibacterial agent. Some ice machine manufacturers now provide a suitable place to store the ice scoop.

A good maintenance overhaul or new ice buckets, tongs, scoops and containers, coupled with good operational hygiene procedures could ensure that your customers can expect good quality ice, free from any harmful bacteria, in their food and drinks.

Refrigerators, cabinet coolers

The back bar areas of most contemporary bars are completely fitted out with cabinet coolers ensuring that all bottled products, however big or small, are served chilled to the customer. This increased interest and usage of these cooling systems in bars highlights the need to understand the function, care and maintenance of refrigerators and cabinet cooling systems.

Environmental awareness (the influence of hydrocarbon)

The need to choose refrigerants and cooling equipment according to their energy efficiency is becoming ever more important. Most of the major refrigerator companies in the bar industry have pioneered the use of hydrocarbon, which is fast becoming accepted as the most energy efficient refrigerant available. It can reduce energy consumption by up to 15%, is less 'aggressive' material and extends the life span of the compressor. Hydrocarbon also provides a quicker 'pull time' when doors are closed meaning more efficient recovery. A lower compressor operating temperature means less heat is emitted and less noise emanates from the compressor. Modern refrigerated units are now fitted with helium leak detection and double coated coils, which dramatically reduce gas leaks.

Power consumption and equipment faults: blocked condensers increase power consumption by 23%, a faulty door seal 11%, incorrect temperature setting 6%, a 15% loss in refrigerant gas increases power consumption by 100%.

Refrigerator stock rotation: always use stock rotation techniques and check regularly the 'best before' dates on all beverages.

Factors to consider when purchasing refrigerators and cabinet coolers:

- A forced air-cooling system which forces cold air into the fridge ensures efficiency.

- A digital temperature display enables you to see at a glance that the cabinet is running at the correct temperature, ensuring food safety.

- Thermally efficient CFC-free polyurethane foam insulation helps maintain temperatures.

- Make sure the units are made from a quality material, such as Optisheen 304 grade stainless steel, with an aluminum interior shell to ensure efficiency.

- Self-closing doors keep cold air inside, and doors fitted with magnetic gaskets created an airtight seal.

- Make sure that the unit is easy to clean with coved internal corners and removable shelving. Castors allow for easy movement and cleaning of the cabinet's complete exterior.

Hot drinks and coffee making machines

Choosing the right type of machine for the bar is an important component of getting your hot drinks and coffee offering right. The majority of major coffee suppliers now supply machines and offer advice and, in some circumstances, barista training in the coffee making skills and techniques.

Figure 3.1: Double group handle barista coffee machine

There are many different types of hot drink and coffee making machines, which include:

■ Pour over machines: usually consists of two hot plates used for making filter coffee, which accounts for over half of all coffee currently sold today

■ Automatic machines: ranging from traditional Brasilia coffee machines (for smaller premises) to Nuevo Simmonelli automatics (for big and busy premises) which can make 200 cups per hour.

■ Semi-automatic machines: do everything except froth the milk.

Cleaning coffee machines and training

Manual espresso machines

These need the most training but automatic machines also need attention, especially when it comes to cleaning and maintenance. If this is not done properly you make a mess of the coffee. If you don't clean coffee machines properly, old rancid (smelling or tasting like rank stale fat) coffee oils are left in the handles where they cannot be seen. Special detergent tablets are used for cleaning, which should be done every night. It is only a 15-minute job. Training should cover areas such as:

■ The workings of the coffee grinder (doing a 'test shot' to evaluate the grind and the quality of the espresso)

■ Checking the cake of coffee for consistency

■ Flushing the 'group head' of the machine

■ Cleaning and drying the filter basket before dosing

■ How to avoid spillage and waste

■ How to get the critical dosing and 'tamping' (compressing the ground coffee) right

■ Cleaning the porta filters on the machine.

Water quality

The quality of water is also important as 98% of any cup of coffee is made up of water. In hard water areas a filter should be used to prevent build up of lime, which makes an inferior cup of coffee and causes blockages in the machine.

There are so many things other issues which contribute towards making of the perfect cup of coffee: the beans, machine training (barista skills), cleaning and techniques for creating the coffee experience to maximize sales in the bar. These topics are covered in comprehensive style in the *Drinks Handbook,* under 'Tea and Coffee'.

3.3   Bar area – small equipment and utensils

Figure 3.2: (Back, left to right) pineapple corer, ice crusher, selection of bar spoons, (front, left to right) lemon juicer, lime juicer, fine strainer, hawthorn strainer, winged strainer, julep strainer, melon baller, citrus peeler, double melon baller, canella knife, small and large apple corers.

Bar spoons

Bar spoons (stainless steel) are mainly used with the mixing glass set. They are 10 inches long. When stirring cocktails, you should stir 20 times to the left and 20 times to the right. At the top end, there is usually a disc called a muddler which can be used to muddle, or crush pieces of fruit, herbs, sugar cubes or extract essential oils; the middle shaft section is spiralled and ideal for mixing drinks. The bottom end gives you a bar spoon measure (same amount as a standard kitchen teaspoon), and the rounded back of the spoon is also used for slowly pouring layers of liqueurs into a glass when you do not want the layers to mix (Figure 3.2).

Bar condiment units

These provide individual hygienic storage space for your garnishes, spare slices of fruit, olives and cherries when they are out of the cool refrigerator. Available in the 3, 4 or 6 piece setting; the white plastic inserts can be purchased separately.

Figures 3.3: 4 and 6 piece condiment units

Boston cocktail shaker (2 cones)

Favoured by professionals because it is easy to clean and to open, and because its capacity enables you to get a better throw of ice, which helps the cocktail mixture and head creation. This shaker consists of two cones – one half glass and one half stainless steel. Sometimes both cones are stainless steel – this type is referred to as a French shaker). One cone always overlaps the other. To lock or close the shaker tap the top cone until you feel the shaker is closed. To open the Boston shaker, place it on the work surface and tap the middle of the shaker near the overlap until you feel it release. Be careful not to pressurize this area.

When using this shaker, fill the glass cone three quarter full with ice, then pour all the ingredients on the top of the ice, pouring the cheapest ingredients in first in case of mistakes. Next, pour the contents of the glass into the steel half, close the shaker, and shake for ten seconds vigorously. Open as stated above, lifting the glass half off first, then use a winged or lugged strainer to strain the cocktail.

Figure 3.4, 3.5: French Shaker and Boston Shaker

Canelle knife

This takes its name from the French word for a 'channel' or 'groove', and is used to obtain peels from fruits and vegetables. To use, apply pressure to the fruit or vegetable, being careful of your accuracy when cutting. Try to stay in an even circular pattern for spirals, or straight horizontal lines for a wheel design patterns. The solidity of the fruit or vegetable is crucial (Figure 3.2) .

Chopping boards – colour coded

These can be made of plastic, wood or marble, and in different shapes, and are mainly used for chopping fruits. For health and safety and HACCP purposes, you should always use the appropriate colour coded chopping boards. The colours commonly available are white for dairy products, red for raw meat, blue for raw fish, brown for vegetable products, green for salad and fruit products, and yellow for cooked meats. You can also purchase a stainless steel rack for storing your chopping boards.

Classic hawthorn strainer

Made of stainless steel, this is the most famous of the coil rimmed strainers, which adapt to the circumference of most mixing glasses or cocktail cones. Strainers can have longer handles, and two or four side wings or lugs (referred to as winged strainers). They are best used when pouring cocktails from the cocktail shaker or mixing glass to separate the drink from ice or fruits, or to let the liquid through without clogging, especially when pouring thick textured cocktails. (Figure 3.2)

Julep strainers carry out the same function but they do not contain the coil springs, and fine strainers, contain a very fine straining mesh, are used to hold back pips, pieces or fine pieces of ice when double straining cocktails. (Figure 3.2)

Dash and bitter bottles

These are advisable for small quantities of bitters. Dash bottles are usually small with a plastic nozzle recessed in the neck. A dash is equivalent to about one third of a teaspoonful. Ideal for a dash of Orange Curacao, Anise liqueur or flavoured bitters which are used to enhance the flavour profile of cocktails.

Figure 3.6: Dash bottle.

Electric blender and liquidizers

Blenders and liquidizers are available from numerous manufactures and most have variable speeds. The stainless steel commercial types are the best. Some practitioners favor the glass see-through blenders with the measurements listed on the vessel side. They are best used for preparing cocktails that require fruit to be pureed, for example fresh fruit Daiquiris. Although most professional electric blenders have specially toughened blades, it is best that crushed ice is used whenever possible; this reduces the stress on the motor, therefore increasing its longevity. When using the electric blender simply pour in all the ingredients – again the

cheapest first in case of mistakes. Ice should always be added last when blending. Blend to reach the desired consistency – it should be smooth. Blend for 20 seconds maximum, being careful not to over-blend, as this can turn the ingredients sour or thick, spoiling the taste of your cocktails.

Figure 3.7, 3.8: Rio Bar blender. Commercial bar blender.

Electric drinks mixer

This is used for making cocktails that do not need liquidising. The types of drinks created in this are similar to the ones created in the cocktail shaker. The mixer is usually used for mixing milk shakes. Always use crushed ice, as whole ice cubes will damage the blade paddles, which are not as strong as blender blades.

Ice tongs and ice shuffles

Made of stainless steel or plastic, these are available in various capacity sizes, and the sizes should reflect the bar's volume of business. Don't overload your scoop as you end up dropping ice, and always keep it sterile and free from any bacteria.

Ice crushers

Two main types are available: manual (vice Scripps type or plastic container with rubber base for locking the ice crusher to the work surface) and electric, which is ideal when large amounts of ice are required quickly. The ice is fed into a hopper above an electrically driven crusher, which delivers crushed ice into a large stainless steel bowl.

Figure 3.9: Manual ice crusher

Electric juice extractors

When you need natural juices, an electric juicer helps separate the pulp from the juice. There are three types of juicers, which vary in price.

- **Centrifugal juicers:** at the lower end of the price range. Coarsely chopped ingredients are fed into the machine, which grates them into tiny pieces and spins them at high speed. The liquid is extracted by centrifugal force, leaving the pulp behind. As the ingredients are exposed to the air throughout the process, juices made by this method have the lowest nutritional content.

- **Hydraulic juicers:** at the top end of the price range. Extreme pressure forces the juice out of the ingredients, through a strainer and into a pitcher, leaving the pulp behind. Juices pressed by this method are very high in nutrients.

- **Triturating juicers:** larger than the other two and in the middle of the price range. A rotating cutter tears up the ingredients and presses them against a strainer. The juice they produce is in the middle of the nutritional range.

Manual citrus fruit squeeze or juice extractor

These can be made from stainless steel, glass or plastic, usually made with an inbuilt serrated compartment for the juice collection.

Figure 3.10: Juice extractors.

Mixing glass

The glass is like a jug without a handle, and the best have a pouring lip. It is used for mixing clear cocktails, which do not contain juices or cream. Cocktails are usually mixed with the long bar spoon, briskly, and then strained with a Hawthorn strainer. The glass half of the Boston shaker can be used as a substitute here.

Figure 3.11: Mixing glass.

Muddlers

These are made of glass, plastic or wood. The wooden type, usually made of lignum vitae which is the hardest wood known, is favoured as it does not scratch glassware. Muddlers vary in size and are used to extract essential oils from herbs, mint leaf or to press sugar cubes or fruits for flavour in cocktails. Muddlers should be used like a pestle in a mixing jug. They can be purchased with interchangeable heads (i.e. smooth or serrated edges) for mashing or grinding.

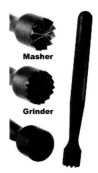

Figure 3.12: Muddler head types.

Nutmeg grater

A tiny grater with small holes, ideal for obtaining fresh nutmeg for egg-noggs, frothy and creamy drinks. To use, run the nutmeg firmly to and fro over the grater. Special tiny nutmeg graters are easy to source.

Paring knife

Used for cutting fruit and shearing off fruit rinds, this is an absolute necessity, and quality and sharpness is important. Non-stainless knives is easiest to keep sharp on a whetstone, but acid juice turns then black. When cutting fruit always hold the knife firmly and cut horizontally along the line to correspond with your finger nails, arching up your hand. This minimizes your chance of cutting your fingers.

Save-or-serve juice containers

These plastic containers will take screw top lids or pouring nozzles for usage in bar and cocktail operations. A colour coded system of save-or-serve is used for storing and serving for your bar mixes, juices, salad dressing sometimes even salt. They are traditionally sold in 3, 1 or ½ litre sizes.

Standard cocktail shaker (cobbler shaker)

A stainless steel three piece shaker with an in-built strainer, with 60cl capacity. It's ideal for mixing ingredients for cocktails containing juices, egg whites, cream and sugar syrups. Its usage is as follows.

1 Insert the fresh ice and products.

2 Secure all parts of the shaker together and using both hands, place the thumb of one hand over the top of the shaker and the forefinger of the other hand under the bottom of the shaker.

3 Grasp the shaker fully around the middle and move the wrist and forearm together and in an arc rhythm shake briskly (15 to 20 times).

Figures 3.13: 3 piece cocktail shaker.

Standard cocktail shaker: points to remember

■ Develop your own shaking style, make it short and snappy (no more than 10 seconds) and hold the cocktail shaker above your shoulder when shaking.

■ Shake vigorously and in an arc rhythm style. Don't rock the cocktail to sleep, but wake it up. Never shake towards the customer in case of an accident.

■ Using a cocktail shaker to prepare your drink inflates the final result, so always allow your glass size for this practicality.

■ To avoid the possibility of leakage or the accidental separation of the cocktail shaker, wrap a clean napkin around the cocktail shaker before shaking.

■ The art of shaking good cocktails depends on attention to detail, experience, use of the best ingredients and a good stainless steel cocktail shaker.

■ The larger the cocktail shaker the better, because this ensures a good movement of ice for a good mix and head creation.

■ Never put an effervescent ingredient (fizzy) into your shaker or blender.

Spirit measures (hand held)

These come in various types and sizes, in glass or stainless steel, double ended measures, cups, and easy to read glass measures. Sample quantities of spirit measures include the jigger (1.5oz), pony (1oz) and the dash (1/8 teaspoon full). Government controls can dictate the standard sizes of spirit measures for use in your country. The art of using a hand held spirit measure should not be understated. With the proper use and pouring accuracy, you will minimise spirit waste and maintain professional bar standards.

Figures 3.14, 3.15: 25ml, 35ml, 40ml, 50ml and 70ml stainless steel and glass measures.s.

Spirit pourer

Long stem, fast or exact measure (stop cock) are the most common pourers and are usually made of stainless steel or plastic with rubber or plastic inlays to adapt to different bottle sizes. The provision of good quality pourers in a busy professional bar helps to eliminate waste and bad measurements.

Speed bottle rails

Made of stainless steel, used to store the house (or most popular) pouring or well spirits and liqueurs. Usually mounted at waist level on the front rails and behind the bar, and allow the bartender to perform bar service while facing the guest. Available made to measure and in 5, 8 and 12 bottle configurations (Figure 3.17).

Figures 3.16, 3.17: Optics. 12 bottle Speed rail.

Spirit optic brackets

Spring loaded optic brackets (Figure 3.16) may be mounted to the wall or shelves, usually located behind the bar. You can obtain rotary optic stands which can store up to 6 bottles together. Optics are particularly useful for inexperienced bartenders who lack the professional skill required to use hand held spirit measures efficiently and correctly.

Stacking rimming trays

These open out into three compartments. The top layer contains the watered sponge for moistening glass rims, middle layer contains usually the granulated salt for rimming cocktail glasses (i.e. Margarita cocktail) and the bottom layer is used for sugar, chocolate or coconut pieces for rimming glasses for sweet or non-alcoholic cocktails.

Wine knife

This is the bartender's individual tool of the trade. The wine knife has a blade for removing bottle coils, a good corkscrew for opening wines and a bottle opener.

Figure 3.18: Selection of wine knives.

Zester

This has a row of tiny holes that remove the top layer of skin off a citrus fruit when dragged across it. Excellent when you require a good aroma for your cocktails.

3.4   Glassware

Glassware is without doubt one of the most important elements which directly contributes to the overall enjoyment of all drinks. Their shapes, sizes and colours add a certain theatre to the drinking and dining experience. Most of the glasses which we use in the bar are produced by the blow and press method. After the glass is shaped, it is put into a warm oven to cool slowly, which is called annealing. The slow cooling stabilizes and strengthens the glass and removes any stress points that may have developed during shaping.

Glassware selection

The quality and condition of the glassware, which you use in your bar, should be considered as an element of your overall décor and concept, plus a firm commitment to the good glassware hygiene standards of your bar. Glassware has a subtle but crucial impact on your customer's perception of your bar's style, quality, and personality. The kind of glass you choose for your bars drinks can have a surprising amount of impact on how the beverages look and taste. Some styles of glass have what is known as a 'chimney', so that the aroma of the beverage is concentrated and wafts up towards the nose. As more than 90% of taste is smell, a glass that can optimize the bouquet is worth using.

The only way to realize this is by placing two glasses side by side with the same beverage. The difference will be immediately apparent and once you try the right glass it's difficult to go back. Although some traditional beverages are served in standard glassware, the final choice is ultimately yours but always ensure the following:

- Glasses should have brilliant clarity, good balance and a fine rim.
- Allow room for a generous amount of drink, ice and garnish (as appropriate)
- Make sure the glass is completely free of any detergent or odour. If glasses are stored upside-down, the air trapped in the bowl will become stale and affect the taste and smell of the drink. Rinse these glasses before using.
- If you have a large refrigerator or freezer, it's a good idea to chill your glasses before using them.
- Use real glass and not plastic glasses, so as not to affect the taste of drinks. Remember too, that multicoloured designs on glasses tend to detract from the drink you are serving.
- Wash and rinse glasses in very hot water, then dry with one cloth and polish them with another.

Appropriate glassware selection in relation to the size and shape for a drink, indicates that the bar knows its business, and signals a respect for that tradition to your customers. Glassware can also be a merchandising tool, stimulating sales for your bar.

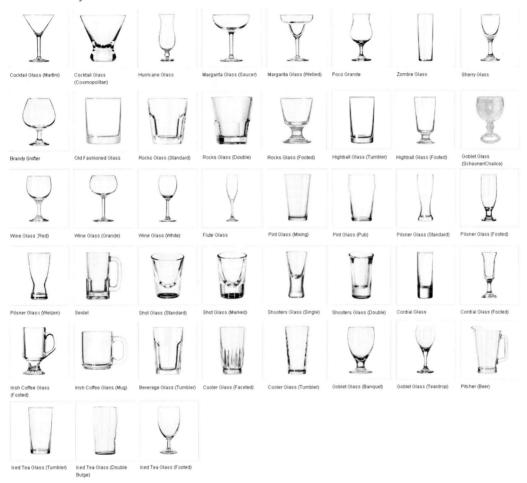

Figure 3.19: Glasssware selection.

Handling glassware (care and attention)

Bar staff handling glassware should be advised of the fine qualities of glassware and how it should be treated and handled.

Improved handling leads to fewer breakages, and this means higher productivity and less chance of injury through accident.

For safety and profitability:

■ Never pick up glasses in clusters

■ Never put silverware into glasses

- Never stack or 'nest' glasses inside each other
- Never use a glass for scooping ice
- Be aware of sudden temperature changes and their impact on the glass (glass shock)
- Always hold glasses near the base for hygienic purposes
- To rim a glass, wipe the glass rim with lemon or dip the glass into a saucer of egg white, water or different colored syrups, then dip in salt, sugar or coconut.
- Glassware should always be clean, not smelling or sticky, and free from lipstick
- Never fill a glass to the brim; spillage will result in soiling clothes and bar counters.

Standard bar Glass types / Styles	Range of Sizes
Brandy balloon (snifter)	5oz - 7oz (15cl - 20cl).
Bottle & draught Beer (pilsner, lido, conical, nonic, tulip)	6oz – 20oz (18cl – 60cl).
Champagne flute	7 ½ oz -1/2oz (21cl).
Goblet or Poco	8oz – 12oz (24cl - 36cl).
Highball (slim Jim / tumbler / sling)	10, 12, 14, oz (30, 36, 42cl).
Irish Coffee (heat resistant)	8oz (24cl).
Old-Fashioned	7oz - 12oz (21cl – 36cl).
Rocks / Granity	8oz – 12oz (24cl – 36cl).
Martini	3, 5,7oz - (10cl,15cl, 21cl).
Shot (gin tumbler, granity, heavy, islande, carvella)	1 ¼ oz – 2oz (3.5cl - 6cl).

Systems used for cleaning glassware

Always hand wash new glasses to remove the film residue left by the glassmaking manufacturing process. Listed below are the crucial considerations involved in the manual and machine-washing systems for your glassware.

Washing glasses by hand

- The detergent chosen must be specially designed for washing glasses
- Rinse the glasses thoroughly in clean hot water
- Leave clean glasses to drain on clean plastic gridding on top of a suitable draining surface for hygiene and ventilation, ideally 5-7mm high glass care mats will allow for proper air circulation
- Wash the gridding thoroughly after each draining session
- Do not clean the gridding and draining surfaces with strong smelling detergent
- Do not dry or polish the glasses with a glass cloth – drying with a tea towel or glass cloth is superfluous and may even damage the glasses
- If the glasses have been used for milk, rinse them with cold water before washing them with detergent.

Figure 3.20: Glass washing brushes suitable for manual glass washing

Evaluating bacterial build up on glassware

This simple system can be incorporated to check the hygienic condition of your draught beer glassware. The 'water break test' consists of a four-step process:

1 Rinse the glass in cold water.

2 Dry the outside of the glass, leaving some water inside the glass.

3 Invert the glass over the sink, pouring out the water slowly.

4 Examine the glass. If it contains spots and dots on the inside, this can indicate pour washing and a dirty glass. If the glass contains a continuous film, this means the glass is clean.

Remember choosing the correct cocktail glassware for your bar and combining this choice with an active integrated glassware management training system for the care and condition of these glasses will pay dividends in customer confidence and overall satisfaction.

3.5 Food service equipment

When your customer enters the food service area of your bar their initial thoughts and feelings may be based on the interior design, atmosphere and the equipment and furnishings which you chose for the bar's décor. It is therefore very important that the style and design of these items is in line with the bar's image. In this section we will explore food service equipment, which includes the main cutlery and tableware items currently in use in the majority of bars that offer food. The variety and style of these items is endless, and each bar will base their section on their food offering, size of the food service area, their turn-around rate and their ability wash these items at pace.

Accepting these initial considerations we will only concentrate on the most popular items used for food service.

Basic and special cutlery equipment

The focus here is on the major varieties and their relevant use in the food experience in bars. It is important that all the staff members involved in food service understand these cutlery items and can use them in a professional and appropriate manner at the dining table.

Table 3.1: Basic and special cutlery equipment

Cutlery item	Relevant usage
Basic cutlery equipment	
coffee spoon	coffee
fish knife	fish, also used for serving large items
fish fork	fish
dessert/pudding spoon	desserts, sometimes also pasta
service spoon	service of large items (i.e. bread rolls) when coupled with a fork
soup spoon	soup
steak knife	steak
small knife	side knife (buttering bread or spreading pate or preservatives), can be used also as a cheese, entrée or fruit knife depending on the circumstance.
small fork	dessert fork (can be used as a pasta, salad, dessert, fruit or entrée fork)
large knife	table knife (the main or joint knife of the table)
large fork	table fork (the main fork or joint fork knife of the table)
teaspoon	for stirring cocktails (i.e. Caipirinha), also for ice creams, sugar spoon, tea
Special cutlery equipment	
butter knife	serving butter, when portions are requested
bread knife	carving bread (usually on a bread board)
cheese knife	used with the cheese board for serving your cheese selection
corn-on-the-cob holders	pair of plastic or stainless steel items (used to pierce both ends of the cob)
carving knife	long extended knife for carving joints at the table for guests
gateau (cake) slice	lifting and serving slices of cake or pastries
ice cream spoon	ice creams served in coupes
lobster pick	two styles (used to extract the meat from the lobster claw)
lobster cracker	to crack (break) the lobster claws
pastry fork	for cakes and afternoon sweets
preserve spoon	used with the preservatives dish (jams, marmalade, etc.)
sundae spoon	long narrow spoon, served with ice cream in tall glasses
snail (escargot) tongs	to hold snail shells
sugar tongs	small spoon tongs used for sugar cubes
tea strainer	long handle with strainer head for straining tea when tea leaves are used

adapted from Lillicrap & Cousins (2010).

Figure 3.21: Cutlery equipment: Top row: (left to right) soup spoons (1-3), dessert spoons, tablespoons (5-7), sundae spoon, gourmet spoon, preserve spoon, coffee spoon. Bottom row: (left to right) Soup ladle, sauce ladle, gateau slice, service fork (4-5), large forks (6-7), pastry fork, snail fork, service knife, steak knife, large knife, small knife, fish knife, butter knife.

Cutlery

There is an accepted way of laying the cutlery so as not to confuse diners, especially where four or more courses are being served, and formal place settings usually adhere to the basic principle. Knives and spoons are laid on the right hand side of the place setting and forks on the left hand side. All the cutlery should be placed in the order in which they will be used, so the first item, usually the butter knife which will be used for bread rolls or similar, should be on the right hand side furthest from the plate, then the second item - perhaps the soup spoon - on the inside of the butter knife and so on until eventually you will have the dessert spoon right next to the plate. The same applies to the forks on the left hand side of the setting. All knife blades should be facing towards the plate and forks should be placed with their prongs facing upwards.

Specialist cutlery such as escargot holders or shell fish picks can be brought to the table with the relevant course.

Serving cutlery can be placed on the table close to where the serving dishes will be set, depending on whether diners will be allowed to help themselves, and condiment sets should also be placed strategically on the table. See also Chapter 14 on formal and informal place settings.

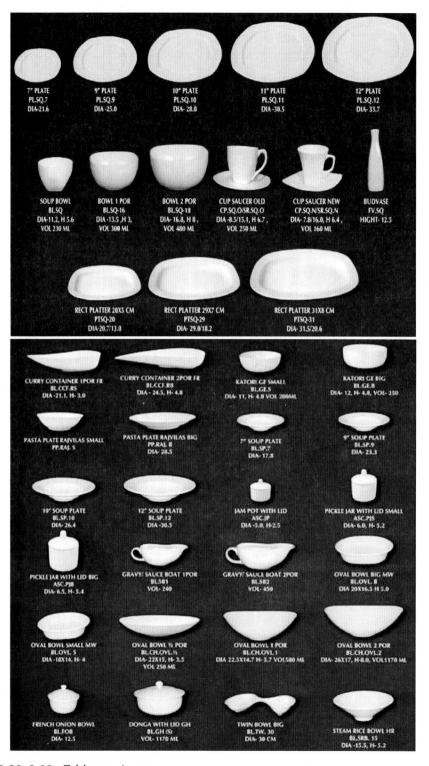

Figures 3.22, 3.23: Tableware items

Basic and special tableware (crockery)

Although the choice and variety available to you is again endless, you must consider the durability (dishwasher proof) and shelf life of the tableware. Be careful if you choose patterns because they can wear quickly.

Table 3.2: Traditional and additional items of tableware

Tableware (crockery) items

Tableware item	Relevant usage
cover plate	presentation or show plate purposes on table, could be basic design, also used as an under plate for service (usually 32-35cm diameter)
large (dinner) plate	main course plate, different shapes and styles (usually 25-30cm diameter)
fish plate	fish, desserts or sweets (usually 16-20cm diameter)
side plate	small plate for bread, small rolls or sometimes pastries(usually 5-7cm diameter)
soup plate	bowl plate for soups, pasta or cereals (usually 7-10cm diameter, 40cl)
sweet plate	desserts and sweets (usually 6-8cm diameter)
tea cup and saucer	multiple sizes, traditionally larger for tea service (20-24cl)
tea pot	stainless steel or porcelain, sizes vary (24cl – 120cl)
coffee pot	glass or porcelain, sizes and styles vary according to the method used to prepare the coffee (percolated, cafetiere)
sugar bowl	stainless steel or porcelain, open or closed, sizes and styles vary (6-10cl)
butter dishes	small flat or bowl type
sauce boat	used for sauces and gravies
cruet	salt (single or double holes) and pepper set (multiple holes)
jugs (steel or porcelain)	small and medium sized used for pouring cold cream, hot milk, hot water.

adapted from Lillicrap & Cousins (2010).

Conclusion

To deliver food and drinks with excellence and quality, management and staff members must understand how to identify and operate a wide variety of large and medium sized food and beverage equipment. This equipment can retain bacteria and become contaminated, which can lead to customers becoming ill. Local government agencies are charged with the responsibility of inspecting bars and licensed premises to ensure that all equipment is spotless and in good working order. Although the variety and functionality of this equipment depends on the products sold and can differ from bar to bar, all staff must master the best practice procedures and maintenance of all food and beverage equipment and understand their importance for effective food and beverage service for customers.

4 Serving Alcoholic and Non-Alcoholic Beverages

Aims and learning outcomes

This chapter introduces the reader to beverage service procedures, and provides a sound basic knowledge about alcohol and how to serve it responsibly. On completion of this chapter the learner should be able to:

- Explain and apply the service procedures for alcoholic and non-alcoholic beverages.
- Determine their legal and moral responsibilities in relation alcohol service.
- Explain the recommended safe levels of consumption for alcohol.
- Know the techniques used to prevent intoxication and to identify intoxicated guests.
- Describe the potential effects of a hangover.

4.1 Beverage service procedures

Always make your customers feel welcome, greet them with a smile, even if you are busy serving a drink order to someone else (Bamunuge, Edwards & Nutley, 2010). This helps to establish a rapport between the customer and the bartender. Whenever possible customers should also be escorted to a bar table or bar counter and seated, as this not only creates a good impression, but also helps you to maximise your seating arrangements. Upon seating a customer, show them the beverages or cocktail, wine or beer lists, explain to them any specialities of the bar or of any promotions that you are currently offering.

You should also take a customer's order as soon as possible and prepare and serve beverages to your bar's agreed standard for customer satisfaction and of course cost control.

Types of alcoholic and non-alcoholic beverages

Alcoholic drinks can be classified into five categories and are served accordingly to your bar's agreed standard or according to the customer's specific request (e.g. coffee as espresso, or whiskey on the rocks).

- **Wine**: still, sparkling, fortified (e.g. sherry, port, madeira) or aromatized – see below for service suggestions.
- **Beer**: ales, lagers, stouts.
- **Cider and perry**.
- **Distilled spirits:** vodka, gin, rum, whiskey, brandy and others – served straight, with water, with ice, within cocktails or speciality coffees.
- **Liqueurs**: flavoured with fruit, citrus, herb, kernel, flower, cream, berry – best served either straight, or with ice, within cocktails or within speciality coffees.

Non-alcoholic drinks can be classified into four categories:

- **Hot drinks**: Tea, coffee, chocolate – see below for service suggestions.
- **Fruit juices:** freshly squeezed or prepared juices – best served mixed with sprits or consumed straight with or without ice.
- **Mineral waters**: natural mineral water – best served chilled or at room temperature with no ice; or manufactured mixers – best served mixed with spirits or straight with ice.
- **Cordials/Syrups** (sirops, squashes) – for sweetening and flavouring mixed drinks or diluted with water to make a 'soft' drink with or without ice.

Note: Please refer to the *'Drinks Companion'* created to accompany this book for a comprehensive review of these beverages.

Still wine service

Initial considerations

Wine service procedures can differ, depending on the number and variety of wines and food which bars and restaurants offer. Each location will have its own procedure for procuring the bottle that the customer has ordered, as well as the number of glasses required. The process begins when a customer orders a particular bottle of wine. Make sure you heard them correctly by repeating the selection back to them. If you don't understand which bottle they are requesting, ask them to point it out on the menu. Less formal restaurants will allow you to ask how many people at the table will be drinking the wine, so that you will know how many glasses to bring. For example: If you have a table of three and some of the people have other drinks, ask the person who ordered the wine 'will you need three glasses?' More formal restaurants will not ask the customer, and just bring a glass for each diner. They will signal you when you are pouring out the wine if they do not want any.

Note: The bottle should never be opened prior to service, nor should any labels or foils be removed.

Glasses: The wine glasses should be spotless. If they are not, clean them. Holding them top down over a steaming bowl of hot water works well. Hint: use a coffee filter to polish the glasses dry – these leave less lint than bar rags or paper towels.

Ice buckets: If the customer ordered white wine, make sure you have a wine bucket with ice in it. (Not too much as the bottle will go in the bucket, displacing the ice and ice melts – you don't want water pouring over the top of the bucket). Don't put the bottle in the bucket yet as you don't want the label to be wet.

Equipment: Bring glasses, wine knife (corkscrew), wine, and wine bucket (if needed) to the table. (Each restaurant is different. Some put the wine bucket on the table; some have clip-on or stand alone wine stands that can be placed nearby.)

Service temperatures: White wines, light and grassy (8-10°C), white wines, robust and with a strong bouquet (10-12°C), rosé wines (10-12°C), red wines, new (12-14°C), red wines, high quality old (14-17°C).

Decanting: Certain old red wines have deposits (lees) in the bottom of the bottle. Do not decant a wine without the approval of the customer. Display the wine to the customer and decant in front of them. Leave the bottle and cork at the table. The carafe should always be at the same temperature as the wine, clean and fresh. It is advisable to place a stopper in the carafe to avoid the wine being in contact with the air too long.

How to open and present a bottle of still wine

1 Present the wine to the host (the person who ordered the wine) with the label facing them. State the name of the wine, the grape (if applicable), the vintage (if applicable) to confirm that the wine is the one that was ordered by the host, who will then accept or decline the wine. If they decline then the correct wine should be sourced and presented immediately.

2 Open the bottle in front of the customer, holding the bottle by the neck in your left hand, with the label facing the customer. Carefully cut the foil below the lip of the bottle with the blade on your waiter's knife and remove the foil. Insert the corkscrew into the bottle, and carefully extract the cork. Ensure that you have your waiter's cloth draped over your forearm so as you can wipe the top of the bottle.

3 The cork is presented to the customer. This is for the customer to examine the cork for defaults as this is sometimes the reason for faulty wine. If it is a screw cap there is no need to present the cap.

4 Serving from the right, pour a little wine for the host to taste. When pouring the wine, hold the bottle behind the label and not by the base of the bottle, so that the host can read the label again.

5 When pouring wine, twist the bottle to ensure that no drops of wine will fall onto the table and then wipe the top of the bottle with a waiter's cloth.

6 The host will then accept or decline the wine.

7 Pour wine for the ladies first, then gents, and the host last. If the host is a lady, then you still serve her last. Consider also age, rank, and social position.

8 A bottle of wine will comfortable serve five people a medium sized glass each. When pouring wine for a party of six or more, ensure that they all receive the same amount of wine. When filling the glass, a general rule is to two thirds of a glass full for white wine and a half glass full of red wine. (This also depends on the size of the glass because some modern wine glasses can be huge.)

9 If the host orders another bottle of the same wine, the host must receive a clean glass to taste and then the remainder of the table are served.

10 If the host orders a different bottle of wine, i.e., a different type of red wine, then everyone at the table should receive clean wine glasses.

11 You must finally check that the host and their guests are happy with the service, ensuring also if they require other products and services of the establishment before you leave the table.

4

Figure 4.1: Carrying a drinks service tray.

Champagne and sparkling wine service

Opening and presenting a bottle of Champagne or sparkling wine

1 Ensure that the Champagne or sparkling wine is at the right service temperature (see below).

2 Remove the foil around the top of the bottle.

3 Carefully unwind the wire restraint keeping your waiter's cloth tightly on top. (With about one in 20 bottles, the cork is forced out as soon as the wire is released, so be careful.)

4 Point the bottle away from anyone sitting near by.

5 Holding the base of the bottle in one hand and the cork in the other hand, gently twist the base of the bottle.

6 You will feel the cork starting to lift up.

7 Keep pressure on the cork, you will hear a gentle 'pliff' as the cork eases out. There should be no 'pop'. It is bad taste and dangerous to allow a Champagne cork to 'pop' on removal.

8 Pour immediately into chilled glasses, using the same service procedures as when serving wine, i.e. let the host taste first, ladies and then the gents and always the host last.

Service temperatures: For Champagne serve at about 8°C in a dry flute glass, as dampness spoils the head formation. If the Champagne is too cold the bouquets will not be released and if it's too warm you get head formation problems also. For Sparkling Wines: The same as above but serve at 6°C.

Cocktail service

To create excellent cocktail service such as you find in a good cocktail bar it takes time, effort, incredible staff training and, above all, practice. Remember cocktails are the fine dining of the alcoholic drinks world. They represent the highest skill a bartender can possess. Today's cocktail flavours run the taste gamut, from the sweet through the exotic, to savoury and dry. The cocktail maker of old has metamorphosed into the modern self-proclaimed mixologist, a sort of consulting Michelin chef on taste combinations and colour, a master of flavour, ingredients and the art of shaking.

Mixed drinks are increasingly offered as gastronomic delights. Making a good cocktail is about getting the balance of flavours right. Cocktails are about three things, balance, style and consistency. If you can get those right, everything else will fall into place. The service also involves strategic decisions regarding the methods used to prepare the cocktails. These decisions depend on several factors:

- If the cocktail contains a cloudy ingredient such as fresh cream, egg yolk, lemon or orange or a similar opaque item it should be shaken.

- If the ingredients are all clear and/or contain CO_2 (fizzy) then the cocktail should be stirred using a mixing glass set.

- If the drinks involved are of different specific gravity and the bartender wishes to keep the layers separate then the cocktail be built slowly over the back of a spoon or just over ice.

- If the cocktail requires freshly extracted oils or juices then the cocktail should be muddled.

Our sister publication the *Drinks Handbook*, provides a comprehensive review of the best practice procedures involved in cocktail service and explanations of all the significant cocktail equipment. The *Handbook* also contains an extensive set of detailed cocktail recipes, which can be adapted for your establishment.

Coffee and liqueurs service

Learning to personalise your fresh coffee offerings can bring new customers and increased business. This area of your business is crucial because customers are fascinated with coffee and they will always purchase well made, good tasting coffee at any time of the day at the bar (by the barista or bartender) or in the restaurant (by the waiter at the end of a good meal)

1 Find whether the customer wants black or white coffee, or if your location offers a range of styles, e.g. Americano, Latte, Espresso, Cappuccino, Latte Macchiato, Caffe Mocha, find which type of coffee your customer requires. For further comprehensive information on personalising your coffee offering see the *Drinks Handbook*.

2 It's important to ask each customer how much sugar they want, when pouring out the coffee at the table, i.e. from a coffee pot.

3 Offer milk, or cream separately, as appropriate.

4 Always serve coffee in very warm cups. The ideal service temperature for milk is 68°C

5 Serve the coffee from the right hand side of each customer. Ideal service temperature for coffee is 82°C

6 Ensure that the coffee has a good flavour, aroma, body and colour with the milk, not grey.

7 When serving coffee, offer customers a choice of alcohol or liqueurs. Place the appropriate glasses, i.e. Cognac or liqueur glass to the right of the customer (see also *scalding* below).

Tea service

Pre-heat teapots and cups with hot boiling water, which is discarded prior to service. Place the teapot to the right (handle pointing inwards) of the guest on an under plate with a tea strainer and a small napkin. If tea bags are used (omit the strainer) and ensure that the tea bag string and label clearly identifies the tea type.

Brewing China tea

This involves getting the amount of tea, the water temperature and the steeping time just right. Generally, a light, airy tea such as white tea requires two heaping teaspoons for an 8-ounce cup. For stronger, more densely packed black teas, use a level teaspoon. White and many green teas should be brewed well below the boiling point, 70-80°C. The stronger and darker the tea, the closer to the boiling point the water should be. Lighter teas steep longer (3 to 5 minutes) than black teas (2 to 3 minutes). Lighter teas may also keep their flavour through multiple steepings. Black teas lose their flavour and much of their caffeine after one or two steepings, although the taste of Pu-erh (a fermented dark tea from China) can last for several steepings.

Brewing other teas

Indian or Ceylon Blend: usually made in either china or metal teapots. Both are offered with milk or sugar.

Russian or Lemon tea: Made similar to China tea, served in heat resistant glasses which stand in a silver holder, with a slice of lemon.

Iced tea: made strong, sometimes strained and always chilled. Served in a tumbler glass on a side plate with a teaspoon and lemon slice.

Speciality teas

Assam: rich full and malty flavoured tea, suitable for breakfast, served with milk.

Darjeeling: the Champagne of teas, delicate with a light grape flavour, served in the afternoon or evening with lemon or milk.

Earl Grey: blend of Darjeeling and China tea, flavoured with oil of Bergamot. Served with lemon or milk.

Jasmine: green (un-oxidised) tea, which is dried with jasmine blossom and produces a tea with a fragrant and scented flavour.

Kenya: consistent and refreshing tea, served with milk.

Lapsang Souchong: a smoky, pungent and perfumed tea, delicate to the palate, which may be said to be an acquired taste. Served with lemon.

Sri Lanka: pale golden tea, good flavour. The Ceylon blend is still used as a trade name. Served with lemon or milk.

Tisanes: Tisanes are fruit flavoured teas and herbal infusions, which are often used for medicinal purposes.

Hot chocolate service

Drinking chocolate is very popular and may come sweetened or non-sweetened and as a powder or soluble granules. It may be mixed with hot water or hot milk. Whipped cream, from a whipped cream dispenser, marshmallows or a sprinkling of powdered chocolate may be added upon request. Hot chocolate is most often served individually in special (heat resistant) glasses that fit into a special holder with a handle. It can also be served in a mug. Hot chocolate may also be presented in a pot or jug for the customer to pour into a tea cup. Usually white sugar and sweeteners are also offered. For details of hot chocolate service see Section 9.10 of *The Drinks Handbook*.

Distilled spirits and liqueurs service

These unique drinks represent the tastes, environments and customs of the whole world. Their irresistible appeal offer delightful sensations as aperitifs, disgestifs, within long drinks with ice and fresh lemon or lime and carbonated beverages or straight up. Although at times these drinks can be quite strong, their gustative qualities are ideal within the food and beverage experience. Adopting modern service techniques for these drinks can help to intensify and enhance the enjoyment of these drinks for your customers.

Modern service styles for spirits and liqueurs

Floating liqueurs (pousse café, layered shooters): Start with a single or double shot glass (ensure that the glass is not wet or hot) and always pour the heaviest liqueur first then by specific gravity weights float the next least heaviest liqueur and so on, do this by tilting the glass slightly inserting a teaspoon bottom side up and pour the liqueurs or spirits over the rounded surface. The best ingredients listed should be used, as substitutes never have the same effect.

For the best results, allow at least five units difference in specific gravity between each liqueur or syrup.

4

Flambé: Flaming a spirit should be done carefully. Ignite a long match and hold it close to the surface of the spirit. Don't let the spirit flame too long. Flambé garnishing on cocktails is also very popular. Cut a slice of lime, lemon or orange peel, hold it between your thumb and forefinger and squeeze close to the flame over the top of the cocktail. This procedure will release flammable citrus oils and a brilliant burst of flame will flare up.

Frozen drinks: Liquor and flavored liquids are mixed in a blender with ice. Many frozen drinks are garnished elaborately and served in fancy long drink glasses.

Frosting (rimming) glasses: You can use superfine sugar, fine salt, or dry unsweetened coconut to decorate the rim of a glass. Rub the rim with a little lemon or lime juice and then dip the glass upside down into a rimming tray of your chosen decoration.

Frappé: One or two measures of liqueur poured over crushed ice in double cocktail or old fashioned glass.

Free pour: Pouring spirits by eye (no measures involved). There's knack to this, which must be practiced.

Chilled spirits: When freezing spirits, only use those above 40% alcohol by volume, which will remain fluid. Spirits below 40% ABV will take on a temporary oily weightiness which may or may not be appealing to your customers.

Mist: One or two measures of spirit served over a shaved ice filled glass.

Martinis: Martinis are short, low ball cocktails made by mixing flavoured liquids and spirits with ice, then straining and pouring the liquid into martini glasses. From straight vodka martinis to elaborate cosmopolitans, appletinis and fresh fruit daiquiris, martinis are still rising in popularity.

On the rocks: One or two measures of spirit poured over cubed ice into an old fashioned glass.

Highballs: Highballs are made with one or more shots of liquor poured over ice, then mixed with a liquid for flavoring and dilution. Some of the most familiar highballs are the rum and cola, the gin and tonic, and the vodka and orange juice.

Scalding: Preheating a Cognac or heat resistant glass with warm water prior to pouring the Cognac, this practice helps release the unique qualities of the beverage.

Straight up, neat: One or two measures of spirit poured into an old fashioned or small glass. It is traditional to offer ice or water on the side.

Shots: Shots can be either the most simple drink ever poured or an elaborate concoction, chilled, layered or shaken, but all shots have one thing in common: they are served in a shot glass. Shots are served in either single (1 1/2 ounces) or double shots, but never contain ice. Whether the customer sips the shot or gulps it down in one is up to them. Distilled spirits, liqueurs and chilled shots are very popular.

For further and more comprehensive information in relation to individual distilled spirits, beers, liqueurs, cocktails, tea and coffee, soft drinks and wine recommendations, preparation and service procedures please refer to the sister publication, *Principles and Practices of Bar and Beverage Management: Drinks Handbook*.

4.2   Responsible service of alcohol

In the bar business, management and staff have the task of serving and dealing with all types of people from all walks of life and status of society. Whilst in the main this is an enjoyable and rewarding part of the job, there are many occasions when they have to deal with people who may well have for various reasons consumed too much alcohol. This situation requires considerable patience, tact, firmness and above all experience. Alcohol awareness and responsible service can ultimately lead to informed and wise decision making by all staff.

4.3   Beverage service and the law

The laws relating to the provision of alcohol differ from country to country and sometimes even region, state or village. The bartender may be held responsible for injury to others that is caused by an intoxicated customer who has been served unlawfully. It is therefore crucial that the bar owner (license holder), management and staff members develop ways to monitor the service of alcohol. It is important that you learn which laws which apply to your country or area.

Once someone has consumed alcohol to a level that they are showing signs of drunkenness, their normal judgment is impaired. Therefore, it is up to the bartender, not the customer, to decide whether they should be served or not. Failure to act responsibly in the service of alcohol can result in accidents or even death. If negligence is proven against the bar or bartender, the court may allow substantial damages to cover loss, medical fees, loss of income, pain and suffering. If more than one party is involved, the compensation will be assessed as to what degree each member of the party has contributed towards the loss, and the damages will be allocated accordingly. Responsible alcohol service practices can also lead to better business practices, which contribute to improving the atmosphere of the bar, and ultimately to achieving greater profits.

In summary, bar owners should improve their responsible service of alcohol practices and training to:

- Maintain a good reputation
- Increase customer satisfaction
- Decrease damage done to the bar
- Avoid potential legal cases
- Reduce police attendance
- Improve morale, boosting productivity and reducing staff turnover.

4

4.4   Alcohol's role in modern society

Did you know, the Swiss Alchemist Paracelsus (1493-1541) was the first person to use the word 'alcohol'?

All ancient cultures had their own form of alcohol, and it played its own role in each society, be it religious or cultural. Enjoying alcoholic beverages has been a part of many societies over many centuries. In most countries, as alcohol consumption continues to grow, trends in the brand and types of alcohol consumed change. In many, the production and sale of alcohol is a very important part of the economy, as the taxes and government levies collected can be substantial. The attitude of governments towards alcohol can vary from country to country. In some cultures, the consumption of alcohol is closely associated with many social activities, such as holidays, dining out, celebrations and business.

It provides for most consumers a great deal of pleasure and causes little or no harm, however there is a small minority (small in percentage terms but large in number) with problems directly linked to their drinking habits. In some cases, drinking guidelines are incorporated into general nutritional guidelines or into a national drug strategy. In other instances, they stand alone as guidelines on alcohol consumption. Information included in guidelines offers recommendations on low risk drinking levels for men and women, but may also define a standard drink or unit and offer advice to particular populations deemed to be at increased risk for harm. Alcohol is considered to be society's most prevalent and accepted legal recreational drug; it is generally accepted as a component of our daily life.

For further information on world consumption, laws, advertising regulations please refer to the World Health Organization (WHO) Global Status Report, Alcohol Policy reports. All the major World drinks companies have joined together to form Social Aspects organizations to promote sensible and responsible drinking and to combat abuse. Other groups include the International Center for Alcohol Policy (ICAP) and the Center for information on Beverage Alcohol (CBA).

4.5   Recommended safe levels of consumption

Recent research studies indicate that customers and individuals are drinking no more than their parents were drinking 15 years ago but the frequency, strength of drinks, and number of drinks consumed per session has increased. These irrational drinking patterns have created a binge drinking culture and large numbers of individuals consuming at home prior to arrival at a bar. This practice is commonly referred to as prinks or pre-drink drinks.

Scale units of alcohol for standard drinks

The agreed convention for standardising drinks is based on grams of absolute ethanol. This means that a 'standard' drink will always contain a given amount of absolute ethanol, regardless of whether it is beer, wine or distilled spirits. Having a standard enables bartenders and consumers to be able to assess the risk levels for consumption. However, different countries have a different standard drink, ranging from 8g to 13g and certain countries may not have such a thing as a 'standard drink'.

Do not assume therefore that each drink, be it a pre-packaged bottle of beer, a standard glass of wine or a measured spirit, to be a standard drink. Recommendations on drinking levels considered 'minimum risk' for men and women cover a range of values as daily limits, or as weekly recommendations. In general, values given for men are higher than for women. You can always calculate how many units of alcohol are in a drink, if you know the amount of drink in millilitres (ml) and its strength in alcohol by volume (abv). Both are usually stated somewhere on the label or in the packaging, with abv usually expressed as a percentage.

To calculate the units of alcohol in a drink, use the formula:

Alcohol percentage by volume × litres = units of alcohol

1 unit of alcohol is equivalent to 10 ml (approximately 8 grams of ethanol)

Examples:

Cider (strength: 5% abv) × (1 bottle: 0.33L) = 1.7 units

Lager (strength: 4 % abv) × (1 pint: 0.568L) = 2.3 units

Alcohol, acute and long term effects

- **1-2 units daily:** Acute effects: a mild alteration of feelings and a slight intensification of moods. At two units, possible bad driving habits could be slightly more pronounced. Long-term effects: regular daily consumption reduces levels of LDL (bad), cholesterol in the blood, cutting the risk of heart disease.

- **3-4 units daily:** Acute effects: You may become more cheerful; feel warm, relaxed or slightly sedated. Emotions and behavior are exaggerated and you take slightly longer to react. Long term effects: no significant risks to health.

- **5-8 units daily**: Acute effects: Euphoria feeling, impairment of mental abilities, dangerous to drive. Long term effects: you're on the slippery slope.

- **9-14 units daily:** Acute effects: Loss of self-control, slurred speech, and double vision is common. Long-term effects: Some risk of breast cancer and liver cirrhosis can be expected.

Official guidelines on alcohol consumption are generally produced by government bodies, such as the Ministry of Health or other departments responsible for alcohol issues. Find out what the applicable laws are in your country by contacting your local government department dealing with trading standards or licensing issues.

The full recommendations on the (upper) drinking levels for most countries are also published by the Centre for Alcohol Policies (ICAP).

4

4.6   The body and alcohol

Alcohol breakdown all depends on the availability of enzymes in your body to break down the alcohol. These enzymes help to turn the ethanol to acetaldehyde, which is then converted into acetic acids. People of Asian origin tend to get flushed after 1-2 drinks because they lack this crucial enzyme. Alcohol is distributed rapidly to the various tissues of the body. It enters the body water but very little alcohol will enter the fat area. The effect and speed of this distribution differs with the sexes.

For men, because of their higher body fluid volume weight (usually 60-80% of body weight) this distribution is usually slower. For women, because of their lower body fluid weight (usually 50-70%) this distribution is usually faster. Women have fewer enzymes in the liver and gut wall to break down alcohol before it enters their bloodstream. Therefore women alcoholics do more damage to their bodies than men. Liver disease, brain damage and mental defects like memory loss and reduced ability to solve problems start earlier for them.

Removal of alcohol

Alcohol is predominately removed from the body by metabolism in the liver cells. The detailed removal is: skin (sweat) 2–6%, lungs (breath) 2–4%, liver 90%, kidneys (urine) 2–4%. The elimination rate is 5–9g e/h per hour, i.e. approximately one unit of alcohol per hour. Vomiting, perspiring, hyperventilating, consuming black coffee or urinating have no effect on the removal on the amount of alcohol in the blood, and have little effect on the degree of intoxication. So you must be extra careful the morning after, for example if you operating machinery or driving.

It is important to note that, the blood alcohol concentration (BAC) increases when the body absorbs alcohol faster than when it can eliminate it. The body can only eliminate about one dose of alcohol per hour, so drinking several drinks in that time will increase your BAC.

BAC levels and tolerance to alcohol

Humans develop tolerance when their brains adapt to compensate for the disruption caused by alcohol in both their behavior and their bodily functions. There are two main types of tolerance – chronic and acute.

Chronic tolerance develops over a long drinking span. Chronic heavy consumers show few obvious signs of intoxication even at high blood alcohol concentrations. It has been found, for example, that the ability of heavy consumers to handle normal situations was only reduced by about 1%. Moderate drinkers, on the other hand, were five times more affected when drinking the same amount of alcohol. Sometimes, in moderate drinkers, the effect is incapacitating or can be fatal. Experience also suggests that tolerance to alcohol is retained for long periods. For instance, alcoholics who have been abstaining for months can return to very high levels of tolerance in a much shorter time than non-alcoholic subjects.

Acute tolerance can happen within a single drinking session. Alcohol-induced impairment is greater when measured soon after beginning alcohol consumption than when measured later in the drinking session, even if the BAC is the same at both times. A person with acute tolerance does experience intoxication after alcohol consumption, but may not exhibit all the effects of alcohol consumption. This may prompt the drinker to consume more alcohol. Acute tolerance to alcohol has important implications for the patron who will drive. For instance, when the BAC is rising, the driver may well feel sufficiently intoxicated to refrain from driving. As the BAC passes its peak and starts to decline, the degree of intoxication may appear (and, in fact, be) much less and self inhibitions about driving may disappear. Blood alcohol concentration is measured as milligrams of alcohol per 100 milliliters of blood. Large people, who have greater blood supplies, can drink more alcohol than small people and yet have the same blood alcohol level. Listed below is a guide on the general effects of alcohol at different BAC levels. Because alcohol affects different people in different ways it should be remembered that this is only a rough guide.

■ BAC 40: you begin to feel relaxed, there is an increased chance of an accident

■ BAC 60:   you are cheerful, you have poorer judgment and decisions may be affected

■ BAC 80:   you have a feeling of warmth and well being, there will be some loss of inhibitions and self control. Slow reaction time, driving ability definitely worse

■ BAC 120: you are likely to become more talkative, excited and emotional, you are inhibited and may act on impulse

■ BAC 150: you are silly and probably confused, speech is slurred, may be aggressive

■ BAC 200: drunk, staggering, double vision, loss of memory

■ BAC 300: possibly unconscious

- BAC 400: unconsciousness likely, death not unknown
- BAC 500: death possible
- BAC 800: death probable.

4.7 Management responsibilities in beverage staff training

Management must clearly state their expectation of staff and give them the authority to make decisions. Management must consider how to support the decisions made by their staff. This can be achieved by having a written house policy, staff meetings, an incident log and reviewing particular incidents. Staffs need to know they have the backing of management. With this support, staff will be more comfortable with the strategy of responsible service of alcohol.

4

Consider safe transport options

- Staff offering to call a friend or family member of a customer, or to call a taxi;
- Making a phone available and the phone numbers of taxi companies;
- Offering to include the cost of mini-buses as part of the costs of a function and starting a designated driver programme

Avoiding conflict and violence

- Removal of glasses, containers and litter regularly
- Adequate numbers of licensed crowd controllers (hosts)
- Adequate toilet facilities
- Video camera surveillance in large bars and clubs
- A good ratio between the men and women attending the premises
- Non-aggressive staff monitoring the door – these staff should vet underage persons
- Ready availability of attractive, keenly priced food, low alcohol and non-alcoholic drinks
- Well trained staff, excellent customer service, variety of spaces and activities
- Adequate seating arrangements

4.8   Preventing guest intoxication and identifying over-consumption

Strategies to prevent guest intoxication

Stepping in to stop someone from becoming intoxicated stems from a concern for their safety and the safety of others. The following actions should be taken by staff to avoid guest intoxication:

- First and foremost, notify management of potential problems (i.e. guests drinking fast).
- Keep track of how many drinks are being consumed and in what time frame.
- Engage your guests in conversation; ask questions that would be a good test of mental alertness (i.e. recent news, sports events).
- Suggest some food (especially high protein food, e.g. fried cheese, potato skins).
- Promote healthy non and low alcoholic drinks/events. Attractive signage and price incentives are useful.
- Bar staff can influence a customer's decision regarding drinks so try to avoid unacceptable serving practices.

Techniques for identifying guest intoxication

Some people are very clever at hiding intoxication, so how do we identify over-consumption? Listed below are some of the signs to help you in your decision making process. These signs must not considered in isolation to each other because rash decisions can also cause you major problems – a person with disability might display some of the signs below.

- A noticeable change in your customer's behavior , becoming loud (heightened voice volume), erratic, entertaining, animated, boisterous, using bad language, annoying customers, slurred speech, argumentative, mean, obnoxious, over friendly to strangers – wants to converse or buy them a drink, sudden quietness.
- A lack of judgment, careless with their money, making silly, irrational or repeated statements, boasts about their financial situation, 'conquests', physical or mental strength, drinking faster, complaining about drink prices.
- Clumsiness, losing muscular control, becoming clumsy, spilling drinks and difficulty in picking up change.
- Loss of co-ordination, swaying and staggering, difficulty in walking straight, bumping into furniture.
- Decreased alertness, becoming drowsy (heavy eyelids), delays in responding to questions and paying attention, hearing, concentration and focus 'glazed eyes', or becomes detached, brooding.
- The smell of alcohol (an important indication).

Code of Practice for the Responsible Naming, Packaging and Promotion of Alcoholic Drinks

First introduced in April 1996 to regulate alcohol marketing. It applies to all alcohol marketing in the UK which is not subject to regulation through the ASA or Ofcom. Its sole purpose is to ensure that alcohol is marketed in a socially responsible way and only to adults. The Code is recognised as a gold standard in effective self-regulation at global, EU and UK levels. For further information on codes of practice see The Portman Group 'Marketing Alcohol Responsibly' (www.portmangroup.org.uk).

Drink Aware (UK)

Drink Aware works at increasing awareness and understanding of the role of alcohol in UK society, enabling individuals to make informed choices about their drinking in innovative ways to challenge the national drinking culture to help reduce alcohol misuse and minimise alcohol-related harm. (www.drinkaware. co.uk). You should check your own local government agency or relevant trade bodies 'Code of Practice' and ensure that you and your staff members are familiar with your responsibilities in your own market.

4.9   Delaying or suspending service

Bartenders must be empowered to delay, suspend or stop service. When a customer has reached their maximum number of drinks, service can be delayed; if the customer showing signs of intoxication, service of alcohol may be stopped for the duration of the evening. This decision can be easily determined by a customer's actions.

- Alert management of potential problems before any decisions are made. If a problem arises, let security or management handle it. Be prepared to call the police if necessary.

- Explain the establishment policy and use a non-judgmental approach and statements (i.e. 'I'm sorry, but if I served you another drink I'd lose my job', or 'I've served you all that I can') because you want them to return again soon.

- Do not judge or appear to judge by using emotionally charged words such as 'drunk', 'high', or 'you've had too much'.

- Be assertive and polite in dealing with the guest and don't change your mind.

- Be friendly, kind and considerate, yet firm. Do not debate your decision. Make the statement and walk away. It's hard for the customer to argue if you're not there.

- Always communicate that the policies are there for the guest's benefit and that you are personally concerned for the guest's well being. "I'm sorry, but it's against the law for me to serve you any more alcohol."

- Try to keep the guest from leaving, especially if they are driving. Instead, suggest an alternative form of transportation for the customer (i.e. ask his friends to drive them home; offer to call a cab; offer to call a friend or family member or try to enlist the help of a companion of the guest, in seeing to it that they get home safely).

- Make sure that the patron has their personal belongings.

Remember serving alcohol to a person who is already intoxicated is an offence in most countries. Once someone has consumed alcohol to a level that they are showing signs of drunkenness, their normal judgment is impaired. Therefore, it is up to the server, not the customer, to decide whether they should be served or not.

Refusal of service technique (T.A.K.E C.A.R.E)

If you believe that the guest is intoxicated, you are morally and legally bound to take appropriate action, but you must always take care of your personal security and the security of your other customers.

- **Tell them early.** Have a quiet discrete word or use other members of a group to warm the offending person.

- **Avoid put-downs.** Don't be judgmental, or say, "you're drunk", or scold the customer, or appear to be blaming them.

- **Keep yourself calm.** Your tone of voice is very important. You need to be firm without being aggressive. Do not raise your voice. Behavior breeds behavior. You can calm them down if you remain calm yourself.

- **Ever courteous.** Respect breeds respect. You might say, "I'm sorry, if I served you another drink I'd be breaking the law"; or "I'd lose my job"; or "I'm concerned about your safety".

- **Clarify your refusal.** Explain why service is being refused, and focus on the behavior, not the individual. Explain that they are welcome back tomorrow if they behave.

- **Offer alternatives.** Offer to call a taxi, offer low or non-alcoholic drinks, allow them to save face in front of friends.

- **Report the incident.** Make all staff aware of what happened. Keep an incident logbook near the bar and write what has occurred. If the customer injures a third party, after leaving the premises ,the record will be important.

- **Echo.** If the customer is a regular, staff can quietly reinforce the message when they return.

Some other good tips are: never touch the customer, speak to them away from others (the audience) – this is useful as a face-saving measure for the customer – and don't be afraid to involve the management.

(Murphy, 2002)

Responsible service of alcohol: role-play scenarios

Scenario 1

It's 9.45 p.m. when Liam (construction worker with blood shot eyes) orders a drink. What information could you supply to the bar staff to assist them with their decision?

Scenario 2

It's lunchtime, when Mary orders a large gin and tonic from her table, the waiter informs the bartender that this is the customer's second drink in 20 minutes, the waiter has noticed that this customer is exhibiting coordination problems (difficulty picking up change, swaying while returning from the ladies toilets). What information could you supply to the bartender and waiter to assist them with their decision?

Scenario 3

It's early morning, when a small group of guys and girls arrive at the bar to order drinks. The bartender observes that the group are exhibiting different conditions of behaviour (laughing, joking, loud, quite, singing and sleepy). What information could you supply to the bar staff to assist them with their decision?

Scenario 4

A small group of six young business people arrive at the bar and request service of a bottle of tequila and 6 shot glasses, what information could you supply to the bartender to assist him with the decision to be made?

4.10 The hangover

Hangover symptoms are caused by the combined effects of the congeners and the products of the breakdown of alcohol. Someone with a hangover will be suffering the following conditions:

- Dehydration: although the drinker has taken in more fluids, they've expelling them more quickly, altering the water balance in the cells and tissues. This is the major cause of hangover headache.

- Low blood sugar

- Irritation of the stomach lining

- A degree of poisoning: congeners (impurities which give particular taste) are present in alcoholic drinks. Methanol, a type of alcohol found as a congener, is not broken down by most people's bodies until the morning after. It's then that the unpleasant toxins responsible for many hangover symptoms are produced.

- Vessels relax (blood shot eyes): alcohol relaxes blood vessels, which then expand to let more blood through, causing telltale bloodshot eyes.

- Nervous system sensitivity: the body combats the sedative effects of alcohol by making the nervous system more sensitive - hence difficulty in sleeping, sensitivity to lights and noise.

- Brain cell damage: for example, one single measure of whiskey destroys 20,000 brain cells, which will never be replaced.

Conclusion

Alcoholic and non-alcoholic beverages are usually present everywhere in our socializing, entertaining and workplace environments; they enliven our moment of relaxation and generally help to promote lively cultural engagements and a healthy disposition when consumed in moderation and with care. Your food and beverage staff must always seek to provide high standards when serving alcoholic and non-alcoholic beverages at the bar or dining table. Unfortunately abuse or over-consumption of alcohol can bring harmful consequences. Responsible service strategies for managing alcohol consumption need to be adopted by all in-house staff. Management should promote low alcohol and non-alcoholic drinks, support bartenders when refusing service and allocate proper access and time for RSA staff training. The house policy on alcohol should be displayed in a good vantage point within the premises. We can all make the differences that count in making our jobs more enjoyable and our bars safer and socially enhanced.

5 Serving Food

Aims and learning outcomes

This chapter introduces the key elements for creating good food experiences in the bar or restaurant area, and food service procedures. On completion the learner should be able to:

- Respond to consumer decision making in relation to the food experience.
- Identify the significant factors involved in the configuration, presentation and description of food menus, menu items and accompaniments.
- Demonstrate a knowledge of food costing and the benefits of using standardized recipes.
- Explain the importance of customer satisfaction.
- Apply cover settings, service sequences, plate and service tray carrying and clearing techniques to suit the menu type offered.

5.1 Introduction

The bar and catering industry has changed out of all recognition in recent times. Large numbers of consumers are choosing a bar for their food experience in the morning, lunchtime, evening and weekend periods. Creating a good food experience in a bar can be very challenging because of the high emotional value which consumers attribute to food. This experience contains both tangible and intangible elements that are not always easy to define. We can however state that the food experience definitely starts with the feelings of the customer, individually or in group, from the moment they arrive outside your establishment until they leave.

Service includes an entire series of procedures that must be performed before the customers arrive and after they have left the premises. These procedures, and the staff, are the crucial link between the establishment's products and services and its customers. The technical knowledge, product knowledge, interpersonal and specialized skills involved in food and beverage service procedures are crucial to achieving customer satisfaction and maintaining a sustainable business.

5.2 Food service in bars

Food is now a crucial component of the bar business and the majority of bars are offering a widening choice in their food products. These increases in food sales in bars have brought about a demand for quality meals and snacks, which are professionally configured, prepared and served with attractive prices. Consumers choose to have their food experience in bars for a number of reasons which include:

- **Social**: the most common reason, social occasions can include events like birthdays, special anniversaries, festive occasions. Bars can offer different styles of dining, pre theatre, cabaret menus, and Sunday specials.

- **Business**: the image and expectation of the bar's food offerings depends on level of business being conducted for business lunches, evening dinners, early working breakfasts and teas. The breakfast period is often a sadly neglected area of the food offering in most bars.

- **Convenience, time, location and access**: the bar's location is crucial, as will be its speed of service for food products, if it is competing for customers with pizzeria, fast food restaurants, take aways, or order and delivery services. Access issues car parks, public transport, passing trade, and good foot flow.

- **Atmosphere and service**: the atmosphere, cleanliness, hygiene and social skills of staff members can be an important factor for certain groups of customers. If a bar's prices are considered dear, the customers will expect a high level of service, which incorporates additional services.

- **Price and perceived value for money**: if customers consider that a bar's food is cheaper, tastier and of great quality, then they are less likely to want to cook for themselves regularly.

- **The menu:** a bar's menus should be adventurous and interesting, creating different food experiences, e.g. tasting menus, food and beer or wine pairings. It should include healthy choices, vegetarian and a good variety of ethnic choices, to cover recent emerging trends in consumer tastes.

- **Quality of the food and beverages:** freshly prepared and homemade have great appeal, but consistency in quality is crucial.

- **Sensory experiences:** there should be a range of tastes, textures, aromas and colours offered by a food dish or drink.

- **Presentation and recommendation of the food and beverages**: the visual presentation and knowledgeable recommendations in relation to menu choices are significant in increasing the appeal.

- **Expectation and identification**: Some customers need to be able to identify and associate themselves with a particular bar and restaurant for a particular meal occasion. They may not always identify with the same restaurant, as their needs and expectations may vary from one food experience to the next. These alternating needs of customers should be identified by a bar owner and catered for appropriately.

- **Interior and exterior design**: A successful bar will have a design that enhances the food experience and creates the environment that will encourage customers to return.

5.3   Food menus

Menu configuration

The menu is the single most important element of your food offering. Its primary goal is to encourage your customers to purchase your food. It is the first contact that your customers have with your food, it is a major sales tool for your business, and it must therefore receive careful consideration. The food choices which you make for your menu are crucial, as they must deliver your customers' expectations and needs at a fair and reasonable price.

Before you plan and print your bar's food menu, you must take into account your marketplace. Consider this in relation to its location (rural, urban, small village), the local clientele (students, mixed, business type, family orientated), the foot flow and access by transport, and trading hours of other local businesses. The size and atmosphere of your dining areas, and the storage and preparation areas for your products must also be considered. Your staff members' skills and knowledge, your furnishings and your ability to secure good quality products for sale will also form a significant part of your menu's configuration.

Menu design

- Food groupings should be clearly separate and the overall menu design should be pleasing
- The food groupings should reflect the bar's character (e.g. Tex Mex, traditional, old world charm, rustic)
- Cold and warm dishes should be presented separately
- Light dishes should be proposed first, followed by the more substantial items on the menu.

Menu engineering: the food and profit matrix

In general, the menu should be designed to encourage sales. Kasavana & Smith (1982) argue that menu engineering concepts can help you to use a scientific approach for your food products based on customer demand, sales mix, and their contribution to the bar business. We must consider the way items appear on our menus and their relevant prices.

The positioning of items on a menu can increase their popularity. Guests' eyes usually move first to the upper centre of the menu space. Here is where specialties and high profit items should be listed.

As you try to find ways to increase profits from your food offering in the bar the easiest way to do that is to maximize the profits from your existing customers. In other words if you have the exact same number of people eat in your premises in a given sales period (for example a year, 6 months or 3 months), you still have the opportunity to achieve higher profits by encouraging your guests to order more profitable items. Using these tools listed below will help allow you, as a bar owner, to take the emotion out of decisions you or your management team make pertaining to your menu and allow you to base those decisions on data and facts.

Each item of your food menu will fall into one of four distinct categories.

Category 1: Gold

These are premier items of the menu that have a high gross profit and are very popular. The more you can influence the consumer towards these items, the more profitable your operation will be. Strategies to enhance their profit potential include:

- Give these items the best placement on your menu. Customers tend to order items which stand out. Make sure your gold items present themselves well.

- Use these items in sales promotions and contests.

- Don't change the price too drastically, but test for price elasticity. Be proud of gold items. If the customer is willing to pay more without affecting your total demand, logic says, increase the price but be careful.

- Don't change the presentation or recipe. Special attention should be given to these items to ensure they are of the highest quality. Your customers like it the way it is.

- Encourage your staff to suggest these items to your customers.

- Highlight these on your menu as house favourites or signature dishes.

Category 2: Silver

These items trudge along doing a great deal of work (sales) while actually doing very little towards making profits. They reflect good volume sales, but generate little profit compared to the gold items. A silver item is a good candidate for stock control. Strategies to enhance their profit potential include:

- Don't offer them as a special. If a silver item does not exceed the average contribution margin, why offer it as a special? Instead, turn the demand to high profit items, the gold and bronze dishes.

- Don't raise the price on these items above what the local market can bear, but test for price elasticity. Will raising the price significantly reduce the demand?

- Reduce portion sizes slightly, which will reduce food cost, and in turn help to increase the contribution margin. This can sometimes turn silver into gold.

- Look at alternative products and ingredients to decrease the food cost without compromising the quality. Remember that silvers sell well, so your customers like the item.

- Hide these items on your menu, so it is easier for the customer to be drawn to more profitable items.

Category 3: Bronze

These are the most misunderstood items on the menu. They manage to make above average contribution margins, but are weak in demand. The issues that arise are twofold: why aren't they selling well and how can we increase demand without sacrificing the high profitability? Strategies to increase your profit on these dishes include:

- Get staff and customer input on the menu item. It might not sell well because it doesn't taste good or fit the market.
- If you determine that the item is a good one, highlight it on your menu to increase sales and use it in sales promotions and contests.
- Offer as daily specials – a quick and easy way to attract consumer attention and increase demand is to offer an item as a special.
- Give the item high menu visibility, make it stand out on the menu.
- Reduce the price. The item may be overpriced, so test for price elasticity.
- Drop from the menu, especially if it has a poor shelf life, or it is difficult to prepare.

Category 4: DQ (DisQualified)

DQs are low in popularity and low in contribution margin. Basically they are difficult to sell and when you do they are not all that profitable. Strategies for these dishes include:

- Get staff and customer feedback on the menu item to find out why it doesn't sell well
- Rename and describe to make more attractive. A catchy name and description may be all it takes to increase demand and turn a DQ into a silver or gold.
- Consider removing these items completely since they do not positively contribute to the profit or popularity of your business. By dropping them you can free space, reduce clutter and inventory, and concentrate on more profitable items.

The need for analysis

Only when you have all this information can you accurately determine which items should remain on your menu, and make an informed decision about how and where each item should be placed on the menu to have the maximum impact on your profitability. Conducting a menu analysis is not an easy task, but it is a necessary one that should be performed monthly. However, all the analysis in the world is of no use unless you act upon the information and apply it to your menu. Every month you fail to change your menu loses more profit!

Menu presentation criteria

- Menus must be attractive, inviting customers to read. They should be clean and neat, without handwritten corrections, and with durable covers.
- Menu items should be correctly spelled. Whenever appropriate, the menu should be written in different languages.
- Oversized menus annoy the guests and cause problems for the premises.
- If the menu is short, the size of the type should be large. Avoid small type and too many fonts or styles – you do not want it to look like a phone book!
- Specialities and signature dishes should be highlighted, with bold or colourful print or coloured pointers.
- Daily specials and meals that are part of the regular menu should be identified and easily exchangeable.
- Make sure your descriptions of the dishes are appealing.
- Prices directly next to or under the text are most visible. Make sure they are competitive and that you adopt suitable pricing strategies for your food options.
- Numbering dishes makes ordering and tabulation easier. Numbering is essential when an electronic data system is used.
- The nutritional and calorific values of low-calorie dishes should be stated and the menu should also reflect trends in eating habits and dietary requirements.
- If a dish may take more time to prepare, this should be noted on the menu.
- Large meat dishes, to be served to more than one person, should list the minimum number to be served.
- Be sure that the menu language is in keeping with the style of the bar. Try to keep your customers comfortable when they are making their menu selections.
- Variety and freshness are crucial, keep a healthy sales mix of products to suit your various customers.
- Liven up your menu regularly. Customers get bored, and you must introduce new options to keep the menu fresh and vibrant.
- One menu should be provided for each guest

Types of foodservice operations in pubs

Pubs and bar establishments offer numerous types of food experiences which range from hot and cold snacks to fine dining. The type of food your pub or bar should offer as we discussed earlier will be based on the needs of your customers. So remember to ensure that you know what your customers want, whom they are likely to have their dining experience with, the time period they have allocated, their budget, the occasion and of course their tastes and preferences. The answers to these considerations will help you to plan the most suitable type of foodservice operation for your pub and food menus which focus on satisfying your customers' needs.

Elliott (2006) highlights some examples of pub food operations which range from cold back bar catering (cold sandwiches) to premium dining (upmarket restaurant).

Style of food operation	Food offered
Cold back bar catering	Cold sandwiches.
Hot back bar catering	Pies, ready prepared burgers, wraps and hot sandwiches.
Simple catering	Hot sandwiches, wraps, burgers, chips, soup, tapas.
'Pub grub'	Traditional, value for money meals, hearty, rustic.
Family dining	Value-for-money menu attracting families (buffet, children's menus)
Premium dining	Upmarket restaurant quality food (A la carte, Table d'hote menus)

adapted from (Eliott, 2006)

Consider carefully the type of foodservice operations you decide to adopt, because each style will require specific foodservice equipment, facilities and the appropriate skilled staff members.

Describing food menu items

In the majority of countries, to mislead consumers with false descriptions of food especially on menus, internal or external advertising boards or electronic signage, can carry a fine, caution and possible other sanctions. You must therefore be careful with descriptions like 'fresh' or 'homemade', or mentions of weights or of suitability for food intolerances, e.g. vegetarians. Misleading descriptions have the ability to do immense reputational damage, through bad publicity, and undermine your customers' confidence in a bar and its food.

5.4   Standardized recipes for food

Using standardized food recipes provides many benefits to bars engaged in food-service operations. These benefits include:

Consistent food quality: the use of standardized recipes ensures that menu items will be consistent in quality each time they are prepared and served.

Predictable yield: the planned number of servings will be produced by using standardized recipes. This can help to reduce the amount of leftover food if there has been overproduction, and will help to prevent shortages of servings on the line. A predictable yield is especially important when food is transported from a production kitchen to other serving areas.

Customer satisfaction: Well-developed food recipes, which are consistent in every detail of ingredient, quantity, preparation, and presentation, provide the consistency and quality which results in increased customer satisfaction.

Consistent nutrient content: Standardized recipes will ensure that nutritional values per serving are valid and consistent.

Food cost control: Standardized recipes provide consistent and accurate information for food cost control because the same ingredients and quantities of ingredients per serving are used each time the recipe is produced.

Efficient purchasing procedures: Purchasing of stocks is more efficient because the quantity of food needed for production is easily calculated from the information on each standardized recipe.

Inventory control: The use of standardized recipes provides predictable information on the quantity of food inventory that will be used each time the recipe is produced.

Labour cost control: Written standardized procedures in the recipe make efficient use of labour time and allow for planned scheduling of foodservice personnel for the work day. Training costs are reduced because new employees are provided with specific instructions for the preparation of each recipe.

Increased employee confidence: Employees feel more satisfied and confident in their jobs because standardized recipes eliminate guesswork, decrease the chances of producing poor food products, and prevent shortages of servings during meal service.

Reduced record keeping: A collection of standardized recipes for menu items will reduce the amount of information required on a daily food production record. Standardized recipes will include the ingredients and amounts of food used for a menu item. The food production record will only need to reference the recipe, number of planned servings, and leftover amounts.

5.5   Customer satisfaction

'to be hospitable is to care'

Customer satisfaction and the quality of food service

The distinction between customer satisfaction and quality of food service is a very important one. The level of customer satisfaction is the result of a customer's comparison of expected quality of the food service with the one they actually perceived. Customer satisfaction is a subjective concept, not only because of the perception filter but also because the expectation will vary from customer to customer. The golden rule for customer satisfaction is to never lose a customer. Dissatisfied customers tell their friends and family. Your business and staff members will face many challenges in food service, the majority of people are usually very emotional about their food and the opportunity for second chances is limited. It is crucial that you believe in your food offering and your staff members. The **BELIEVE** acronym is a useful business tool to assist you in this on-going work:

B. The **Boomerang** principle – make your business decisions on getting your customers back, taking the long term approach.

E. Lead by **Example**. The behaviour of the owner and managers is crucial, and should foster mutual respect amongst your staff and customers. Aim to instil a sense of what is right, ethically and morally.

L. Listen to the customers and staff. Organise customer and staff panels meetings to brainstorm new ideas and to obtain feedback.

I. Information. Use loyalty cards or other means to collect data, but be careful of how you collect and use this.

E. Elevate. Make heroes of your staff. Give them a sense of satisfaction – your staff should always want to go to work. How do you achieve this?

V. Value. Don't forget the business you are in. Remember to look after your existing customers, and don't spend too much time driving for more.

E. Enjoy. To succeed you must enjoy your success and share this success.

(Quinn, 2006)

Expectations

Customer expectations of the level of service they regard as satisfactory are rising. Many food service premises are looking closely at just what their customers want. This focus has placed increased demand on food service staff members to perform, not just in terms of productivity, but also in terms of customer satisfying behavior. The focus of attention in all successful food service premises is on individuals (hospitality staff members) and their behavior. Therefore from each staff member's point of view, the difference is you. If you want to work for successful food service premises and enjoy your job, you have to commit yourself to providing the highest levels of service in every aspect of your duties and responsibilities.

The hidden differences

The major hidden difference between people is their personalities; similarly the hidden difference many products and services is the employees who make, sell and serve them. Food service staff come in many shapes and sizes, but when they are supplying something to us only two categories count: those who are concerned with our satisfaction and those who are not. Food service staff who are concerned with customer satisfaction achieve superior results; they also derive more job satisfaction from what they do, which is good for them.

Seeing the customer's point of view

Imagine putting yourself in your customer's shoes. Remember your customers want to feel that they matter and that they will enjoy the experience of contact with you and your colleagues or associates. With this thought in mind use the box below to list all the things that could be done to satisfy them, especially the little things; seeing your customers points of view

Table 5.1: The customer's point of view

My customer's criteria: list all the things that your customers want from you.	Bad actions: list all the bad things that could be done to dissatisfy your customers	Good actions: list all the things especially the little ones, that could be done to satisfy your customers

(Murphy, 2010)

Customer complaints

No matter how hard we work, things can go occasionally wrong, for example the food gets burned, orders are forgotten or new staff members neglect to practice the skills and knowledge from their training. Irrespective of the type of complaint, the most important thing is to try and please the customer and send them home knowing that, yes there was a problem, but it is not typical of your bar. Let them know that you, the owner, or your staff members value their comments and their business. Remember how you handle customer complaints will determine if the customer comes back. Here are some tips to help you field your next complaint and send your customer home with a smile.

■ **Listen:** Listen to what the customer has to say. Even if you can't solve the problem immediately, you still need to listen. For example, perhaps a customer is displeased because of the waiting time for their meal.

■ **Body language, posture**: The way your staff members stand and look at a customer can speak more than words. Ensure that they maintain eye contact and don't cross their arms over their chest, if they are feeling defensive.

■ **Avoid the urge to roll your eyes**, if you are feeling exasperated. Instead, nod and smile, no matter how irritated you may feel. This shows you value their opinion and their business.

■ **Apologize**: Offer an apology, 'I understand that you are not happy about whatever the complaint was about, sir/madam, but we are working hard to sort this out immediately. We really appreciate your patience and co-operation; perhaps you would like to have a drink at the bar until your table is ready.' Demonstrate that you understand their frustration and are working diligently on a solution.

■ **Complimentary offer, compensation**: If a customer has problem that could have been prevented, such as an overcooked fish or an ignorant staff member, then the best route to take is to apologize and to offer them some sort of compensation. You might offer one or other of the following: a drink or a round of drinks, depending on the group size, free dessert or coffee, or a reduced price for the meal.

Occasionally you will have a truly angry customer (perhaps justified, perhaps not) who declares, 'I'm never coming back!' If that is the case, there probably isn't any compensation which you can offer to change their mind. Calmly assure the customer you understand their frustration, and offer an apology (again) and let them know if they change their mind you would love to see them again. By sending them off on a courteous note, there is a very good chance, once their anger has cooled, they will try your bar and restaurant again.

Table 5.2: Customer satisfaction and its measurement with food

Restaurant, bar service				
Category: This is the area covered i.e. (pub service) (restaurant service)				
Premises: (enter here the exact bar location)				
Date and time: (enter here the exact date and time of arrival)				
Standards evaluated		**Meet**	**Below**	**N/A**
Standards: arrival, seating				
1	Was the guest greeted or acknowledged within 30 seconds upon entering the restaurant?			
2	Was the guest greeted in a friendly and pleasant manner?			
3	Did the host ascertain guest's name and use it during interactions?			
4	Did the host ask guest to follow them to the table?			
5	Did the host seat the guest within 1 minute of their arrival?			
6	Did the host seat the guest at a fully laid table?			
7	Did the host present the menu and wine list?			
8	Did the host explain any specials of the day where applicable (i.e. soup, fish etc) or any items not available?			
Standards: product- menu and food				
9	Was the menu clean and in good repair?			
10	Did the restaurant menu offer a varied selection of dishes (i.e. starters, main courses and desserts)?			
11	Were at least two vegetarian options available?			
12	Was the food presented in an appealing manner?			
13	Did the food directly resemble its description from the restaurant menu?			
14	Was the food fresh and of good flavour?			
15	Was the food served at the correct temperature?			
16	Were the texture and colour of the food acceptable?			
17	Were portions of acceptable size?			
18	Was the food cooked as requested?			

5

	Standards: product – table layout			
19	Were all the set tables in the restaurant consistently laid up?			
20	Was the tablemat clean and in good condition?			
21	Was the correct cutlery used for its intended purpose and was it clean and matching in pattern?			
22	Was the crockery clean, not chipped and matching in pattern?			
23	Was the glassware clean, not chipped and matching in pattern?			
24	Was the ice bucket clean and polished?			
25	Was the butter provided (portion packets are acceptable)?			
26	Was a branded (outlet) serviette as opposed to a company/group serviette provided and was it clean and fresh (if applicable)?			
	Standards: product – physical condition of the bar and restaurant			
27	Were the salt and pepper cruets available and if so clean and full?			
28	Did the sugar selection include white, brown and sweetener?			
29	Were the carpet/tiles free and clean of any stains or debris?			
30	Were the light fixtures fully illuminated?			
31	Were all walls clean and free of any chips, scuffs or marks?			
32	Were all mirrors polished and free of any smudges?			
33	Were all windows clean and free of any streaks or spots?			
34	Were all plant and floral decorations fresh (if applicable)?			
35	Were the sides stations clean at all times?			
36	Was the table steady?			
37	Were the table /chair legs free of any scuffs/ scratches and matching in colour?			
38	Was the chair's upholstery clean, matching and in good repair?			
39	Was the restaurant free of noise and odour from the kitchen?			
40	Was appropriate music played at a pleasant level (if applicable)?			
	Total number of standards:	Meet	Below	N/A
	40 - to be evaluated			
	(Enter your total percentage score here out of 100%) This score is based total number of standards to meet. Disallow the not applicable ones for your bar and write your report based on these experiences. You may decide to change and adapt this tool.			

(Murphy, 2010)

5.6   Food service procedures

Place settings

Formal and informal place settings

Place settings at the dining table or dining area of the bar should be laid to suit the type and style of menu offered and the estimated number of guests attending each sitting.

Always base your decision in relation to place settings on how many courses are being served. In general, at a formal dinner, the cutlery will be placed at the sides unless the space is limited.

Positioning and placement of the cutlery and crockery

Place settings at a dining table can be confusing for some guests. What are all these plates, glasses, and utensils? Which ones are to be used and when? Improper use of dishes, glasses, and utensils can be embarrassing for some guests, so remember that the meal experience is intended to foster and build friendship and conviviality. Try to help your customers to dine with confidence and concentrate on enjoying themselves, which is the focus of the meal.

The bread plate and butter knife are located on the left, and the glasses are on the right. A basic cover setting (sometimes referred to as a la carte) includes the cutlery, crockery and glassware most commonly used for the meal. When your customers have ordered, this cover setting is corrected to suit the specific order.

Figure 5.1: Basic cover setting

The place setting is the guide to the meal ahead. The dining table will be pre-set with most of the items needed and the soup spoon can already be set. If the guest doesn't require soup, then the waiter removes the soup spoon and so on with other courses. If the place setting does not include a necessary item, the server will bring it with the course (for example fish or steak knife). The placement and choice of the cutlery and crockery sends an indication to the guest of what will be served during the meal and the order in which these foods will be consumed, for example: soup first, salad second, main course third, and dessert last.

Formal table setting

If you bar is located within an upmarket hotel or restaurant you will require some formal table setting knowledge. At a formal business or evening function, a five or four-course meal may be served. The table setting will have more items. The crockery and cutlery laid out in Figure 5.2 illustrate some of the different utensils and their placement. Note that the napkin could be placed to the left or in the centre of the dinner plate.

The placement and choice of the crockery and cutlery should indicate to the guests what will be served during the meal and the order in which the food will be consumed.

The easiest way to assist a guest in determining which items to use is to start with the knife, fork, or spoon that is the farthest from their plate and tell them to work their way inwards using one utensil for each course. If you advise the guest to remember the rule to work from the outside in, them they will be fine. Also as the meal progresses, the used silverware for each course should be removed as that course is finished.

Figure 5.2: Formal cover setting

Service sequence

The sequence of service can differ from one establishment to another depending on the location's style (classic, formal, contemporary or casual). The most important consideration here is that all staff members involved in the food service areas follow the best practice procedures for food service set down by the owner or their management.

Listed below are some recommended skills and techniques to be followed during food service. These ensure that all staff members understand their responsibilities from the moment the guest arrives at the establishment.

Best practices for food service

5

1 Give a warm and genuine greeting when seating the party and guest.

2 With napkin service, ensure it is placed on the table or opened for the guest.

3 Offer bottled or tap water. Serve the water chilled, and only offer ice on request.

4 Take the drinks order, suggest appropriate aperitifs.

5 Serve the bread, rolls and butter.

6 Present the menu and advise the guests of chef's specials, signature dishes and seasonable offers. A short decision period is needed, so leave the guest to decide on their choices.

7 Return to the table and take the order for all courses up to the main course.

8 Present the wine list, suggesting the specials and appropriate wines. Be discrete.

9 Source the wine, checking the vintage, brand, etc. Present it to the guest and open the wine at the table, placing the cork on a side plate and offering the host a sample taste. If it is approved, pour to all the guests, ladies first, gents next and the host last.

10 Remove cutlery and crockery items not required on the dining table.

11 Serve the starters and after a short period of time remove starter cutlery and crockery and crumb down the table, carefully.

12 Top up the guests' drinks, wines, beers, bottled waters. Open new bottles (on request) and serve any further starter and salad courses.

13 Remove the crockery and cutlery of the remaining starter courses.

14 Serve the main course. Ask the guest if their main course is fine and if they need any additional sauces, etc.

15 Remove the main course crockery and cutlery.

16 Present the dessert and cheese menu, and advise on any house, chef's or seasonable specials. Take the order.

17 Remove cutlery not required for desserts and cheese.

18 Suggest tea, coffee, liqueurs, listing the menu if needed, and take the order.

19 Serve teas, coffees, liqueurs and sweets, offering top ups.

20 Assemble the bill (when requested) and present it at the table, on a side plate or in an enclosed folder.

21 Collect payment and return change with thanks and an invitation to return.

22 Thank the guests as they leave the bar or restaurant.

adapted from Brown, Hepner & Deegan (1994)

Carrying and clearing plates

In silver service style, food should be served to the left of the guest and drinks to the right, however plated food is always served from the right side as plates are cleared from the right. Plate carrying and clearing, although a pre-requisite to food service, can be a tricky endeavor. Staff members responsible for this work should be skilled and it is recommended that no more than four plates should be carried at any one time for health and safety reasons. The main methods adopted for carrying plates and glasses in the dining area are shown in Figures 5.3 – 5.5.

Figure 5.3 5.4: Two and three plate carrying.

Figure 5.5: Glass carrying.

Carrying a service tray

It is easier to carry a tray with one hand underneath. It seems logical that using both hands would be more stable, but in reality one hand is best, depending on the load and the variety of food and beverage items to be carried. You may already know this if you have carried bar trays full of drinks. If you are carrying an oblong shaped tray (which are common for food service because they are quite large) always position the tray lengthways onto the forearm and support it by holding the tray with your opposite hand. Position the heaviest items on an oblong tray nearest the server, this assists the balancing of the service tray.

Best practice procedures for carrying a service tray

- Load the heaviest items in the middle of the service tray, and put the lighter items closer to the edge.

- When carrying a loaded oblong tray, position the tray lengthways onto the forearm and support the tray with the other hand. Always organise the heaviest items, e,g. empty large dinner plates, nearest the body to help the balance.

- Hold the service tray balanced on your palm, wrist straight, and part of the tray over your forearm.

- Always carry larger trays filled with plates (entrees, main courses, etc) higher. Position your open palm under the centre of the large tray, and rest a side of the tray on your shoulder. Remember to bend your wrist so that the tray is on your flat hand; if you support the tray with the tips of fingers, you may hurt yourself.

- Irrespective of the tray's size , consider it an extension of your body and move your body and the tray as a unit. You should therefore not swing the service tray around your body while you stand still, but turn your entire body with the tray in one single motion.

- Move as close as possible to the person you are serving, and transfer the plate from the tray to the guest (remembering that food is always served to the left of the customer and drinks to the right).

- Bars and restaurants will also provide small fold out stands which can be assembled easily to support the larger trays beside the customer's table. The server carries the tray on one side of her body, and holds the little stand with their other hand. Clever food and beverage managers will usually strategically position the small fold-out stands in convenient spots in the dining area for staff members to reduce their carrying loads to the customer's table. The server just grabs the little fold-out stand with their free hand, places the stand on the floor and rests the tray on the stand.

- Bend at the knees. Do not bend over at the waist while lowering the tray onto the stand, as this will cause back strain, similar to lifting very heavy loads.

- When transferring lots of food and beverage items from the bar or kitchen try not to carry the 'lazy man's load'. It is just as easy to make two trips.

5

Conclusion

In the past, food in the bar was designed to be simple and salty to keep customers drinking. These times have changed and the food produced and served in bars can be top quality. Many bar owners have invested a lot of money, training and research into their food offerings and now offer quality meals, well thought-out menus and attractive prices. Consumers still enjoy the traditional bar, but now selling fantastic homemade food or, for the young and lively, contemporary twists on classic dishes. Modern food trends, which include food sharing and grazing, have lead bars to offer small taster or sharing plates at reasonable prices, and these have become really popular. But irrespective of their choices, consumers are always looking for value for money, even in gastro pubs. Your customers are looking for restaurant quality food at below restaurant prices, so you must keep a tight control on costs, portions and profit margins.

Be careful not to over-complicate your menu offering, but keep it simple, local and fresh. When things go wrong with your food offering and customers complain, always try to see their point of view, and act quickly.

Finally you should remember that the golden rule is to 'never lose a customer' because dissatisfied customers tell their friends and family and their lifetime value to your business must never be underestimated.

6 Customer Care in Bar Operations

Aims and learning outcomes

Successful customer care is really about keeping the customer satisfied. On completion of this chapter the learner should be able to:

- Apply customer care techniques in the bar.
- Observe and anticipate customer requirements.
- Anticipate and respond to particular requirements of customers' children, elderly and disabled persons.
- Explain the importance of culture and its influence on food offerings in the bar.

6.1 Introduction

The bar industry today is faced with increased competition from a variety of entertainment sources, and bar owners also recognize that other establishments are providing a similar offering, sometimes at lower prices. This realization has brought about an increased focus on the care of customers and their viewpoints. When customers leave bars unhappy, it is usually because they encountered attitudes of indifference from staff and poor service. Dissatisfied customers usually talk to others about their dissatisfaction and the negative effect of this outcome can paralyze all your best pro-active customer and marketing efforts. It costs, on average, five times as much to win a new customer as it does to keep an existing one. Unfortunately, bars put enormous efforts into winning new customers and very little into customer care and retention.

6.2 Customer care

Stone & Young (1993) argued that 'customer care is not a veneer to be applied to an organization to make it look good for customers'. In the bar industry it should be a core value and should be built in to the very fabric of your offering – you should always seek to underpromise and overdeliver. But how can you deliver on your customers' expectation time after time? The starting point must, of course, be with yourself. You must seek to see yourself as others see you in all your glory, which includes all your faults. As you go through your daily duties, it is very difficult to stand back and ask, 'what can I do to improve our customer care techniques and improve business and profitability'? The first answer must always be to improve the quality of your service. A good bartender needs job crafts, people-handling skills, a positive attitude, good business procedures, communication and teamwork, and a commitment to continual learning. To get it right for your customer in the bar, you have to know what to do, and how to do it in thoughtful, appropriate and efficient ways.

6.3   Making the difference

So much has been written and spoken about customer care, customer service, and even customer delight, but what does it all mean to your bar?

Peter Drucker (1954) once wrote 'there is only one valid definition of business purpose: to create and keep a customer'. How your customers feel about you and supporting your establishment, largely reflects how they think you feel about them. You have to have a real passion for your customers; passion and the ability to impact on your customers are the two major factors in the bar industry today. You also have to be able to convey your enthusiasm and to surround yourself with employees who buy into it. If everything that you and your employees do sends a consistent message to customers that they are valued and respected, your chances of retaining their business increase immeasurably. Impress your customers through sincerity and enthusiasm, and delight them with your product and service.

Customer care does not work unless people are committed to it.

- **Expectations:** customer expectations of the level of service they regard as satisfactory are rising. Bars are constantly exploring just what their customers want. This focus has placed increased demand on all staff to perform, not just in terms of productivity, but also in terms of customer satisfying behavior. The focus of attention in all successful bars is on individuals (bartenders, sommeliers, waiters, chefs) and their behavior. Therefore, the difference is you.

- **Commitment:** commit yourself to providing the highest levels of service in every aspect of your duties and responsibilities.

- **The hidden differences:** the major hidden difference between people lies, of course, in their *personalities*. Similarly the hidden difference between the many products and services offered in your bar is in the employees who make, sell and serve them.

6.4   Creating first impressions

Do you believe first impressions are important? How can we improve these first impressions in the bar industry? A prospective customer will be won or lost by their first impressions of you and your bar.

You will usually have only one chance to make a first impression, so the initial impression is vital. These first impressions can be vastly improved by adopting the following techniques.

Creating a good first impression – face to face

1   A natural smile, a welcome expression
2   Immediate acknowledgement of the customer's presence
3   Undivided attention, with a courteous, hospitable and efficient manner adopted at all times
4   Use eye contact
5   Address customers by name if possible
6   Present a smart, neat appearance
7   Customers should be advised of any delays in service
8   Do not drink or eat in front of your customers while on duty.

Creating a good first impression - over the telephone

1   Answer the telephone promptly
2   Clearly identify the bar
3   Speak clearly
4   Try to use the customer's name
5   Always let customer ring off first
6   Avoid holding up the customer without explanation
7   Give customer telephone calls priority over personnel calls where possible.

Improving on those first impressions

Now that you have hopefully created a good first impression, you need to concentrate on improving on these first impressions. Consider adopting the following techniques to make them feel special.

1   Anticipate your customer's requirements
2   Co-operate with customers or groups in a hurry
3   Pay attention to the needs of special groups (i.e. the elderly, young children, or disabled)
4   Treat all customers equally

5 Use a tactful approach to problems and awkward situations

6 Do not impose on customers conversation among staff

7 Remember that a good team spirit leads to a pleasant atmosphere for the customers

8 Avoid being over familiar with customers.

Grooming and social skills

It is crucial that the bartender's image is always presented in harmony with the professional image that the bar wishes to portray to its customers. The bartender must remember that they are always in the public eye and must therefore pay special attention to the following areas. In addition to following the grooming rules laid out in Chapter 2, the bartender should also foster these social skills:

1 **manners**, bad manners should be checked

2 **facial expressions**, sincere and welcoming

3 keep a **good eye contact** (implies honesty)

4 **listening** and really hearing

5 **speech**, your projection and volume is crucial (it's not what you say it is how you say it).

Finally staying cheerful even when you are tired, agitated or in a bad mood, you must always try to not let your personal feelings and negative feelings affect how you deal with customers or work colleagues.

6.5   Customer care encounters

Bartenders regularly face an increasingly knowledgeable and sophisticated customer with broader tastes and experiences than ever before. These customers demand satisfaction but are increasingly difficult to satisfy. The key to success for your bar in this competitive environment lies in the quality of the service offered; this vital mechanism can be used to achieve a competitive advantage. Quinn (2006) contends that 'customer driven people in companies always have to fight with people who have other priorities'. Listed below we highlight a short series of customer care scenarios which revolve around retail and services business encounters. Each one of individual scenarios is concluded with two possible endings which you should carefully consider for reflection and possible discussion with your hospitality colleagues. The key to customer satisfaction, loyalty and retention is to consistently deliver a level of customer service that exceeds and even anticipates the customer's expectations for value (also see Appendix I).

Scenario A

A party of three people has booked a table at a restaurant. When they arrive, the restaurant owner apologies and informs them that the table will be another twenty minutes.

- *First ending*: he asks if they would mind waiting in the bar area.

- *Second ending*: he will understand if they wish to cancel the reservation but if not, perhaps they would care to enjoy a drink in the bar area with his compliments.

Scenario B

A man in a supermarket has bought a small number of very heavy items. At the checkout, an assistant operates the till while another assistant places the goods in a bag.

- *First ending*: the packer ensures that the heaviest items go at the bottom, fills the bag and hands it to the customer.

- *Second ending*: before he begins packing, the packer places one bag inside the other saying 'We don't want the bag to break in the car park'. He then packs the bags heaviest items first.

Scenario C

An engineer has just finished a routine service on the domestic central heating boiler of an elderly widow and informs her that:

- *First ending*: "all is done, if you sign here I'll be away, I've got a really busy day today!"

- *Second ending*: "OK, that's all done, no problems there, it's all in good condition. I also checked the pipe work out to the oil tank; that's fine too. Oh, and by the way, the cupboard door was a bit loose so I tightened up the hinge. No problem, it only took a second."

Scenario D

A young man has been saving money for two years. Every month he takes his pay cheque to the same bank, pays it in and transfers the same amount of money to a savings account. On this occasion there is a new cashier who:

- *First ending*: smiles, accepts his pay cheque, affects the transfer to the savings account and wishes him a nice day.

- *Second ending*: smiles, accepts his pay cheque, notices that he is a regular saver and asks 'will you continue this rate of saving into the future Mr. Murray because if so you can switch to this other account especially designed for regular savers. It would pay you a lot more interest.

You should now consider the first endings of each scenario. In what way did these businesses gain or lose?

6.6   Cultural diversity and intercultural awareness

Over the last decades, the majority of countries around the world have gone through considerable social and economic changes, which have seen them move being traditionally rural people to becoming predominately urbanised. The bar industry worldwide has been part of this amazing economic evolution. Its customers and staff members now originate from every continent in the world. The diverse intercultural environment in the bar has brought about a significant impact on bar owners to provide intercultural awareness training for their staff members, focusing on the following areas: the intercultural environment, cultural difference, dangers of stereotyping, sensitivity to racist attitudes, prejudice and discrimination, cross cultural communication and working in multi-cultural teams in the bar.

Cultural diversity and intercultural awareness, also known as multiculturalism, is the acceptance and promotion of the variety of human cultures and their different value systems in a given society (the society in this case refers to the bar). Cultural diversity and intercultural awareness in the bar industry recognises the importance of native languages, dress, traditions, and beliefs that govern self-identity. There is a compelling business case in the bar industry for the effective management of cultural diversity (CD) and intercultural awareness (IA) in every bar establishment. CD and IA can help bar customers, pub groups and hospitality organizations to:

- Identify and capitalize on opportunities to improve their products and services
- Attract, retain, motivate and utilise human resources effectively
- Improve the quality of decision-making at all organisational levels
- Reap the benefits from being perceived as a socially conscious and progressive business.

To achieve the above, CD and IA must be both managed effectively. This requires leadership commitment, the establishment of priorities and realistic objectives, the assessment and development of procedures to meet the particular needs of the bar and the provision of management and employee training and support processes. The rapid globalisation of the bar business and the changing demographic characteristics of the local population mean that the pursuit of diversity in the bar industry is everyone's concern.

6.7   Understanding culture

Cultural models

Geert Hofstede, cultural onion model

The model consists of three layers around a core. The core stands for the inner cultural values, e.g. good vs. bad, dirty vs. clean, ugly vs. beautiful, unnatural vs. natural, abnormal vs. normal, paradoxical vs. logical, irrational vs. rational. These core values do not change much and are therefore interesting to learn about from history. Even if something seems to be outdated, it still can subconsciously play a role in a modern society.

In the first layer around the core are the rituals, which are the way people do things, personally, inter-personally and as groups. A ritual can be the way of personal hygiene (most Asians shower in the evening, Europeans in the morning), or of greeting – German people like to shake hands often, Malay people tenderly touch the fingertips and then point to the heart. Those rituals are changing slowly.

In the second layer around the core are the heroes. A hero can be a fictive person, but has influence on the culture. A nice example is *Dracula* (written by Bram Stoker, published 1897). Since this book was published, many people in the Western world developed a fear about vampires, even if it never existed in their culture before. Heroes can also be national heroes, photo-models or scientists – all people who act as role models in that society.

The third layer is about the symbols. Nowadays most symbols appear as brands like BMW, Apple or Louis Vuitton. Those symbols usually move according to the momentary fashion. All three layers can be trained and learned through practices except for the core's inner cultural values.

E. T. Hall, iceberg model for understanding surface and deep culture

The iceberg model of culture lends itself to the idea of looking below the surface, or inward. It is a useful metaphor for locating one's own culture, most of which is hidden from us for those elements that are below the surface are those that are most difficult for us to access and verbalize. We often find it easier to spot the foreign behaviours, but even when noticing them, we fail to get below the surface to where the important cultural information lies. We rarely look, however, even at the surface of our own culture; there is so little need to, as it is all so familiar and normal to us. To further stress the notion of unconscious and hidden culture, you could also turn your attention to the first model, taken from the work of Geert Hofstede.

Tip: You can obtain some excellent illustrations for training purposes of Geert Hofstedes (cultural onion model) and E.T Halls (iceberg model) for understanding culture from a simple Google images search, but please be mindful of copyright.

You can generalise the information from these two models for understanding culture and state that culture can be basically seen as consisting of three elements:

- *Values*, the ideas that tell what is considered important in life
- *Norms*, the expectations of how people should behave in different situations
- *Artefacts*, those things or material culture, reflects the cultures values and norms but are tangible and manufactured by man.

6.8   Intercultural communications

Intercultural communication generally refers to face-to-face interactions among people of diverse cultures. It entails the investigation of those elements of culture that most influence interaction when members of two or more cultures come together in an interpersonal setting, e.g. in hospitality industry, specifically in the hotels, restaurants and licensed premises sectors.

Barriers to intercultural communication

Learning the norms of every culture and subgroup would be an impossible task. A more practical way is to understand general barriers as suggested by Barna (1994) who developed a list of six such barriers to effective intercultural communication.

Anxiety: Being anxious because of not knowing what you are expected to do, for example in a new job, conscious of being new and out of place, therefore your focus of attention centres on this feeling which can cause common mistakes. Anxiety felt during normal everyday life is much higher than that of people living in their country of birth (Brislin & Yoshida, 1994).

Assuming similarity instead of difference: False assumptions bring unawareness of important differences between cultures. It's better to assume differences and anticipate ways in which different languages and norms will affect communication (Jandt, 1995).

Ethnocentrism: This belief in the superiority of one's own culture leads to a rejection of the richness and knowledge of other cultures.

Stereotypes: These impede communication when they leads us to assume the stereotype is true of the group and of the individual, and to explain an individual's behaviour on the basis of the stereotype.

Prejudice: Refers to the suspicion or hatred of a group, race, religion, or sexual orientation. Racism is prejudice against individuals of a particular race. Hate crimes grow out of fear of difference and in hostility toward those who are perceived as different on the basis of race, religion, gender, or sexual orientation.

Awareness of these barriers to intercultural communication may not provide rules for behaviour or concrete answers to dilemmas, but they do provide clues as to where the problems may lie, much as a list of symptoms may help doctors to diagnose an illness.

6.9 Implementing an action plan for bars

Managing cultural diversity and intercultural awareness can be identified in terms of a bar that:

- Is free from discrimination and harassment of all ethic and non-national staff member groups
- Accords value to cultural diversity and intercultural awareness and takes steps to accommodate their practical implications
- Takes steps to achieve full equality in practice for non-national and minority ethnic employees and customers

The bar's action plan must address some key practices to promote a cultural diverse workplace.

Providing induction training to non-nationals

This will give staff members an understanding of the local practices and their role in the bar. This should provide assistance to foreign national workers in settling in and dealing with problems of adapting to an unfamiliar cultural environment. This helps reduce stress and isolation for foreign nationals and helps to support them to be more involved in the bar and the local community. Non-nationals receiving induction training are more positive and productive in the bar. To implement this key practice you will need to address four specific areas:

- **Preparation**: Get feedback from existing non-nationals on the types of information and other assistance they needed on first joining your bar. Check with HR officers or local bar owners of other pub groups and bars as to what they have found useful in setting up induction training for non-national workers. Consult representative organisations about the needs of their particular minority ethnic constituencies on joining the bar and hospitality industry, and on the design of appropriate induction programmes.

- **Delivery**: Train all your groups together because some non-nationals may be reluctant to raise their specific problems outside the group. Involve them in the delivery of the training (if possible), and include opportunities for them to raise questions. Provide the training as close to the starting date as possible, use understandable appropriate language as necessary.

- **Content**: Should include employee rights and conditions, workplace policies and procedures, settling in including information of support (transport, local community, leisure activities), basic language training.

- **Follow up**: Provide follow up meetings to identify emerging problems, assign mentors (or buddies) for support, provide staff manuals and workplace documents in appropriate languages.

Making cultural allowances

This helps to create a bar in which non-nationals feel recognised, respected, appreciated, welcomed and at ease. It helps to develop a culturally competent bar with a capacity to operate effectively in cross-cultural situations. To implement this key practice, you will need to do your research and develop strategies for your staff. Get feedback from existing non-nationals workers, cultural groups and HR personnel in other bars on the cultural and religious needs, obligations and expectations, and what they found useful in making flexible cultural allowances for foreign nationals. Practical strategies could include providing flexible holidays, acknowledging, accommodating, celebrating, or giving time off to celebrate relevant national, ethnic or religious holidays or festivities, catering for their dietary needs, accommodating dress code requirements, providing visual displays, maps, flags, and art which represent ethnic cultures, in public areas of your premises.

Changing the attitudes through diversity and intercultural awareness training

This can help to create a harmonious working environment where all employees can contribute to their full capacity. This enriches the working environment by improving relationships, communication and contact across diverse cultural identities. This cultural diversity and awareness training programme might involve:

- Provision of information regarding legislation, workplace policies and procedures
- Review of attitudes through exploring definitions of culture, approaches to cultural diversity and facts, figures, myths, assumptions about foreign nationals
- Development of skills in the management of diversity.

Changing rules and procedures

Review your employment systems, policies and procedures in consultation with employee representatives and other relevant parties to access the operation, appropriateness, ease of understanding, ease of access to, ease of use and effects of those systems, rules, policies and procedures for your bar.

Active recruitment and promotion

This will help to create a more inclusive bar, and to increase the range of talent, expertise and creativity of your workforce. To implement this key practice you will need to address the areas of:

- Job applications: you can encourage more non-nationals to work for your company by translating portions of your applications forms, placing advertisements in designated community media, using outreach programmes to target schools and other training and educational institutions, and to target ethnic community groups.

- Improving employability of job applicants: support school programmes and special training schemes including cultural programmes; provide management and leadership training for ethnic employees to support them to qualify for promotion; set up a mentor system.

- Selection procedures: ensure due weight is given for qualifications obtained abroad; include foreign nationals on the interview boards; arrange for translation facilities at interviews; provide feedback following interviews.

6.10 Cultural influences on food offerings

Your customers represent a great variety of cultures, each with their own ways of cooking and enjoying food. It is therefore essential that bars understand and cater for these cultural influences in their food offerings.

The influence of religions

Religion still plays a major role in affecting what and when many people eat. Some people's diets are restricted daily by their religion; others are influenced by what they eat on special occasions. Fasts, feasts, celebrations and anniversaries are important events in people's lives. It is necessary for those involved in the bars catering area to have some basic knowledge of the requirements and restrictions associated with religion.

Buddhist: Strict Buddhists are vegetarians. Vesak in May is the festival to celebrate the life of the Buddha.

Christians: Eating habits are not affected, though some will be vegetarians, usually for moral reasons, and some will refrain from eating meat on Fridays. Some sects, for instance, Mormons, have many rules and restrictions regarding eating and drinking, for example complete abstinence from tea, coffee and alcohol, and an emphasis on wholesome eating. Many Christians refrain from eating certain foods during Lent – usually something they like very much. Other religious days often observed are:

Good Friday: hot cross buns are often eaten as a reminder of Christ's crucifixion.

Christmas (25 December): celebrated with feasting, with roast turkey today often replacing the traditional roast beef and boar's head, followed by Christmas pudding and mince pies.

Other predominantly Christian countries celebrate different saints days by special events. For example, St Nicholas, patron saint of children, is celebrated on 6 December in Holland, by eating Dutch St Nicholas biscuits. In Spain the Three Kings are remembered with a special crown cake on 6 January. The fourth Thursday of November in the USA is Thanksgiving Day, when traditionally turkey and pumpkin pie are served.

Hindu: Most Hindus do not eat meat (strict Hindus are vegetarians) and none eat beef since the cow is sacred to them. Holi is the Festival which celebrates the end

6

of winter and the arrival of spring. Raksha Bandhan celebrates the ties between brothers and sisters at the end of July or in August, and Janmashtami celebrates the birth of Krishna, also in August. Dussehra is the festival of good over evil; Diwala is the festival of light, celebrating light over darkness, held in October or November. Samosas (triangles of pastry containing vegetables), banana fudge and vegetable dishes of all kinds, as well as favourite foods, are eaten to celebrate.

Judaism: Jews have strict dietary laws. Shellfish, pork and birds of prey are forbidden. Acceptable foods are fish with scales and fins, animal that have 'cloven hoof' and birds killed according to the law. Strict Jews eat only meat that has been slaughtered in prescribed ways, known as kosher meat. Milk and meat must neither be used together in cooking nor served at the same meal, and three hours should elapse between eating food containing milk and food containing meat. The Jewish Sabbath, from sunset on Friday to sunset on Saturday, is traditionally a day of rest. In the evening, plaited bread called chollah is broken into pieces and eaten. Matzo, an unleavened crisp-bread, is served at Passover as a reminder of the exodus of the Jews from Egypt. Pentecost celebrates the giving of the Ten Commandments to Moses on Mount Sinai; cheesecake is now a traditional dish served at this celebration. Hanukkah, the Jewish Festival of Lights in December, is a time of dedication when pancakes and a potato dish, latkes, are usually eaten.

Muslims: Muslims celebrate the birth of Mohammed at the end of February or early in March. Alcohol and pork are traditionally forbidden in their diet.

Only meat that has been prepared according to Muslim custom by a halal butcher is permitted. During Ramadan, which lasts for one month and is the ninth month of the Muslim calendar, Muslims do not eat or drink anything from dawn to sunset. The end of the fast is celebrated with a feast called Eid-al-Fitar, with special foods. Muslims from Middle Eastern countries would favour a dish like lamb stew with okra; those from the Far East, curry and rice.

Sikh: Sikhs do not have strict rules regarding food but many are vegetarians. Baisakhi in April celebrates the New Year and is the day Sikhs are baptised into their faith.

Conclusion

Customer care training is not an optional extra but an essential part of all bar establishments' business strategy. The success of any bar depends on the minute-by-minute performance of its staff members. To manage customer care successfully, staff members must know what to do and have the ability to do it in thoughtful, appropriate and efficient ways to please the customer, because each encounter is different. This care begins with creating and improving on the first impressions, which includes the bartender's grooming, appearance and social skills.

Globalisation and international travel have brought international customers and multinational business operators to all parts of the world. The impact of these changes, added to economic changes have resulted in significant numbers of nationalities working outside their home country. Unfortunately a lack of understanding of different cultures and nationalities has lead in the past to ineffective management techniques in directing and motivating these staff members, particularly in older, traditional businesses with a homogeneous workforce. The challenge today is clear, that bars must implement action plans to stimulate cultural awareness, value workplace diversity and encourage a welcoming atmosphere for their new diversified staff members and customers.

6

7 Health, Safety and Security in the Bar

Aims and learning outcomes

This chapter introduces the areas central to health and safety, and security. It also explores how to manage waste in bars. On completion the learner should be able to:

■ Explain the rationale for food safety, HACCP and personal hygiene and its effect on food safety.

■ Explain the importance of labelling foods.

■ Act on safety statements and the essential safety and security issues in bars.

■ Apply best practice procedures for reducing risks and handling potentially violent situations in the bar

■ Explain techniques for improving safety in pub cellar operations

■ Compare and contrast insurance premium covers for bars.

■ Outline the challenges of waste in bars and broadly explain prevention techniques for reduction, reuse and recovery.

■ Conduct a waste audit for identifying waste and managing waste streams

■ Identify energy saving innovations for their bar.

7.1 Introduction

In the majority of countries around the world it is a legal requirement that all staff involved in a food environment, which includes bars, are adequately trained and supervised commensurate with their work activity. The responsibility for the training and supervision of staff lies with the proprietors of the bar and food businesses. This is the case for all staff members whether they are part-time, full-time or casual, and whether they are employed in the public or private sector.

Bar owners also have to be more concerned about their establishment's safety and security issues. This is the result of a variety of factors, most notably recent legislative changes at national and international level and the subsequent high costs of accidents (including costs relating to litigation and compensation). Poor safety and security standards place staff members and customers at risk of serious injury if not death; employers suffer in terms of lost productivity and potentially higher premiums; and the morale of the staff, as well as the industrial relations climate in the bar, can be adversely affected. At a minimum, bar owners should have a practical understanding of the local and national legislation in this area. They should also ensure, if necessary by enforcement, that their staff members follow proper safety and security standards.

7.2   Rationale for food safety

Food safety and hygiene is a subject which is taken more seriously by bar owners nowadays. The concerted efforts to improve hygiene standards has been brought about by outbreaks of food poisoning, resulting in sickness and in some circumstances fatalities. Government agencies have tightened up local and national rules and regulations on food hygiene for licensed premises in line with international standards, and these regulations are now enforced more strictly than in the past.

Bars, because they are traditionally regarded as high risk, have started to receive more visits from the local environmental health officers (EHOs) with new owners, or owners switching their food offerings, coming under particularly close scrutiny. The EHOs are charged by the local government with the responsibility of carrying out the evaluation of procedures for compliance with the relevant legislation for food safety and hygiene in bars. EHOs will generally arrive at a bar unannounced and will want to ask lots of questions and look at all aspects of the food and beverage operation. They will also assess in detail the maintenance procedures which the bar uses to set the high standards of food hygiene which are required by law.

7

Enforcement and closure

EHOs usually have a contract with the local government health boards and they can issue enforcement orders ranging from:

■ Closure orders

■ Prohibition orders

■ Improvements orders

■ Improvement notices

Bars with a high volume of food will be inspected on a more regular basis. A typical EHO during their visit to a bar will:

1 Announce themselves – by warrant

2 Take detailed contemporaneous notes and temperatures, any particular problem will be photographed for file

3 Visit the kitchen

    4 Look for signs of infestation

    5 Ensure correct storage of products

    6 Check ice

    7 Carry out a general inspection of the premises and check HACCP and training documentation and notices.

    They will then return to the office to write up their report.

Closure orders

A closure order is normally served where it is deemed that there is or is likely to be a grave and immediate danger to public health. Typical causes include:

- Poor hygiene
- Inappropriate storage or refrigeration
- Inadequate cooking or re-heating
- Cross-contamination from raw to cooked food
- Infected food handler
- Inadequately trained or supervised staff.

7.3   The bar layout

You must constantly examine the layout of your bar in relation to the products and services which it offers. The objective of your workplace study is to ensure that you always have the correct products, equipment and stock for use and in the right place to avoid excessive and unnecessary movement or action for yourself and fellow hospitality staff members. This examination is also of critical importance in relation to the care of your customers, as it helps to save you time and energy and to improve the overall speed of service.

The famous French culinary genius Auguste Escoffier (1921) preached 'Le mise en plaice', which translated simply means 'everything has its place', and this statement applies to all areas of the bar. This professional approach to organisation helps to improve the method and speed of how we can work, which results in increased customer satisfaction. A rigorous study of yourself and your bar surroundings is crucial to customer care and health and safety. The study should include all equipment layout and design, and how you and your fellow members of staff work in relation to your efficiency and effectiveness, for example, within certain time periods.

For a further discussion on the bar layout and design issues see Chapter 1.

7.4   Steps critical to food safety and hygiene

Good hygiene results in good health, which results in good business and increased profits. Money invested in hygiene pays great dividends. If the publican or bar manager is not committed to good hygiene practices it is unrealistic to expect the staff to give hygiene the priority the public expects.

Food protection, best practices

- Buy from an approved source with good standards
- Check all deliveries for damage, infestation
- Stock rotation, F.I.F.O (First In, First Out)
- Clean delivery van and personnel
- Separate storage areas (raw meats, vegetables, dry goods, cooked foods) keeping raw foods and cooked foods apart
- Handle food as little as possible in preparation
- Clean as you go
- Cook for the time and temperature required
- Thoroughly thaw frozen meat/poultry before cooking
- If re-heating is essential, thoroughly re-heat
- Serve hot food hot, serve cold food cold.

7

HACCP – a systematic approach

Hazard analysis critical control point or (HACCP) is a preventative system of food control and a systematic approach to the identification, assessment and control of hazards.

Hazards

A food hazard means any kind of contamination which could cause harm to the consumer; these hazards can be grouped into three categories:

1 Microbiological contamination, bacteria or other micro-organisms that cause food poisoning
2 Chemical contamination cleaning materials or pest baits for example
3 Physical contamination, hygiene, foreign material such as bits of glass.

Hazard analysis

This is the systematic examination of the steps involved in the production of food. These are: purchase, delivery, storage, preparation, cooking, assembly, exposure for sale and service. It is from these points that you need to control your critical points (CCP).

Control points

Once all the hazards have been identified then control measures to limit the risk of food poisoning can be put in place.

The bar's task is to analyse and identify the possible areas of the shop or stages of production which could be hazardous, and to take appropriate steps to eradicate the risks. Having identified potential hazards, you need to introduce systems to deal with the hazards and monitor these systems for continuing effectiveness.

Process steps, identifying hazards and controls

The manager should designate appropriate staff members to carry out the controls and check the monitoring sheets to ensure the controls are working. They should check that the staff are comfortable with refusing food deliveries or disposing of spoilt food. This system should be regularly reviewed.

Table 7.1: HACCP - control of hazards, using ham sandwich as an example. (FSAI, 2013)

Step	Hazard	Control
Purchase	Contaminated cooked ham due to cross contamination with raw meat or inadequate cooking at the meat production premises.	Detailed purchase specification ensures that produce is purchased from reputable firms with quality assurance programmes.
Delivery	Growth and multiplication of bacteria on the cooked meat due to the failure to refrigerate the meat during transportation.	Use of a refrigerated vehicle for delivery. Temperature checks on goods being delivered. Goods above 5°c degrees should be rejected.
Storage	Growth and multiplication of bacteria on the cooked meat due to the non-use of refrigerators during storage at the delicatessen.	Chilled storage of high-risk food until such time as they are needed. Regular monitoring of chill temperature. An air temperature above 5°c degrees is unacceptable.
Assembly	Transfer of bacteria onto the cooked meat due to cross contamination from soil, raw meat or dirty surfaces, utensils while making the sandwich. Bad personal hygiene practices.	Staff training in basic food hygiene. Adequate provision of utensils, space and cleaning chemicals and equipment.
Exposure for sale	Growth and multiplication of bacteria as the sandwich is stored at the incorrect temperature.	Chilled display for food, regular monitoring of chill temperatures, a limit of 2 hours on display for sale, hygiene standards of food workers and practices.
Service	Contamination of the sandwich due to poor handling techniques by food workers while serving the customer.	Hygiene standards of food workers and practices.

Controlling temperature

A hazard can also relate to the survival of undesirable micro-organisms or the persistence of toxins after heating, and the multiplication of micro-organisms when food is held at incorrect temperatures. Examples of these are:

■ Food kept at room temperature for several hours

■ Food kept warm, but not in a hot holding device

■ In cold storage facilities, but in large quantities at an insufficiently low temperature.

Food poisoning bacteria

In order to grow, bacteria require: food, moisture, warmth, time and some oxygen. Food poisoning bacteria grow best at body temperature, i.e. 37°C. Raising the temperatures above 37°C slows down the rate of multiplication. At 63°C degrees or above the bacteria will die. Common food poisoning organisms are not able to multiply below 5°C degrees (therefore all refrigeration units operate below 5°C degrees. Deep freeze units must keep food below -18°C degrees).

HACCP - documentation and record charts

It is good practice to keep written records for your HACCP system. The diagrams given below can be reproduced on a basic computer. These hard copy records will help you to demonstrate that you have exercised 'due diligence' in food safety and hygiene for your bar.

7

Figure 7.2: Food delivery record sheet. (FSAI, 2013)

Date	Supplier	Food	Date code	Temperature	Physical condition	Corrective action	Signed

Temperature of chilled food deliveries shall be between –1oC and 5oC.

Temperature of frozen food deliveries shall be less than –18oC.

Figure 7.3: Basic cleaning schedule sheet. (FSAI, 2013)

Item to be cleaned	Frequency	Chemical	Chemical preparation	Person responsible

In this schedule sheet you record the equipment to used or cleaned, the areas which require regular cleaning, the personnel available to clean, the cleaning chemicals to be used and records of when and by whom the task was completed. Good cleaning schedules should always be part of your customer care programme and all staff should adapt a 'clean as you go' policy. A lot of businesses use service providers to assist them in identifying the appropriate chemicals to be used for cleaning their bar. Listed below are just some of the benefits of employing these individuals.

Cleaning chemical supplier

The cleaning chemical supplier should have:

- A knowledge of your food operation and the range of cleaning chemicals suited to the premises and equipment to be cleaned
- A knowledge of the appropriate health and safety legislation and requirements
- The expertise and ability to conduct an audit to determine cleaning needs
- The time to demonstrate the use of the product(s) to obtain maximum benefit
- The ability to provide relevant, easy to understand documentation (health and safety data sheets. product specifications, cleaning schedules, cleaning records, etc.)
- The ability to replace non-conforming stock.

Figure 7.4: Refrigerator temperature record sheet. (FSAI, 2013)

Week commencing	Time	Temperature	Corrective action	Signature
Monday	am			
	pm			
Tuesday	am			
	pm			
Wednesday	am			
	pm			

Refrigerated stores shall be maintained at between −1°C and 5°C (ideally less than 3°C). Deep freezers shall be maintained at or below −18°C.

Figure 7.5: Master sheet of food control - cooking. (FSAI, 2013)

Date	Food type	Start time	Finish time	Core temperature	Signed

Cooking: core temperature minimum 74°C for a minimum of 2 minutes.

Reheating: core temperature minimum 70°C and served within 30 minutes unless it is maintained at above 63°C.

Figure 7.6: Master sheet of food control – hot holding

Food type	Time in	Temp after 30 minutes	Temp after 60 minutes	Temp after 90 minutes	Corrective action	Signed

Hot holding: all food must be maintained at or above 63°C

Reheating: core temperature minimum 70°C and served within 30 minutes unless it is maintained at or above 63°C

Figure 7.7: Master sheet of food control – cooling. (FSAI, 2013)

Date	Food type	Time finished cooking	Temp after 90 minutes	Refrigerate & check temp after	Corrective action	Signed

Cooling: Food shall be placed under refrigerated conditions within 90 minutes after cooking and shall reach a temperature of less than 10°C within 150 minutes after cooling has commenced.

Figure 7.8: Staff training record. (FSAI, 2013)

Name	Position	Date of employment	Induction training	Basic hygiene course	Advanced hygiene course	Refresher training	Signed

7

Figure 7.9: Thermometer calibration check. (FSAI, 2013)

Year	Date	Temp. Hot	Temp. Core	Corrective action	Signed
January					
February					
March					

Cold temperature check: Place the tip of the thermometer into a container of crushed ice and a little cold water and leave for five minutes. Take the reading. A temperature between −1°C and +1°C is fine.

Hot temperature check: Place the tip of the thermometer into the steam emitting from a free boiling kettle of water. Take the reading. A temperature between +99°C and +101°C is fine.

A competent company should calibrate the thermometer once a year and certify its calibration and accuracy.

7.5   Personal hygiene

If food workers have bad personal hygiene it is unlikely they will have good food hygiene. To facilitate personal hygiene, separate sanitary conveniences with hand washbasins, mirrors, soap and towels should be provided wherever possible. A sign advising staff to wash their hands after using the toilet should also be pinned up beside the toilet. Undesirable habits such as nose picking, finger licking or smoking should be prohibited when dealing with food. Minor illnesses should be notified to the manager particularly diarrhea, vomiting, sore throat and skin infection. Food workers are deemed to have a good standard of personal hygiene, when they have a clean body, clean appearance, clean outer clothing, and follow a code of good hygiene practices when handling food. It is important that strict personal hygiene is observed for the following reasons:

- **Possible contamination of foodstuffs:** People carry bacteria such as staphylo-coccus aureus in their hair, ears, nose, throat, skin and in septic skin conditions. other bacteria such as e.coli and salmonella can be found in human intestines.

- **Legal obligation of food handlers:** Food workers have a moral and legal responsibility to ensure that they do not spread bacteria to food for example Article 24 of the European Communities (Hygiene of Foodstuffs) regulations 1998 places specific obligations on food workers to observe strict hygiene.

- **Customer awareness:** Personal hygiene is the one area of hygiene that all customers can notice; attention to this can have a direct impact on your business. A customer must also comply with the Food Hygiene regulations while in a food premises, and may not cause a risk to food while in such premises.

Food workers must:

- Keep their person clean
- Wash hands regularly, before starting work, after using the toilet, after handling refuse, after using a handkerchief, after handling or preparing raw food, prior to handling cooked or ready-to-eat food, after cleaning duties and after smoking
- Wear clean outer clothing
- Keep equipment clean
- Not handle food unnecessarily

Figure 7.10: Hand sanitizers.

- Not exhibit any unhygienic practices - picking their nose and ears, picking at spots and septic sores, touching their mouth, hair, smoking, spitting, coughing / sneezing over exposed food

Food workers must do without:

- Long nails
- Nail varnish or false nails
- Watches and jewellery
- Perfume and aftershave.

Food workers and illness

The following must be reported by food workers to their superiors:

- Skin cuts and infection
- Vomiting and diarrhea
- Scheduled infectious diseases - typhoid, paratyphoid, dysentery or salmonella
- Flu

Staff facilities and food workers

It is crucial that bar owners organize areas for their staff to change into the appropriate protective clothing. Bar owners must also have in place specific training and policies which address, brushing and combing hair – grooming skills in the food area, eating and drinking while on or off duty and smoking.

Cross contamination

Cross contamination describes the process by which food poisoning organisms from a natural source, for example raw meat or soil, transfer onto food which was previously free from all harmful bacteria. Bacteria are not mobile. They depend on human beings, insects or animals to provide them with transportation onto high-risk foodstuffs. Examples of cross contamination.

Direct contact:

- Blood from a raw chicken drips down onto cream cakes in the fridge.
- Raw and cooked meat stored side by side in the fridge touch one another.
- Soil from unwashed vegetables lands a roast left to cool in the kitchen.

Indirect contact:

- A chef uses the same wiping cloth to clean a raw meat knife and then a cooked meat knife.
- A waitress makes a cheese sandwich using a cutting board that has not been cleaned after dirty potatoes were put on it.
- A chef uses a fork to test whether the joint is fully cooked. He later uses the same fork again, introducing bacteria from earlier into the joint, which is now fully cooked.

Good storage principles – fridge layout:

Top shelves   = Dairy produce, cooked and ready-to-eat foods.

Bottom shelves = Raw foods and defrosting products.

Pest control

In most countries there is a legal obligation on bar owners to have rigorous pest control programmes in place and to have a formal pest control contact with an approved independent pest control company. The pest control service provider will provide:

1 A complete survey of the premises to determine the level of service required.
2 The contract outlining the frequency of the inspection, and contact details.
3 A plan of the bait point locations.
4 Information on the pesticides, and rodenticides used for pest control treatment
5 Written reports on each visit

Food safety and ice

Regular surveillance of ice for contaminants is vital for the protection of public health and consumer confidence. The production of good quality ice has also important economic implications in an increasingly competitive hospitality industry. Ice must be clean and fresh and free of any flavour save water. The sampling and testing of ice from food premises and bars is traditionally supervised by the local health boards and governed by national and international regulations.

Precautions to avoid contamination and improve the quality of ice in bars: Bacteria can build up if ice machines and equipment are not sufficiently serviced and maintained, but contamination is most likely caused through the handling of ice by serving staff or customers. Precautions to avoid contamination and to help improve the quality of ice cubes are covered in Section 3.2.

Case study

A study of the quality of ice in bars explored a random selection of nine bars in a major European city. The outlets included hotels, Michelin Star rated restaurants and traditional pubs.

Testing procedure: All samples of ice were brought to the local chemical analysis laboratory. Bacteria in water are usually tested at two temperatures in order to separate bacteria levels of environmental origin and animal or human origin. Testing at 22 degrees reveals levels of environmental bacteria, while testing at 37 degrees establishes levels of human or animal bacteria, which are more likely to cause illness.

The study results

- Coliform bacteria at levels well in excess of recommended safe limits
- Evidence of probable human bacteria was discovered in eight of the nine samples (possible handling of ice)
- Levels of bacteria discovered in ice hundreds of times higher than the bacteria in the toilet water at the same venue (safer to drink the toilet water)
- Thankfully no e. coli bacteria was found in the samples

Due to the coliforms found in some of the research samples, three bars in this study faced sanctions by the local health board in accordance with the microbiological guidelines for ice intended for human consumption. (Clarke & Hanley, 2006)

7

7.6   Labelling of foods

The regulations surrounding the labelling of foods can be quite complicated. In the EU, the rules are governed by the 1997 EU directive 'QUID (quantitative ingredient declarations) regulations'. The regulations aim to enhance and assist consumer choice when buying food, by providing information about the ingredients of what they are buying. The main result is that manufacturers have to include on the label the percentage of all of the principal ingredients, these being the things that influence your customer to purchase the food product. Presently these regulations do not apply to foods sold on the premises where they were made, or on other premises owned by the producer. However it is likely that in the near future, these regulations will also begin to apply to these areas. It is especially important to be aware of the current regulations if you buy in pre-packed foods (i.e. sandwiches) as the regulations would apply to these. If you decide there is a market for you in making foods for other, separate outlets, then the foods you supply to them must be correctly labelled.

7.7 Health and Safety

General regulations on safety issues

In every country or state directives, are incorporated into legislation through regulations (normally referred to as acts). These are enforceable by penalties and apply to employees (bartenders, waiters, etc.) and employers (bar owners and managers). The main regulations that bar owners and staff members should be properly trained and aware of are those relating to:

■ **The physical environment of work, safe use of equipment**: It is mandatory for bar owners to provide the right equipment, which must, of course, be in working order. All equipment should be fitted with safety devices and warning notices, in accordance with the manufacturer's specifications. Such equipment should be properly maintained and regularly checked. Bar owners must also ensure that their staff members are properly trained to use it.

■ **Personal protective equipment (PPE)**: It is a requirement that PPE be provided to and used by staff members where needed, normally one piece of equipment per individual member. PPE may include, but is not limited to, headgear, eye glasses, earplugs, gloves and safety shoes. The PPE must be suited to the task, used properly, and properly maintained. Employees must be trained to use PPE, and are required to report any defective equipment.

■ **Manual handling of loads**: It is obligatory on bar owners to minimize to amount and degree of manual handling that must be done by their staff members. Where handling is done, it is a requirement that risks be minimized by having proper equipment, and by strict adherence to safety procedures. Employees of the bar should be provided with information on weight, center of gravity, and any special handling requirements for any load, in addition to being trained to handle equipment properly.

■ **Visual display units (VDUs)**: An employee constantly using a VDU is entitled to adequate rest periods, free vision tests and eyeglasses if required.

■ **The use of electricity**: Electrical sockets may not be overloaded, and faulty wiring must be replaced. A proper identification system must be used with each piece of electrical equipment along with the proper marking scheme. All new electrical equipment has to be installed by a qualified person and staff members have a duty to report faulty electrical requirement.

■ **First aid**: All bars are required to have minimum first aid equipment. Arrangements regarding first aid must be recorded in the safety statement.

■ **Emergency procedures:** Bar owners are legally required to have emergency plans that include provision for the safe evacuation of employees and the provision of notices relating to such. Emergency plans may be attached to the safety statement and must be in located in full view of all staff members.

Summary of employees' obligations for health and safety

- Take reasonable care to ensure the personal safety of themselves and others
- Co-operate with the employer
- Use protective equipment, operate machinery properly and follow the correct procedures
- Report any hazards as soon as possible, usually to their immediate supervisor
- Report any injuries/accidents immediately
- Recognise their obligation in the promotion of a safe working environment.

Safety statements

Every bar owner is obliged to have a safety statement, which must be made known to all employees, this safety statement should:

- Specify the manner in which the safety, health and welfare of staff employed shall be secured
- Be based on an identification of the hazards and an assessment of the risks to which the safety statement relates
- Specify clearly the co-operation required from staff and the names of the persons responsible for safety in the bar.

It is the duty of every bar owner to make each staff member aware of the safety statement and allow them access to it. Government agencies normally provide guides which help small businesses prepare their safety statements in line with the local regulations. Staff members have a right to be consulted in regard to any proposed changes in the safety statement, and to information as to whether the introduction of new technology or changes in the organization of work in the bar will affect their health and safety.

Summary of employers' responsibilities for health and safety

- Employers must provide a safety statement
- Employers must consult with employees with respect to health and safety
- Employers must obtain specialist advice on health and safety
- Employers must ensure:
  - ❑ a safe working place
  - ❑ safe access and egress
  - ❑ safe systems of work
  - ❑ competent supervision.

Young worker safety in restaurants

- Avoid awkward postures if you must carry trays, plates, or beverages. Serving with awkward postures such as unsupported elbow and finger postures can increase your risk for injury.

- Limit the number of plates or items you carry, realizing that carrying more than a couple puts excessive strain on your arms and back and may lead to injury.

- Use both hands to carry items such as coffee pots or water jugs and carry them with your elbows close into your body.

- Move the glass or cup to you, when pouring, rather than over-reaching with a heavy coffee pot or water jug to fill a glass.

- Carry plates with your elbows close into your body to lessen the strain on your arms and back. Avoid bending at the wrist or extending upward at the fingers. Your shoulder, arms, and hands should be in a neutral position rather than bent at the wrist or extended upward at the fingers.

- Balance the tray on both your arm and hand.

- Alternate carrying tasks from hand to hand.

- Balance the load evenly, placing heavier items in the centre of the tray.

- Make sure trays are serviceable and clean and dry and without defect before using.

- Stand by the person you are serving if possible, rather than reaching across tables and over people. In booths, pass the plates along, requesting that the people sitting closest to the edge of the booth assist you in passing the plates.

- Get help to move tables and chairs, rather than lifting alone.

Source: http://www.osha.gov/SLTC/youth/restaurant/strains_serving.html.

7.8   Identifying the hazards to reduce risks

The following areas must be considered in preparing a safety statement:

1 **Floors**: wet areas, the entrance, lobby, kitchen and bar areas, non-slip surfaces, floor washing and degreasing, trip hazard mats, 75% of tripping accidents caused by obstruction, importance of good housekeeping.

2 **Stairs**: non-slip surfaces, handrails and appropriate lighting systems, keep access routes clean and clear, careful of uneven surfaces.

3 **Bar and restaurant**: non-slip floors, furniture and stools, drink dispensers, hot lamps

4 **Lounge**: access to overhead planters, single steps, furniture, glazed doors

5 **Glassware and crockery**: cracks, chips, glass stacking, glass washing machines, careful of polishing and cleaning, separate container for broken glass/crockery.

6 **Beer kegs**: stacking height, manual handling, beer line cleaning, gas cylinders, keg delivery, keg tapping

7 **Kitchen**: vegetable slicer guard, bowl cutters, gravity feed slicer, planetary mixer, deep fat fryer, food processor, switch off procedures, extract ventilation, fire extinguisher, fire blanket, transport of hot liquids, cooler fan guards, knife handling and storage, cutting technique, solid surface, never cut item in your hand, suitability of knife for task, transferring knives.

8 **Gas safety**: lighting up, shut down instructions, flame safeguards, low-pressure cut-off valves, spreader plates, safety shut off valves

9 **Toilets**: non-slip floors, wet floor inspections, door latches, toilet fittings, floor-cleaning frequency

10 **Food**: best before date, cooked and raw meats, cutting boards, refrigeration temperature, food storage

11 **Health and hygiene**: detergent handling, dermatitis notices, barrier creams, reconditioning creams, towels, cloths, gloves, waste disposal, insect traps, rodent poison, kitchen cleaning procedures, no smoking signs.

12 **Store**: shelf stacking heights, safety stepladder, fire detector, combustible materials, clear aisle way signs, shelf rack construction

13 **Manual handling**: beer kegs, crates, cooking oil drums, foodstuffs, flour sacks, use mechanical aids, trolleys, careful of hot & cold items, sharp edges, obscured vision, large items, seek help when necessary.

14 **Office**: trailing leads, swivel chairs, filing cabinets, desk aisle ways, shelf storage heights, shelf construction, waste collection

15 **Building maintenance**: ladders, stepladders, trestles, hot work permits, contractors

16 **Yard**: keg delivery hatch, lighting, trip hazards, parking, ramps, access to fuel tank

17 **Safety**: hold up notices, supply chords and overheating conductor grips, cord grips, periodic equipment checks, distribution boards, RCBs, earth loop impedance tests, bonding of wash areas

18 **Fire safety**: emergency lighting, exits, fire extinguisher training, fire point notices, evacuation procedures, fire detectors, fire alarms, drills, fire brigade calling, escape routes

19 **Incident investigation**: incident report forms, responsible persons, witness interview, photographs, sketch, remedy, incident database.

20 **Burns and scalds:** boiling water, steam, hot and pressurised equipment (i.e. candles, sizzling dishes), serving hot food and beverages.

21 **Chemicals:** safe disposal, storage and usage of appropriate chemicals, proper labelling (not unmarked items, or in inappropriate containers), following instructions (never mixing, dilute accordingly), proper clothing, first aid equipment.

22 **Machinery and equipment**: proper training, risk assessment, safety warning, faulty equipment, firm bases, emergency cut out switches, proper space, use of guards, switch of power.

23 **Natural gas and LPG**: ventilation, proper maintenance, fault reporting, storage, standard procedures.

24 **Employees**: stress (define targets, provide feedback, consistency, worklife balance, rotation of tasks), safety (illegal drug or alcohol consumption), dealing with violence, intruder alarms, lone workers , first aid equipment, shit down procedures).

You should also include an external evaluation which includes any outbuildings, car parks, play areas and grounds which are directly associated with your bar.

For further safety information see the 'Guide on Manual Handling Risk Assessment in the Hospitality Sector' at www.hsa.ie .

Fire

- Ensure all staff know fire alarm locations, escape routes, fire exits and how to contact emergency services.
- Ensure fire escape routes are kept clear and not locked.
- Ensure emergency lighting is provided and maintained in working order.
- Extinguishers and fire blankets to be provided at suitable locations and serviced regularly, staff must be trained to use them.
- Disconnect the electricity at the mains.
- Never throw water at an oil fire.
- If you catch fire, stop, drop and roll.
- Do not store flammable items near heat producing equipment or naked flames.
- Provide smoke and fire detection equipment, provide fire alarms and ensure they can be heard throughout.
- Ensure extraction and ventilation equipment is cleaned regularly to avoid a build up of grease.

Table 7.1: Selecting the right fire extinguisher

class	material	extinguisher type
A	solids such as paper, wood, plastic	water or powder
B	flammable liquids such as paraffin, petrol, oil.	powder and carbon dioxide (CO2)
C	flammable gases such as propane and butane	powder or CO2
D	metals such as magnesium and aluminium	graphite powder
E	electrical fires	carbon dioxide
F	cooking oil and fat	wet chemical

Instructions: each staff member will receive a safety orientation before beginning work, please check off each item that was covered in the orientation, staff members will sign this form once all items have been covered and all questions have been answered satisfactorily.

The staff member (name)_____ has been:

☐ Informed about the elements of the written safety program that outlines the company's safety efforts.

☐ Informed about monthly crew safety meetings.

☐ Told to report all injuries and shown how to do this.

☐ Told to report all hazards to their supervisor and shown how to do this.

☐ Informed about all machinery, equipment hazards and, if less than 18 years of age, instructed about prohibited duties.

☐ Informed about all other hazards and ways to protect themselves, i.e. chemicals, slippery floors.

☐ Shown where the first aid supplies are located and who to call for first aid.

☐ Told what to do during any emergencies that could be expected to occur.

☐ Shown how to operate a fire extinguisher.

☐ Informed of and trained on chemical hazards according to the Hazardous Chemical Program training requirements, including how to read a label and precautions to take when using them.

☐ Trained on the safe methods to perform the specific job the employee was assigned, including any hazards associated with that job.

☐ Provided any formal training required to do his/her job, such as proper lifting, use of knives, grill and fryer operation, spill clean-up, etc.

The signatures below confirm that the orientation was completed on the date listed. Both parties accept responsibility for maintaining a safe and healthy work environment.

Date: _____ Manager, supervisor: _____

Date: _____ Staff member : _____

They will also sign an attendance form for each individual safety briefing attended and a copy of that form will be attached here.

(WCU, 2008)

Figure 7.11: Staff members safety orientation checklist

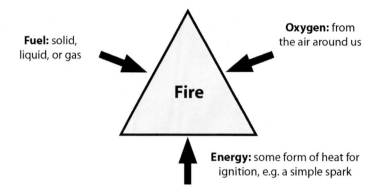

Figure 7.12: The fire triangle. For a fire to occur three elements are necessary. Fire extinguishers remove one or more of these elements.

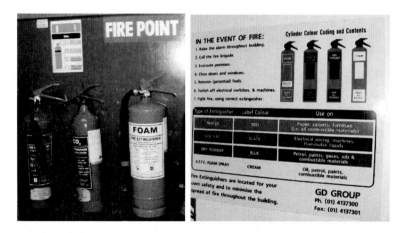

Figure 7.13: Fire extinguishers, instructions of use and evacuation instructions.

7.9   Conflict and violence in bars

Preventing and handling aggressive or potentially violent situations in the hospitality industry, especially in bars and nightclubs, is unfortunately a common area of concern. The most common origins of conflicts between managers, staff and customers occurs when dealing with disorderly customers, many of whom are deemed to be drunk, either individually or in groups. This accounts for nearly two thirds of all the violent encounters which managers and staff experience (MCM, 1990).

Techniques for the prevention of violence

Management skills and style

Firmness and fairness: Managers who are able to deal effectively with potentially belligerent and aggressive customers emphasise the need for firmness, of an assertive rather than aggressive nature, but also insist that this will only be effective if applied fairly. Fairness is developed gradually in dealings with customers and is part of the more general process of winning respect.

Involvement and detachment: While the essentially sociable nature of effective management requires a degree of involvement with customers, effective managers stress that this needs to be coupled with an appropriate sense of detachment. Being one of the lads, in their view, can lead to distinct problems when a manager needs to act in a more formal role and constrain the behaviour of certain customers. Bar managers must therefore always:

- Set clear and consistent standards
- Create a sociable atmosphere
- Combine firmness with fairness
- Be friendly, but professional.

Monitoring and surveillance

Very few aggressive incidents arise spontaneously or erupt 'out of thin air'. They have a distinct pattern of development which, if detected at an early stage, can often be curtailed. The diligence of the manager and his staff in detecting these antecedents is directly related to the number of aggressive and violent incidents which a pub experiences. It is characteristic of effective managers that they rarely stay in one place in their pub for more than a few minutes. During busy sessions in particular they will be seen engaged in apparently trivial activities such as collecting glasses or emptying ash trays. In this way they are able to see and to listen to the conversations of various groups of customers without being too obtrusive and without appearing to spy. Bar managers must therefore always:

- Know the danger signals, e.g. changing behaviours and conduct rowdiness, drunken behaviour and anti-social antics, large groups forming with opposing opinions.

- Use low profile monitoring techniques, e.g. covert CCTV cameras, undercover security personnel, management and senior staff members collect glasses and clean tables

- Combine monitoring with sociability, talking and engaging with your guests relating small stories of current affairs, sport and family events coming up.

- Intervene early but tactfully.

Figure 7.14: CCTV computer based system. Clockwise from top left: Flat screen monitor, dome camera, external LED camera, DVR recorder, signage.

Calming strategies

In addition to the need for the manager to remain calm when faced with aggression, there is an equal need to reduce the level of aggression in the customer before attempting to apply control measures. A highly emotional individual is unlikely to respond to direct instructions or demands. Only when the aggression has been reduced through the use of calming strategies can controls be effectively enforced. Bar managers must therefore always:

■ Get them away from an audience

■ Stay calm, and not respond to provocation

■ Use relaxed non-aggressive body language

■ Be assertive and not aggressive.

Managers should consider what they are trying to achieve when faced with an aggressive situation and what they want the outcome to be. The answer, of course, is always a non-violent resolution, a win-win situation where nobody gets hurt.

Control

Anger control: Successful bar owners emphasise the need to stay calm and use phrases such as 'not adding fuel to the fire'. By taking such an approach they are more able to reduce the anger and emotion in the customer/s with whom they are interacting.

Control strategies: Once calming procedures have been employed, the application of control strategies is likely to be much more effective.

At this stage there is a need for managers to make clear what they require of the offender. Where ambiguities exist, there is the potential for further conflict so effective managers typically use phrases which allow the offender to accept easily the need for control measures. Bar managers must therefore always;

■ Calm before control

■ Be clear about their requirements

- De-personalize the conflict
- Always allow face saving, the more respect you show the more confused the guest becomes and they are not able to sustain the argument.

When refusing service, entry, asking people to leave or removing offenders from the premises, emphasize your legal or professional obligations to make it less personnel.

Frustration

Our ability to think clearly and logically is impaired through intoxication. This, in turn, reduces our ability to employ coping strategies when in situations which are frustrating or aggressive. So you should try to:

- Look at the pub and bar from your customer's point of view.
- Identify and remove potential sources of frustration through good housekeeping and good customer service.

List from your staff or customers the frustration points of your bar. The most common frustration points include; slow or inefficient service, no acknowledgement from bar staff, poor seating layouts spills, no locks on toilet doors, faulty furniture, poor ventilation (hot/cold), last orders or poor signage. The two paths between alcohol and violence interact with each other. Because we can't think so clearly, we come to depend much more on cues in the situation to help us understand what is going on. A heated argument among a group of people, for example, can trigger aggression in others who have been drinking and witness it.

Hostility from managers or staff becomes magnified in the eyes of people who are intoxicated. Levels of frustration can become far more significant.

The police

- Know your limits, no heroics
- Establish and maintain good relations for advice and information
- Don't expect the police to run your pub for you.

Closing time

- Have a clear and consistent message, for example, at last orders, do you flash the lights and call "last orders"
- Maintain a regular routine that everyone understands
- Conduct a gradual wind down
- Be always firm but polite when dealing with the end of the evening session.

A bar which has a friendly and non-aggressive atmosphere is likely to provide an environment in which alcohol leads to increased sociability and well being among drinkers. Many acts of violence among serious drinkers can be avoided if steps are taken to ensure that their mood is not negatively influenced by perceived aggressive cues especially at closing time.

Disorderly conduct and crowd control

The sensitive area of disorderly conduct in bars and its effects on the guests is an emotive area. In most countries, bar owners must not permit disorderly conduct and any individual engaging in this behaviour must leave the bar upon being requested to do so by either the owner, his nominee or a police officer. Your focus must always remain on your customers and you must pay close attention to the total environment in which you place them (Murphy, 2005). You should introduce a system of crowd control which is focused on active monitoring, prevention and intervention at the earliest possible moment. This leads to greater guest security, comfort and enjoyment (as highlighted above). These measures should not be used in isolation; they should form an active integrated approach, which will help create a sociable atmosphere, and happy satisfied customers.

7.10 Principle areas to protect

This section focuses on the principle areas which bar owners must also consider towards implementing a good security policy.

The delivery area

Ensure that you have keep trained personnel, or senior staff members in the delivery area, and that they are familiar with the goods, the documentation, delivery dockets jargon and abbreviations and all the stores and cellar area safety procedures. Big losses can occur through poor systems at the point of delivery. Keep a dedicated separate area for the delivery. This saves new stock getting mixed with old stock which eventually causes confusion. Watch out on your delivery dockets for allowances for short deliveries, any broken or free goods and empties which you returned for credit. Finally ensure that all access doors to the cellar or stores areas are always locked and consider some spot checks on deliver goods.

Staff members

It is crucial that you rigorously check their previous employments. Provide training which addresses the house rules and policies. Consider movement of staff between bars and lounges to keep them on their toes. The bar business is still predominately a cash business, and if your in-house systems are weak some staff will take full advantage.

Customers

Modern designs in bars can create a series of blind spots, which can be used for illegal activities or theft. Insist that customers are issued with receipts for all purchases at the bar. The most common theft occurs through unattended bars.

Fixtures and fittings

Always keep records of all the bar's fixtures and fittings (including all the equipment in your kitchens, cellar, lounges, nightclubs). You would be amazed how many pieces of equipment, fittings and fixtures, go missing especially when staff members change positions.

The security of valuable stock

Expensive wines, Champagnes, etc should be secured in separate locked stores which are only accessed by the owner, manager or charge hand.

Intruder alarm system

A system for a bar should comply with the equivalent national or international standard and ideally shold be linked up to a monitoring station. The bar should have a couple of panic alarm buttons installed in the premises; the location of these buttons should be easily accessible and known by all staff members.

Close circuit television (C.C.T.V)

CCTV is crucial ad a good deterrent against theft, violence and anti-social activity. The CCTV system should have covert cameras and a good computer based network which incorporates recording relayed to a secure area, which staff members cannot access.

Key security

The issue of key holding is controversial. I would suggest that the access to keys to the bar should be limited to the owner, the manager and senior charge hand, or other appropriate person. Consider also a duel key holding system for example the owner carries safe keys and the manager carries the pub keys.

7.11 The role of hosts and private security in bars

A host, door supervisor or bouncer means a person, employed by the bar who, as part of his or her duties, performs any of the following functions at or in the vicinity of the bar where a public or private event is taking place or is about to take place. Their duties and responsibilities include:

- To control, supervise, regulate or restrict entry to the bar or premises
- To control or monitor the behaviour of persons therein.

Removing persons from the bar because of their behaviour

The use of private security in bars has increased in recent years. This demand has been brought about by the anti-social, violent and drunken behaviour of some customers. The majority of local authorities and government agencies around the world regulate and license the private security industry in their own country or state. Bar owners who use these services must ensure that they employ a licensed security contractor or employee. If they contravene this requirement, depending on the local laws, they will be liable to incur a fine or imprisonment.

Licenses issued to individuals who offer private security services to bars are backed by a recognized qualification which ensures that all those working in the industry have been trained to a high standard. In addition, applicants are usually vetted by the local police force before any license is issued. Government authorities will usually maintain a register of both contractor and individual license holders on their website. These registers are a useful tool for bar businesses and the public, who can ensure that their private security provider is licensed by checking the details on the register. Fines can be imposed on bar owners who engage unlicensed private security providers.

Violent conduct or acts of abuse by your hosts can result sometimes in criminal convictions which lead eventually to bad publicity for your bar. This type of behavior can turn people away from supporting the bar.

7.12 Insurance cover

The bar industry and the services that it offers have changed immensely in recent years, and to keep up with customers' expectations nowadays, the bar owner must offer many diverse services which are governed by regulations and costly investments (Elliott, 2006).

Before you delve into this area please remember you should always examine your existing insurance cover to initially assess if the premium you are paying is money well spent in your business. Your insurance brokers should be made aware of all the bar business activity planned for the year, ahead including holding functions, parties, dances, cabaret, festivals, etc.

Business insurance

The main kinds of business insurance which bar owners must consider are;

- **Fire insurance:** This can cover damage by fire to the bar's actual premises and contents, which would be also crucial in the event of rebuilding costs.

- **Burglary, theft insurance**: To replace stolen or damaged assets, theft insurance covers the threat against equipment, stock in hand and cash.

- **Property damage insurance:** This should be on a material damage (all risks) basis, to obtain the widest coverage currently available in the market. The property valuation of the bar should reflect the cost of rebuilding or replacing the buildings and trade contents as new, and stock should be valued at cost. If the valuations on the buildings are based on market values they may be overstated, which will mean you are paying too much premium. If they are understated, they will not provide adequate protection.

- **Public liability insurance:** This covers claims by members of the public (your customers or patrons), or damage to the bar arising through the negligence of the insured or through their employees, or through any defect in the property of the insured. In order to arrange the policy on a proper basis, complete designation of trade should be given, all processes involved, and details of all properties owned or leased by the insured should be made known to the insurance company.

■ **Public liability, interiors and structures:** Designs for interiors and structures to which people will have access must create a healthy and safe environment free from any hazard. Specific legal provisions in your own country will set the minimum standards, types and qualities of materials and methods of construction that must be used to create safe and healthy environments. This essential cover and premium is normally calculated by using projected turnover for the forthcoming year and taking into account the level of activity, particularly entertainment in the bar. Currently, a normal limit of indemnity on the policy would be €2.6 million in respect of any one accident and €2.6 million in any one year for products liability insurance (explained below). The critical areas that need careful consideration are loss of money, theft, personal accident insurance.

■ **Product liability insurance:** This covers claims arising from loss or injury through using defective or dangerous products supplied by the nar. It is very important in food products, which includes beverages. Goods and products must be of merchantable quality, worth their price and reasonably fit for the purposes required. They must function properly and safety, and for a sensible period. Bar owners must equip themselves with sufficient knowledge and understanding of such legislative requirements for goods and services according to the markets in which they will be used.

■ **Employer's liability insurance**: Bar owners must provide a healthy and safe working environment for their employees and visitors. The purpose of employer's liability insurance is to protect employers against claims for damages brought by employees or visitors. An employer may incur legal liability to an employee who, while serving under a contract of service or apprenticeship, sustains bodily injury or illness, which arises out of and in the course of that employment. The premium is calculated on projected wage roll for the forthcoming year and an accurate projection should be given to the insurer. This should include payments to family member's entertainers, stewards, etc.

■ **Motor insurance**: Coverage against driving accidents. A wide range of third party, fire and theft and comprehensive insurances are available to cover transport vehicles used in the business. Third party cover is compulsory by law in most countries. Most insurance companies offer all the insurances listed above, or some combination, in a single office or business policy, which is more cost-effective than separate policies for each.

■ **Goods in transit insurance**: This covers the business against any loss or damage to goods when they are being transported from one place to another, and could be useful if a bar provides off-site services for functions and private parties.

- **Business interruption insurance**: This covers consequential losses, and is essential for a bar because a serious fire will affect its ability to continue to pay overheads and generate profit while the bar is being rebuilt and re-equipped. It is important the sum insured reflects the potential loss of business for at least the forthcoming 12 months, and provision should also be made to select a suitable indemnity period, which is the length of time that business interruption cover applies from the date of the loss. It may be advisable to select a longer indemnity period, 18 to 24 months, if you anticipate it taking more than 12 months to rebuild and get back lost customers. The policy can also be extended to cover loss of business caused by imposed closure by the local authority due to murder or suicide on the premises, food or drink poisoning on the premises, defective sanitary arrangements, vermin or pests on the premises, outbreaks of contagious or infectious diseases on the premises or within 25 miles of same. Cover can also be extended to include prevention of access to or use of the premises following loss of or damage to property in the vicinity of the premises by say a fire.

- **Fidelity guarantee insurance:** This type of insurance covers the risk of dishonesty by an employee. Since insurance companies rate risks differently, it is worth talking to an insurance broker, whose job is to find you the widest coverage at the lowest price. Ask whether you can reduce the premiums by paying an excess (just like motor insurance), and also whether the premium can be paid over the year rather than all at the start.

- **People-related insurance:** If the business is dependent on yourself, or one or two key staff, it is a good idea to take out key man insurance on these people. Then, if they die or are unable to work, the insurance company will pay a lump sum to help overcome the difficulty. It is also wise to look at life assurance, to provide death-in-service benefits, critical illness, permanent health insurance or medical expenses insurance for your staff members. In this instance the cost, and whether your staff value the insurance will be major factors.

- Other areas for which you must consider the protection of insurance include: legal fees protection, credit, bad debt, data and computer, travel and patents insurances.

Your own personal insurance and pension

What insurance you take out on yourself depends on the risk you are willing to take, your budget and your family situation. You may already have some insurance in place, in which case taking out more through the bar business would be duplication. Look at the possible key risks involved in running your bar business, which you need to be covered for:

- You could get sick and be unable to work: you need insurance to provide a replacement income, permanent health insurance.

- You could get sick or die and have no one to take over the running of the business for you: you need a replacement income plus enough extra to pay someone else to run your business, permanent health, critical illness, life assurance.

Life assurance brokers can advise you about coverage against these risks, talk to them also about pensions. A pension can be a tax-effective way of transferring cash from your bar business to yourself.

Assessment for fire insurance premiums

The basis of a fire policy is the sum insured. In deciding on the sum insured it is important to take into account:

- Replacement cost of the building
- Stock
- fixtures and fittings

It is very important to insure for the correct amount, otherwise the 'condition of average' may apply in the event of a claim. This in effect means that should the sum insured at the time of the loss be less than the value at risk, you have to cover the difference yourself. In arriving at the premium the insurance companies take various considerations into account:

- The actual business carried on in the premises is the major factor
- The construction of the building is important. Is it standard construction, i.e. concrete walls, tiled roof, and concrete floor? There are various forms of construction, which would be considered standard. A non-standard one would a building with a felt or thatched roof.
- Is there a mains water supply and adequate pressure available in the event of a fire?
- Fire extinguishers, smoke alarms, sprinklers and fire fighting equipment installed to scale can warrant discounts on your premium.

7.13 Cellar safety management

The responsibility of cellar health and safety lies with the bar owner and their management team. The standard legalisation in this area can differ from country to country, however most will have specific guidelines for the safe working in cellars of pubs and licensed premises, and these guidelines will be set down by the local health and safety authority of the land, backed up with strict laws. Unfortunately in some circumstances, bar staff members are offered little or no proper training surrounding the cellar area, and their knowledge of the hazards and risks associated with all types of cellar equipment, including highly dangerous gas dispense systems, is sadly very limited (Murphy, 2009).

We have read in recent times, in the national newspapers and trade magazines, of some terrible accidents and fatalities occurring in pub cellars. The majority of these incidents have occurred because of unsafe conditions and a serious lack of proper investment coupled with the necessary staff training required in this area.

Cellar safety, examples of some recent fatalities and near misses

- Dublin, Ireland (August 2009): A young assistant bar manager was crushed to death when his upper body became trapped in a cellar goods lift when he was moving kegs.

- Leipzig, Germany (July 2006): This death of a bar landlord due to asphyxiation from CO_2 gas inhalation resulted in major German legislation changes.

Why bother with cellar safety? In the bar industry we face hazards on a regular basis, but we tend not to pay too much attention to them until a major accident occurs, then we or the local Health and Safety Authority have to examine the factors which lead to it. You can request companies to carry out a complete risk assessment based on your individual premises. This review will highlight:

- Identification of all hazards in the cellar area

- Where the hazards actually exist

- Who is in possible danger (employees, service individuals)

- What action should be taken.

A tidy and well ordered cellar reduces safety hazards and enhances the efficient operation of the cellar. To ensure that you continue to meet the highest standards in this area, start by adopting the following safety techniques;

Cellar safety techniques

- Rotate the cellar's stock regularly, check for out of date products

- Delegate staff members to control the organisation and layout of the cellar

- Only stack draught beer kegs two high

- Electrical wiring must be standard and in line with local regulations, also don't overload cables or socket outlets

- All gas cylinders for beer dispensing should be safely stored, upright and placed behind the chains anchored to the wall

- Never tamper with high pressure gas reducing valves

- All detergents must be properly labelled and safely stored, preferably in locked cabinets or high shelves; do not mix detergents

- Ensure a good level of light in the cellar area

- Avoid any build up of litter and keep passageways clear

- CO_2 leaks are highly toxic and can kill; this is why most large bars now have a fixed gas monitoring alarm systems fitted (see below).

Figure 7.15: Typical pub cellar.

Figure 7.16: Kegs commonly found in cellars.

Safety regulations and risk assessments

The cellar area of bars is classified as a confined area. This definition relates to any location that has the potential to accumulate dangerously high levels of gas, as well as gas store or cold room areas (Bamunuge et al, 2010). Under the laws of the land in most countries, employers have a duty of care to their members of staff to provide a safe place of work. This entails carrying out :

- A proper risk assessment where the risks are identified and managed, ideally this assessment should be carried by a competent person, for example a private health and safety consultant.

- The implementation of measures to minimise risks to anyone entering the confined spaces in your bar, which could involve installation of forced ventilation and CO_2 monitor alarms systems.

- Providing training to members of staff, which must be properly recorded.

- Incorporating the risk assessment findings in your company safety statement.
- Making preparations for a possible emergency.

Gas leaks – dangers and procedures

CO_2 is heavier than air. It is odourless, colourless, non-flammable and axphyxi-ant. It is also undetectable to the human senses; you cannot smell, taste or see CO_2. It gathers in unventilated areas and displaces air, reducing the oxygen in the atmosphere. CO_2 leaks are highly toxic and can kill, which is why in most large licensed premises now they have a fixed gas monitoring alarm system fitted.

CO_2 levels up to 0.5% are safe enough; at 1.50% you would feel a shortness of breath and increased heart frequency, between 3-4% you will experience muscular pain, dizziness and nausea and finally at levels 9% and above you will experience convulsions, immediate paralysis and death.

You may be able to identify a gas leak by the sound of hissing from the cylinder, or the appearance of frosted cylinders or sometimes actually a higher than normal usage of your CO_2 stock. (BOC Gases, 2010).

Figure 7.17: CO_2 monitoring system. CO_2 gas cylinders.

Dealing with minor gas leaks

When dealing with minor gas leaks you should:

1 Tell someone you are entering the cellar.
2 Prevent anyone else from entering the cellar.
3 If possible isolate the supply of gas by closing the cylinder valve.
4 Ventilate the cellar by opening doors and trap doors.
5 Once the source of the leak is identified, rectify or call the responsible service provider.
6 Normal operations can only resume once the leak is repaired.
7 Turn the gas supply back on.

These minor gas leaks can develop because the tapping head was not connected properly or the nut was not tightened correctly on the cylinder hose. At alarm level 1, or minor gas leak levels, the gas monitoring alarm system can indicate that there is an 1.5% increase in CO_2 levels (38 times normal levels), this is not immediately dangerous and you can enter the area to investigate the gas leak for a short period, but do make sure no-one else enters until the leak has been fixed.

Dealing with major gas leaks

When dealing with major gas leaks you should:

1 Evacuate the area immediately

2 Call for assistance

3 Do not let anyone enter the cellar area

4 Open all the outside doors and windows to ventilate the area

5 Call your service provider to deal with the leak, particularly for underground cellars.

These types of major gas leaks can develop from a bursting disc rupture on the cylinder valve or an open tapping head in the cold room. At alarm level 2, or major gas leak levels, both lights on the gas monitoring alarm system will flash, indicating that there is a 4% increase in Co2 (100 times normal level).

The most important issue here is not to become a casualty yourself. You must remember that CO_2 is not easily detected by human senses.

In general it is odourless and tasteless and if staff members enter a CO_2 rich environment they must be wearing a breathing apparatus which is crucial to preserve life. Your service provider team can provide full training in this regard and address the issues also of safety systems for the handling and storage of gas cylinders. Your staff members should remember to keep the access areas clear at all times to the gas cylinders. Risks can occur if staff cannot easily access gas cylinders when the pub is busy. Keep in mind that a clean and uncluttered cellar is a safe cellar (BOC Gases, 2010)..

Key questions

Bar managers should ask themselves the following questions:

■ Is the area safe to work in?

■ Is the lighting sufficient?

■ What are the main hazards in the area? Uneven floor, slippy floor, safe storage of stock?

■ Has the cellar area that I work in adequate ventilation or a CO_2 alarm?

■ If something happens to me down here does anyone know that I am here?

■ If I enter the cellar area and find a colleague lying on the ground, do I know what to do?

Finally please remember fatalities could occur in your premises if you do not adopt proper systems for cellar safety, think safety always first.

7.14 Waste management

Waste management has become a significant business issue for bars in recent years; costs have grown dramatically, landfill capacity has become increasingly scarce and expensive while stringent legislation has been introduced around the world to ensure optimum waste management practices in bar businesses. Opportunities have to be found to reduce, reuse and recycle waste streams, while ensuring residual waste is managed in a responsible and efficient manner in compliance with the relevant legislation.

Identifying the challenges of waste

Some of bar owners and management teams might be wondering about the merits of spending precious time considering waste and trying to find methods and techniques to reduce or recycle it.

Why should bars recycle or reduce waste?

1 Recycling can reduce the bar's operating costs by diverting materials from disposal.

2 Waste reduction techniques can reduce purchasing costs as well as disposal costs.

3 Recycling demonstrates a bar's commitment to environmental protection to customers, local businesses and its employees. Most large bars or pub groups have a corporate mission statement which includes environmental protection.

4 Recycling saves raw materials, energy and reduces environmental pollution.

   Some additional considerations:

   - Recycling glass saves 25-32% of the energy used to make virgin glass.

   - Recycling paper uses 60% less energy than manufacturing paper from virgin timber and reduces pollutants by 50%.

   - Recycling steel and tin cans saves 74% of the energy used to produce them from raw materials.

   - Recycling aluminium uses 95% less energy than producing aluminium products from raw materials

Developing and implementing a waste management plan

To assure that your plan will be successful, develop an environmental statement which incorporates your waste management plan into your bar's or company's policies (staff members handbooks, etc).

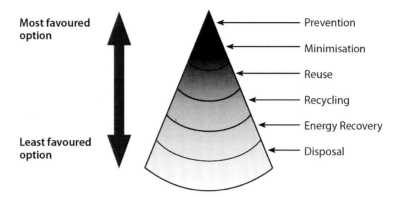

Most favoured option

Least favoured option

- Prevention
- Minimisation
- Reuse
- Recycling
- Energy Recovery
- Disposal

Figure 7.20: Waste management hierarchy. *Source*: Clare Casey, University of Liverpool

1 Write a waste management policy statement that reflects the commitment of the bar owner or top management.

2 Appoint either (a) an individual recycling co-ordinator for smaller bars; or (b) a green team, for larger bars or groups, to champion waste management on site. A co-ordinator should be genuinely interested in recycling and able to interface with personnel in the bar. Chose team members from among those who will be most affected by your waste management program. It is also a good idea to have a spokesperson for the employees.

3 The team should have frequent meetings to discuss how their department is doing and ways of improving the program.

4 Conduct a review to establish the current source, nature, quantity, ultimate destination and cost of the waste generated on site and use this information to identify opportunities.

5 Explore waste prevention and minimisation opportunities such as: reusable, returnable or recyclable alternatives; substitution; reducing waste generated. Talk to your suppliers about reducing/reusing packaging.

6 Develop a plan which selects projects, sets targets and responsibilities and implements them. These targets should include reduction goals that are specific and measureable, such as a 25% reduction in food waste within 6 months.

7 Communicate the plan to all staff members and throughout your bar.

8 Train staff in waste reduction and handling techniques on-site, e.g. through correct segregation, etc.

9 Work closely with your waste contractor to maximise the use of your waste management infrastructure, e.g. balers, bins, etc.

10 Use reputable waste contractors only and retain records of all waste transfers.

11 Review the waste management plan and acknowledge staff achievements.

12 Adjust the plan as new waste challenges arise.

Adopting these practices will lead to greater process efficiency, innovation and a competitive advantage.

7

7.15 Performing a waste audit

What is a waste audit? An audit is an assessment of the type and quantities of waste that the business generates. It can help you decide which materials can be recycled and how many collection containers will be necessary.

Why do a waste audit? Not all bars or restaurants are the same. The amount of waste and recyclables produced is affected by variables that differ from one business to the next. You need to examine your own waste stream before adopting new programs, to assure a good fit with your business.

How to conduct a waste audit

One approach is to sort and weigh several samples of your trash over time. This effort will provide a good accounting of your waste stream composition. Another method involves a review of purchasing and waste removal records. These records can help you to develop a decent estimate of your waste materials. Look for high-volume materials such as corrugated cardboard, and for high-value materials such as toner cartridges and aluminium cans. These types of materials make good candidates for waste reduction and recycling. Walk through the facility noting what type of waste is discarded in each area. A walk-through will help you determine the size and placement of collection bins.

What you will find

The type and mix of wastes that a facility generates will be unique. The level and type of waste generated by a business will reflect the nature and size of the operation. To manage your waste you must understand the quantity and type of waste that occurs on site, the reasons why it is generated and find opportunities to prevent or minimise its generation. Residual waste should then be managed in the most efficient and environmentally friendly manner. Find out what to recycle and how your business may save money by reducing waste. Generally, waste from business arises under one or more of the following categories:

- Office area: office paper, corrugated paper or cardboard, other paper, beverage cans and bottles
- Bar and dining area: beverage cans and bottles, newspaper, uneaten food
- Retail: packaging waste from the off-license area of your bar
- Kitchen: food waste, grease and oil, packaging waste like corrugated cardboard, pallets, steel cans, aluminium cans, glass and plastic bottles
- Guest rooms: newspaper, magazines, bottles, cans.

Types of waste

The amount and nature of waste varies from site to site. Therefore, its management requires a suite of measures depending on the waste stream involved and whether the waste is being managed on-site or off-site. Ultimate responsibility for all stages of waste management rests with the producer. As a result, businesses are finding themselves under ever-increasing pressure to find alternative and more effective ways to deal with the waste streams they produce. Use a chart like that in Figure 7.21 to keep track of your waste audit.

Figure 7.21: types of waste (www.ciwmb.ca.gov, 2012)

Material type	weight per month	rubbish disposal cost	recycle weight per month	overall recycle cost
aluminium				
batteries				
cans				
food waste				
glass bottles, containers				
mixed paper				
other paper (magazines, newspapers)				
plastics				
Others identified:				

Reassess your system

A key reason for starting a recycling program is to reduce waste collection costs. After implementing your recycling program, you need to conduct a second waste audit to see if your program has significantly reduced the amount of waste generated. If it has, you may want to reduce your collection schedule or the size of your container to save money on refuse disposal costs.

What licences are required to manage waste on-site?

Generally, only waste facilities require a waste licence. However, if you are not regulated by the Environmental Protection Agency and you store hazardous waste on-site in quantities that exceed 25,000 ltr (liquid) or 40m³ (solid) at any time, in most countries you would be required to register with your local authority.

7.16 Reduce and reuse – techniques for bars and restaurants

Now that you have finished the initial waste audit, you can identify materials for reuse and reduction. Below are some techniques for bar and restaurants. Identify any waste stream that can be reused, recycled and recovered, and train staff accordingly (Snarr & Pezza, 2000). Make sure to provide recycling bins to promote and encourage recycling in the bar.

7

Purchasing

- Ask all your suppliers to take packaging back
- Ask your suppliers to inform you of products that contain recycled content, have reduced packaging, and are packaged in recyclable materials
- Establish purchasing guidelines to encourage the use of durable, repairable equipment, and reusable products such as linen and tableware
- Buy dispensing systems to replace disposable food and beverage sachets such as sauces, soaps, etc.

Donation

- Used linens, towels, blankets, soap, shampoo and furniture may be appreciated by a local shelter.
- Cardboard and plastic cartons used for fruit and general food items and other materials could be offered to local schools or day care centres for use in arts and crafts activities.
- Flowers which are carried over from parties, functions could be offered to a local hospice or community centre.
- Send un-served food to local food banks. Produce scraps can be composted on site or donated to local farmers for composting.

Waste minimization

- Use straw-style stir sticks for bar beverages instead of the solid style.
- Serve straws from a health department approved dispenser rather than pre-wrapped, and offer only one straw per drink.
- Use pourers for sugar, pitchers for cream and small serving dishes for butter and jellies.
- Use re-useable cloth towels or hot air dryers in the bathrooms.
- Buy beverages in concentrate or bulk form, if possible.
- Minimize excessive use of disposable and non-recyclable packaging.
- Use minimal packaging to wrap take-out items, and offer pre-packaged food in recyclable packaging.
- Buy shelf-stable food supplies in bulk.
- Have staff members use permanent-ware mugs or cups for their drinks.
- Offer customers a discount if they bring their own mugs, containers, or bags.
- Write daily specials on a chalkboard or dry-erase board, rather than printing daily specials on new sheets of paper every day.

Reuse

- Store food in reusable containers.
- Use old paper bags when draining fat off oily foods, instead of paper towels.
- Turn stained tablecloths into napkins and chef's aprons. Use cloth linens and old linens for rags.
- Use reusable coffee filters. Quality cotton, silk or metal filters can replace the cartons of paper filters restaurants go through in a given year.
- Collect and resell used cooking fat (oils) back to a manufacturer.

    Food Preparation and Storage:

- Adjust stock levels on perishables to reduce waste due to spoilage or dehydration.
- Use daily production charts to minimize over prepping and unnecessary waste.
- Whenever possible, prepare foods to order.
- Adjust the size of meal portions if you find they are consistently being returned unfinished.
- Wrap freezer products tightly, label, and date them. Make sure they are used in a timely fashion, to minimize waste due to freezer burn.
- Check your produce deliveries carefully for rotten or damaged product, and return any substandard product.
- Rotate perishable stock at every delivery to minimize waste due to spoilage.
- Clean coolers and freezers regularly to ensure that food has not fallen behind the shelving and spoiled.
- Arrange your refrigerated and dry storage areas to facilitate easy product access and rotation.

Waste management equipment

The correct equipment can help to ensure waste is properly managed. Volumes can be reduced by using compactors, balers, shredders, etc. Colour coded waste bins should be used to assist in segregation. Do not put liquid wastes into compactors.

- **Burning waste**: It is illegal to burn waste.
- **Awareness**: Identifying waste management opportunities and introducing good practice are the first steps. To be truly effective, however, staff must be appropriately trained and protective clothing and equipment provided where necessary. Staff should be regularly updated as to the success of the initiative.
- **Emergencies**: Develop and implement emergency plans and response procedures if handling or storing any waste on-site.
- **Environmental protection agency (EPA) regulated sites**: Business activities regulated by the EPA must comply with the on-site and off-site waste manage-

ment conditions set down in the EPA's licences. All other companies (which includes bars) must comply with the local waste legislation and implement best practice procedures, as outlined here. It is your responsibility to ensure that waste is properly managed in your establishment (www.ciwmb.ca.gov).

7.17 Waste management programs (WMP) and energy saving innovations

Certain areas of the bar and hospitality industry have well established WMPs. There are many examples of the benefits that an effective WMP can have on your bar or pub group. Here are two case studies focused on international hospitality companies, and some energy saving innovations which bar owners can use to reduce costs.

WMP – case studies

Starbucks coffee company

This specialty coffee retailer has its corporate headquarters in Seattle, Washington. The corporation has developed an environmental mission statement for its stores. The mid-Atlantic green team oversees the Washington area environmental effort.

- **Materials recycled**: plastics, corrugated cardboard, and some newspapers.

- **Cost savings**: the most money is saved from the promotion of reusable items like coffee mugs.

- **Waste reduction**: Starbucks provides in-store customers with ceramic mugs, glasses, glass plates, and stainless flatware. It provides a $0.10 per cup incentive for customers to bring their own mug, or customers can purchase a mug at the store and receive a free re-fill of coffee. Customers can also pick up used coffee grounds at the store to use for their backyard composting.

- **Buy recycled**: the store sells a coffee paper note card set made from post-consumer paper containing coffee tree fibres. The store's paper bags, napkins, shopping bags, cardboard boxes, paper towels, receipt tape and tissue paper all contain varying amounts of pre- and post-consumer recycled content.

- **Education**: employees undergo training, participate in community clean ups, which helps the stores improve their recycling, and the store newsletter discusses environmental issues. Starbucks also instituted an internal environmental award called the Green Bean award that is presented to a store or department that meets certain environmental leadership criteria. Customers are educated through signs posted in the store.

- **Keys to success**: the company instils environmental values in the employees through education. It is important that employees at all levels know the company's environmental policy and support it.

Marriott International Conference Centre

Located in Chantilly, Virginia, the Westfield's Marriott International conference centre has 345 guest rooms, three dining rooms and 425 employees. John Huppman started the recycling program in 1991 after Fairfax County mandated it.

■ **Materials recycled:** paper, glass, metal cans, cardboard, motor oil, antifreeze, tires, fat/oil.

■ **Cost savings**: reduced tonnage of regular trash which decreased the amount of pickups overall, decreasing the cost of hauling the trash.

■ **Waste reduction**: includes use of china and glassware in all dining areas and serving beverages from dispensers. Double-sided copying and use of scrap paper helps to reduce paper consumption. Use of cloth towels in restrooms. Pallets and large plastic tubs are returned to vendors.

■ **Buy recycled**: cardboard, steel.

■ **Education**: through meetings, classes, sessions about recycling. Waste containers easily accessible. There are recycling bins next to trash cans for guests to use during coffee breaks from conferences.

■ **Keys to success**: Keep it simple. Get the guest involved because it makes them feel good. Separate at the source.

■ **Challenges**: people putting trash in the recycling bins.

■ **Outcomes:** Recycled: 110 tons; waste disposed: 440 tons; recycling rate: 20%

7

Energy saving – industry examples and innovations in the bars

Light fittings: Energy saving bulbs are offered in a multitude of options (candle and stick shaped varieties) all of which use 80% less electricity than a traditional GLS bulb. Fittings and diffusers should be cleaned regularly. The average GLS lamp last for 1,000 hours while a CFL (compact fluorescent) will keep going for up to 6,000 hours. Lighting companies offer establishments solutions to cut costs.

Fridges: 60% less energy is used by the new models of bottle coolers compared to traditional ones. Look for the 'Low E' symbol on glass doors. Some pubs are advised to invest in smaller coolers and stock them regularly instead.

Ice machines: Those fitted with a new patented system of heat recovery save 20% on energy costs.

Hand dryers: Dyson Airblade uses 80% less energy than normal hand dryers. It works by sucking in dirty washroom air to Dyson's digital motor which then passes it through a hospital grade HEPA filter motor which removes over 99.9% of bacteria while drying your hands. If a washroom uses 200 paper towels per day the cost would have been approximately €1,000 per year, this machine offers a 99% saving and is eco friendly.

Hand soap: One-touch foam soap cartridges each with 3,000 doses instead of the regular 2-3 squeezes of the soap dispenser – saves up to 50% on liquid soap.

Kitchen: Several studies have revealed that different chefs operating the same kitchen with the identical menus can use up to 50% more energy, why? Because of inefficient habits such as turning on ovens too early, leaving cookers on at cooking temperature. Buying in cooking oil from a tanker, using plastic re-useable trays for fruit and vegetable delivery stocks will all reduce waste and save money.

Food waste: The Electrolux waste management system can reduce the volume of food waste in a pub or restaurant by up to 80%. It removes excess water from the waste, allowing that to pour down the drain, while the pulp is stored hygienically in a separate container and is perfect fodder for composting.

Dishwashers: Do not use dishwashers on part load – run them only when full, and use a water softer to prevent scale formation and to minimise energy use. Consider the use of low temperature sanitising liquids.

Extraction: Only used when needed, and consider variable speed extractors, **especially** for larger locations. Ensure filters are cleaned regularly, and consider heat recov ery from exhaust. Ventilation should be linked to gas supply to ensure sufficient air for safe gas combustion appliances.

Car park area: By installing low energy lamps, motion detection, day light sensors, and power correction techniques, savings of up to 40% can be made. One business was spending €70,000 per year and after the installation of this equipment the savings was €28,000 in one year.

Water: Turn on taps changed to push buttons or sensors. Waterless urinals are used by large pubs chains and food companies like McDonalds. This approach is saving up to 100,000 litres of water annually in their restaurants (falconwaterfree.com).

Energy saving schemes for bars

Most countries around the world are promoting energy saving schemes, backed up with tax allowances for businesses. Bar owners can avail themselves of accelerated capital allowances (ACA) which are tax incentives introduced by governments to encourage companies, including bars, to buy energy efficient equipment (Paul, 2004).. It allows a bar to write off 100% of the purchase value of specified energy efficient equipment in the same year of purchase, hopefully translating to double savings and a greener bar all round. Bars usually qualify for energy saving schemes with capital allowances up to 100% maximum on the cost of expenditure such as lighting, motors and drivers and building energy management systems.

Conclusion

Although significant advancements have been made in recent years to help edu-cate food service workers about safe food handling practices, research studies still indicate that there has been no significant change since the 1980s in the top three causes of foodborne illness attributed to food service workers, which are: poor personal hygiene, improper holding temperatures and improper cooling procedures. Food safety and hygiene in the bar is crucial. Food workers must understand the principles involved in correct food storage, preparation and service, and must be aware of the causes of food poisoning. Preventing the cross contamination of foods is paramount to protect public safety. Bar owners must assist staff members through regular training initiatives to apply local hygiene regulations commensurate with their individual work activities.

Workplace safety and security is the bar owner and management's responsibility, it includes the formation and implementation of safety and security programs. Safety and security for your bar and cellar also involves training programs which are meant to teach staff members how to handle the risks and responsibilities involved in carrying out their duties. Bar owners must also implement strict meas-ures to prevent acts of violence, anti social behaviour and drunkenness in the bar to safeguard their staff members against harassment, intimidation or ill-treatment from customers or other employees. Your insurance cover schemes and safety and security policies can help cover all the risks which staff members, customers and the bar premises might encounter in its daily operations, it is imperative that bar owners keep their insurance coverage up to date.

Finally, the problem and challenge of waste management and reducing energy costs has become a significant cause of concern for bars. Through the adoption of more sustainable activities such as energy reduction, waste minimisation, pre-vention and recycling, bars have demonstrated that simple waste management measures can reduced the cost of waste disposal significantly. The introduction of waste management programs is not limited by the availability of technology, as most measures are simple and local governments will provide help to those interested in implementing waste minimisation strategies for their bar.

7

8 Handling Cash and Payments in Bars

Aims and learning outcomes

This chapter aims to introduce the areas central to handling cash and payments in the bar. On completion of this chapter the learner should be able to:

- Explain the principle payment systems used in the bar
- Identify management procedures for the handling, movement and recording of cash and payments in the bar
- Identify the risks which arise from fraudulent and dishonest activities in the bar.

8.1 Introduction

The bar industry is one of the last remaining industries where the predominant method of payment is still by cash. Although in recent years we have noticed the rise of credit and debit cards as the new methods of payments, cash still remains the preferred method of payment. The control and management of all forms and methods of payments bring with them their own challenges to managers, bartenders and owners.

8.2 Payment systems used in the bar

The cash register

Usually operated as the main payment point in most bars, and usually in the centre of the back bar where it is easily accessible by all food and beverage staff members.

The amount of cash registers held in any location usually depends on the volume of business that the location is turning over. Some large bars will provide one cash register per staff members with responsibility for the contents of the cash drawer and float.

Cash register functions

The principle functions which cash registers are required to perform are:

■ **For the business:** they record the sales and total them on a report printout that becomes a master record. They record every transaction producing a printout of the price of food and drinks ordered by customers and the total amount due for the food and beverage orders.

■ **For the manager:** who can operate defined keys to extract totals for all transactions during particular trading sessions (for example the lunchtime period). This is useful for checking cash totals and accounting information for the business.

■ **For the customer:** who can receive a receipt for their food and beverage order. They can witness their order recorded and totalled on the ECR display, which can be projected onto larger screens positioned at good customer viewing vantage points for price, product and transaction transparency.

Figure 8.1: Antique cash register.

Electronic cash register (ECR)

In the majority of bars, owners wanting a more specialized machine order their registers through a distributor, who will work with the owner and management team to understand the specific tasks the register needs to perform. The distributor will design the software for these special functions or have it designed at a software company. The distributor then approaches the manufacturer with the list of needed features. In some cases, the new features can be made to fit in a pre-existing model or the manufacturer's engineers may have to redesign parts and processes. Although bars choose distinctly different ECRs, the greater majority of these ECR systems will contain similar function buttons and facilities.

ECR operation instructions for bar staff

1 Turn the register to the appropriate mode or setting for accepting cash sales.

2 Enter the number, or clerk code, that you have been assigned as an employee. This code allows the owner to see who processed what cash transactions and how much he is responsible for in the drawer.

3 Enter in the price of the first item you are ringing up, using the numeric keypad. Some electronic cash registers also allow you to enter a department code or item number. Press Enter. Repeat the process for each item.

4 When finished, press Subtotal to get the final amount of the sale including tax.

5 Type in the amount of cash received from the customer and press the Change or Cash button. The electronic register should open to allow staff to give change and print a receipt for the customer.

Figure 8.2: ECR system.

Electronic point of sale (EPOS)

There are EPOS systems, also known as management control payment systems, which are designed specifically for the hospitality and bar industry.

Touch screen EPOS systems

These systems are designed specifically for point of sale. Operators are led through transactions, prompting them to select options such as cooking instructions or side orders. Screens can be configured to encourage staff to up-sell or promote sales of high margin products. These systems promote good customer service and significantly reduce transaction times. Multiple operators can concurrently use the system. Simply touch the screen to select any course and you will instantly be presented with a new keyboard containing only those items. The system is ideal for extensive or complicated menus that have a variety of choices and options.

Screen based EPOS systems

Use for operators with large menus, individual buttons (ranging up to 165 buttons) can be set up to display a list of items for selection. Buttons could be set up for any products, food and beverages. These EPOS systems are a good alternative to touch screen EPOS systems where budgetary constraints exist, with virtually identical features to the touch screen systems at lower prices.

Figure 8.3: EPOS system.

Principle features of EPOS systems include: accurate customer billing, reliable order printing, hand held ordering, tighter cash control, customer accounts, detailed management information, improved promotion control, back office software, real time alerts and third party integration.

Contactless payment systems (touch and go systems)

Customers expect other forms of convenient, secure and reliable payment solutions in the bar environment today. This is a crucial part of customer service; in most circumstances it's the last - and most lasting - contact the bar staff make. This is why in recent years contactless payment systems have become very popular. These range from robust, wireless payment machines made to withstand daily knocks, spills and constant handling, through to total payments platforms for end-to-end customised systems (Verifone, 2012). Contactless payment systems are credit cards and debit cards, key fobs, smartcards or other devices that use radio-frequency identification for making secure payments. The embedded chip and antenna enable consumers to wave their card or fob over a reader at the point of sale (Payment News, 2012). Contactless functionality means that customers are able to make payments very simply and quickly by conveniently tapping their credit or debit card on a terminal, without the overhead of entering a PIN. Staff carry portable terminals on a belt clip which means that the customers have the option of paying for their products and services on the go from their desired location. Most contactless systems in bars are also integrated with an iPhone ordering system app which enables customers to order food, drinks and then make payment for these services using the app. Customers are no longer restricted to making payments at their table, or at the bar. Terminals are fully integrated with the till system, removing the need to re-key transactions which will also help to reduce any human error. The lightweight, water resistant terminals, with robust wireless communication to the base station, are carried by every member of the bar staff who interacts with customers, removing the need for bar staff to wait for a terminal to become available. Given the convenience and speed of service that can now be deployed, these solutions are designed to best serve high throughput sales environments, in particular during peak trading activity (Mastercard, 2012).

8

Pros and cons of contactless systems

- *Convenience and speed*: no cash or access to an ATM needed, the card is held near to the machine and registers the payment without typing in any numbers or signing anything. The transaction is quick - perhaps the fastest way to make and receive payments.

- *Safety:* the cards are simply a debit card with a tiny antenna inside that sends the information to the machine in less than five seconds. This means there is zero time for anyone to hack the transaction and a very low chance of any data from the card being captured and used by a fraudster.

- *Security issues:* unfortunately contactless card can be used by anyone, anywhere to purchase goods and services for £15 and less. Technically this would allow anyone who stole or found a debit card to use it as many times as they like as long as the price of their goods were no more than £15. These people could potentially spend a lot of money before the owner even knew that the card was lost or stolen.

■ *The future and true costs*: whether or not as a business owner you decide to accept contactless payments or not, you cannot deny that the way forward is certainly in card payments. Perhaps it depends more upon your location and the actual demand for contactless payments before you sign up for them, but either way you would do well to thoroughly investigate the true costs before deciding to forge ahead.

(Payment Sense, 2013)

Mobile payment systems

Mobile payments are payments made through devices such as mobile phones, smart phones, or personal digital assistants fall under this category. These systems represent a big opportunity for bars going forward which they must not ignore. When deciding on whether to implement remote or in-store mobile payment methods, consider the implementation costs and the relative position of the telecom operators and financial institutions in the market before opting for a particular model (Portio Research, 2008).

■ *SMS Payments*: the mode of payment is a text message. The customer asks for a payment request by means of a text message, once the transaction is completed the payment is charged against their phone bill, the merchant is notified and the goods are released.

■ *Near field communication (NCF) based payment:* NFC payments involve a mobile with an embedded chip which acts as the mode of payment. The technology involves contactless communication between the two devices over a range of 10cm. it enables the mobile to act as a smart contact credit/debit card which can be read by any smart card reader and NFC device. This process is similar to swiping a debit or credit cards but without any contact with the machine much more convenient than the SMS method but this process is generally considered less secure than the SMS based model (www.ntt.docomo.com). NFC based mobile payment system represent the family of contactless payment methods. The other members of the group are RFID (radio frequency identification), Bluetooth and Ir DA (infarred wireless communication) payment models. The methodology remains the same across all members but there are slight changes in the implementation of the technology.

■ *Mobile Web payment:* customer uses online pages on the handset in order to purchase goods or services. This is considered more secure than SMS based payments. This system is reliable but the payment behind the pages differ as follows. With direct operator billing there is a direct connection between the customer and billing operator – these allow fast and secure transactions; with credit card payments users are directed to the 'credit card' page and required to fill their details; with on-line billing through third party players, payment is made through companies like Paypal, Amazon Payment, and Google Checkout. (Portio Research, 2008).

8.3   Procedures and controls for receiving payments in the bar

Rationale for codes of conduct when receiving payments

To protect the business from undercharging problems, which affects profits and the business image.

■ To ensure customers are not overcharged, which saves customer complaints and helps to stop customers from not returning due to overcharging problems.

■ To ensure that customers receive the correct change, to help prevent claims of incorrect change which are not always genuine.

■ To protect staff members blamed unfairly for business losses.

■ To protect staff members against unfair dishonesty and competency claims.

■ To protect the business and its employees from the danger of robbery, as cash-rich businesses are targeted by thieves.

■ To reduce the risk of cash theft by staff or customers.

■ To prevent the acceptance of forged bank notes or dud cheques and credit card payments.

Internal cash controls for the bar

What could go wrong in a business? Many things – for example, the bar manager could embezzle cash due to lack of internal controls. If only one staff member in a large establishment is given total responsibility for collecting deposits from various departments and depositing funds in the bank, and if this same person is also responsible for reconciling the pub accounts with the bank accounts, that is too much control for one person. Some bars operate with no authorizations needed to conduct any of these functions. In some circumstances, staff members can alter receipts, cash details and bank deposits too easily. You must therefore focus on procedures for firming down your internal cash controls.

8

Accountability

Where cash is needed for the daily takings, who has access to it and why do they have access to cash? The business has real accountability when:

■ The cash is secure

■ Pub keys are secure

■ Pub or safe passwords and combination are not shared

■ Transfers of all moneys are fully documented

■ All cash transactions can be traced to a staff member

■ A receipt is given to each customer

- Rigorous background checks are performed
- Properly prepared cash drawers for staff members
- Keys for each cash drawer are easily accessible.

Separation of duties

There are four major cash functions which should ideally be separated:

- Record keeping duties
- Authorization duties (i.e. approving voids, refunds, over- and short registrations, movement of cash)
- Asset custody duties (i.e. access to cash and cheques, checks, keys, cash drawers)
- Reconciliation duties (i.e. drawing up bank deposits).

The real problem occurs when these four major duties are carried out by the same person.

These procedures should also be evaluated regularly but especially when staff member's duties have been reassigned or when employees join or leave your business.

Best practices for handling payments

Receiving payment for food and beverages forms a natural part of the bartender's other exchanges with guests. To minimise the risk of mistakes for customers:

- Always say 'please' when asking for the money and 'thank you' when given it
- Explain the bill or till receipt if the guest looks puzzled or concerned
- Allow your customers the time to study their bill
- Always count the change into the customer's hand, on the counter, table or plate
- Return the change quickly
- Be discreet when checking forged bank notes or stolen cheque or credit cards (and if there are problems, be discrete)
- Total up credit card vouchers (open totals implies that you are encouraging a tip)
- When presenting the bill always offer it to the host.

Applying best practice procedures to cash handling in the bar:

1 Correct cash handling helps to reduce and prevent mistakes and fraud.
2 State the price clearly to the customer. Staff members should serve the drinks or food and quote the price due by saying, for example, 'that will be €8 Euros please'. If the order is part of a running a tab, see point 8 below.
3 State the relevant denomination of the tendered note as it is received from the bar counter, or customer's hand, so the customer, fellow staff member and

any nearby guests all hear the amount stated. That eliminates many instances where customers claim they handed the staff member a larger bill than was cashed.

4   Enter the sale for the stated amount directly into the till after serving the drinks and food. Staff members should be trained to process one sale at a time. Once a staff member is allowed to make more than one separate transaction in the till at one time, you have a situation where an honest or dishonest mistake can be made (for example deliberately not inputting a sale). Your customers should clearly see the amounts being entered into the till (it is bad to have a till where the customer cannot see what is being entered).

5   Remove the change before placing the tendered note in the till drawer: experienced staff members leave the note on top of the till while they remove the change. The note should go into the drawer only after the change has been counted out. The cash-tendered key is useful for helping staff members to determine how much change is to be returned to the customer. (Some very experienced staff skip using this function, but I believe it should be used to eradicate any problems.)

6   Count the change back to the customer: this is the final check to ensure that the proper change for the tendered note was correct to both the staff member and the customer.

7   Thank the customer for the sale, and for any tip (this step is for good manners).

8   For a customer on a tab, the initial sale should be entered immediately onto a blank check and the check placed down near the customer. The customer's name should be written on the check at this time. The employee should enter all sales directly on the check after serving drinks and food, and handle the relevant payment at the end, following steps 2 to 7

You should find that when all of your all staff members with cash-handling duties follow these steps, innocent cash handling mistakes are reduced. When you insist that these steps be followed, it also makes it easier for the publican and management team to watch for any differences in the agreed house procedures which would indicate a potential or existing problem.

Best practice procedures for recording payments

- All monies of the business should be placed in the safe after each trading session or at the end of the day, in most premises. All business safes should be kept locked at all times. The responsibility of the safe keys will lie between the owner and the management team (for example some business will have a number of safes, with access restricted to certain personnel).

- All ECRs must be checked periodically within the day's trading, depending on the volume of business but certainly at least once a day. This can be done quite easily, by preparing drawers with the appropriate cash float in advance.

- Cash loans, IOUs or drinks on credit to customers should be discouraged.

- A house policy for cashing cheques should be instituted and strictly followed (for example if it is clear to staff that it is not the policy of the premises to cash or honour cheques and a staff member disobeys this instruction, it is recommended that the unpaid or bounced cheque should be given to the staff member as part of their wages).

- It is good practice to carry spot checks at any time on the ECRs, checking that the ECR reads and the cash or cheques correctly total up.

- If it advisable to label all items in detail when personal money and valuables are kept in the business safe, it should be also stated that the business accepts no responsibility for such items.

Procedures for handling large amounts of cash

When there is a large movement or handling of cash you should consider the following:

Security of cash: Minimum cash amounts kept, deposits kept in time delay or locked safes, with the use of cash capsules for frequent and regular cash drops.

Cash handling office: Secure location for the cash counting office, with reinforced doors and windows, and entry controlled from within.

Cash carrying, large amounts:

- Only use physically fit, trustworthy and established employees.

- Survey the route before use and establish those vulnerable spots so that extra vigilance can be exercised on approach. Be aware of drivers of vehicles or people behaving suspiciously.

- Frequent changes of times, routes and collection or delivery may offer security advantages. Preferably use a busy route rather than a quiet one, and establish alternative routes, if possible

- Consider a cash carrying case, alarm bag or dummy bag. Fastening the cash cases to the body can increase the risk of injury being caused to the carrier.

- An able-bodied escort should be considered when large amounts of money are being moved.

- The carrier should walk facing on-coming traffic, reducing the risk of a surprise attack from behind. An escort should walk a few yards behind.

- Know the identity of tradespeople on the route.

- Avoid regular or rigid procedures.

- Special care is needed when using a night safe. Any escort should stand with their back to the safe to observe surrounding area.

- If large amounts of money are being banked daily then consider using the service of a security firm.

- If using a private car, keep the doors locked at all times.

- Ensure the time of return is known so an alarm can be raised if necessary.

8.4   Cash counting, floats and cash drawers

Counting cash and cheques

You should always be mindful when counting cash to not allow any distractions, and be watchful for counterfeit notes. Count the cash out of the public view. If possible two people should count the cash. Store your cash in a secured locked receptacle or area. When receiving cheques, examine the cheque details (dates, names, company, amounts and general condition of the actual cheque) and remember that cheques can be stolen. Endorse the cheque promptly with your initials or signature, store in a secure area and deposit daily to reduce the risk of stopped payment on the cheque. Cash drawers should always be left open and empty to avoid possible damage by intruders when leaving the bar unattended overnight. Before leaving the bar check that no person has remained on the premises, checking toilets or obscure hiding places within your premises.

Bar cash floats

As part of the preparation procedures for licensed premises, staff members working behind the bar will be issued with a cash float before their shift starts. This cash float must be checked to ensure that:

- There is sufficient supplies of change for the many various transactions throughout the trading session
- The issued cash float contains the total amount, which the manager in charge claims to have issued to the relevant staff members.

Reserves of additional notes and change will usually be stored in the safe and can be requested in exchange for a similar amount of cash tendered throughout the trading session. Cash floats are returned to the manager in charge at the end of the trading session. The servers, bartenders or whoever is responsible for the cash float should check that the float is correct and, if requested, sign that they have indeed checked the cash floats.

Waiter or floor staff cash floats

As part of the preparation procedures for table or lounge service in licensed premises, the waiting or floor staff members are usually issued with a cash float, which they use to purchase food and drinks on behalf of the customers whom they charge when the food and drinks are discharged.

Waiter or floor staff cash floats are issued to safeguard large amounts of food and drinks being issued without immediate payment. This must not be confused with restaurant service where the guest will usually make payment at the end of the meal for beverages and food consumed.

It is usually the duty of the manager in charge, head bartender or supervisor to ensure that these cash floats are returned to the ECR behind the bar at the end of service before the ECR is totalled up at the end of trading.

8

Cash drawer configuration – the cash compartments

All moneys received throughout the trading period should only be put into the appropriate cash compartments all facing up in the same direction. This action reduces the time required to find change and reduces the risk of giving the wrong value coin or note by mistake.

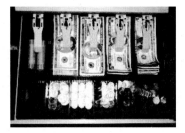

Figure 8.4: Drawer configuration.

Cashing up at the conclusion of trading

After subtracting the cash float which was issued, the total value of cash, cheques, credit card value in the ECR, plus any cash, cheques and bills are moved from the ECR to the safe during the trading session, should agree with the ECR reading for the total sales within the trading period. It is possible that the staff members who are responsible will request to check and count the ECR contents with the manager in charge. The manager in charge keeps a record on the breakdown of payments and any differences with the ECR readings (see daily cashier's checkout sheet documentation below). Differences and discrepancies can arise because customers were given too little or too much change, or because some of the order was incorrectly or not registered at all. If this is the case, the best course of action is to report the incident to the management team immediately. If you allow a period of time to elapse, however big or small, it will look like that you or your colleagues wanted to cover it up. Occasional discrepancies may be accepted, but repeated cash and balancing problems will not.

Coin sorting and counting machines

The majority of medium to large bar operations invest in coin sorting and counting machines, as they do not have the time and labour to count manually all the coinage and notes received by the business on a daily basis.

These portable electronically operated machines are specifically designed to sort and count mixed coins at incredible speed, and can process up to 600 coins per minute of up to 8 different denominations, all counting at the same time, depending on the type of machine model. Sensors identify the value of the individual coins. Operation panels give overall running totals as the coins are being sorted, and will also give individual totals when the sorting is completed.

Figure 8.5: Cash counting machines.

Note sorting and counting machines

Specifically designed to count notes at incredible speeds, note counting machines contain magnetic ink detection, UV detection, infra red detection, AMG detection, width size detection, length check detection and variable counting speeds facilities. Counting speeds vary from between 800 to 1,500 notes per minute.

Cashier's daily checkout sheet

The cashier's daily checkout sheet can vary according to size and scale of the business. For example, one location could contain four bars, one restaurant, one nightclub and an off-license. Below is a sample sheet which you may adapt for your bar, irrespective of its size. The most important issue is that the day's trading (which includes all outgoings) are properly and accurately recorded.

Daily Cash Sheet	Bar:	Day:		Date:		
	bar read	food read		till Z. read	cash total	over/short
Till 1.						
Till 2.						
Till 3.						
Total read:						

Cash:	till 1.	till 2.	till 3.	till float	till float	till float
100						
50						
20						
10						
5						
2						
1						
Coin						
Cheques						
Cash total						
				Cash total	Credit cards	
Paid out					Visa	
Credit card					Laser	
Total						
Ullage:_____ Line cleaning: _____ Complimentary: _____				Paid outs	C. cards total	
Cheque list:						
					Lodgements	
Total cheques						

Figure 8.6: Sample cashier's daily checkout sheet (Murphy, 2012)

8

8.5   Fraudulent and dishonest activities

The problems occurring in this area are generally due to fraudulent or dishonest activities. A very small amount of mistakes can arise from genuine human error.

Cash – counterfeit money

The main risk is from counterfeit money. Thieves who pass off counterfeit notes wait until the bar is busy and the bartenders are concentrating on numerous orders. These notes are worthless; the police will keep them for evidence for future prosecutions, but the business loses out with no compensation. Staff members are never truly sure of the relevant legislation with cash transactions, especially concerning counterfeit cash. This is a big problem for the bar industry across the world in Europe, for example the ECB (European Central Bank) and other world banking centres publish guides for retailers of the security features to look out for when manually checking for forged banknotes. If you suspect a forged note, keep the note in sight of the customer and call the manager in charge to check on your suspicions. Don't give the note back to the customer if it is forged.

Figure 8.7: Counterfeit money – security features.

- Euro scan laser: this is an innovative detector with laser technology, which detects the maximum security measures incorporated into Euro notes. The system is totally immune to the state of a banknote, lined areas, stains, wrinkles, washed, torn notes or notes that have been stuck with scotch tape.
- Counterfeit notes: devices are currently available for the detection of fraudulent notes, for example pen, ultra violet light, personnel checking. The ECB website publishes a list of the products which have been approved for detecting counterfeit notes.

Figure 8.8: Counterfeit money detector.

Cheques, credit cards and vouchers

In most bars the manager in charge or the owner are the only people who are authorised to cash or accept cheques, to avoid problems encountered by staff. Cashing third party cheques (for example pay cheques) can be fraught with problems therefore cashing these cheques is quite rare and only occasionally done for well known customers.

Issues regarding crossed cheques: these cheques must not be cashed because they are intended to be deposited directly into the bank account of the person who received the initial cheque.

Vouchers: These vouchers gives the customer certain items free, or at a reduction. Accepting them can be a useful revenue stream for lunchtime trade (for example luncheon vouchers). Purchases over the value of the voucher must be paid in cash, but usually change is not given if the value of the voucher is not fully used. Always check the validity and date of the vouchers. Under the regulations, luncheon vouchers cannot be used for the purchase of beverages, so be careful and encourage your customers to spend them on food only.

Credit, charge and debit cards

Plastic cards are popular and widely accepted in many premises for payment methods.

- **Debit card**: the amount due is immediately taken out of the customer's bank account. Some customers prefer this. The bank verifies transactions as they are made, provided there are sufficient funds in the customer's account.
- **Credit card**: payments can be settled once a month with one payment to the bank from the customer.
- **Charge card**: payments are settled once a month but with no extended credit usually allowed.

Staff fraud

Why staff commit fraud: The dominant factor behind most staff fraud is greed, and the employee's desire to fund the type of lifestyle they aspire to but cannot afford. In many cases where staff have committed fraud in order to pay off debts, they have continued to undertake fraud after the arrears have been successfully cleared. The continuation of fraudulent activity would indicate that greed is the primary driver.

Three other factors may present in staff fraud cases:

1 **Opportunity**: As a result of the organisational changes, junior and supervisory staffs that comprise modern workforces have never had more opportunity to commit fraud and, conversely, more responsibility to act ethically. Furthermore, senior or long-serving employees often hold a position of trust, which some may abuse.

2 **Motivation and pressure**: The increased susceptibility to targeting by organised criminals and a growth in personal debt has provided a more direct motivation and more obvious source of pressure than existed previously. Generally, fraudsters will be motivated by financial gain, which may or may not be linked to collusion with organised criminals or personal associates.

3 **Integrity and rationalisation:** There is no evidence to suggest that staff members are any less ethical or lacking in integrity than in the past. However, the infiltration of organisations by criminals, combined with a high staff turnover, reduced loyalty, relatively low pay in comparison to the national average and the perception of fraud being a 'victimless' crime with little chance of being caught, means that members of staff will increasingly rationalise the crime they're committing.

The internal culture within your premises: Bar management and senior staff members should promote an organisation culture which establishes through both actions and words the expectations of integrity for all employees in conducting business. It's also vital that staffs are fully aware that, if they committed fraud, there would be absolute zero tolerance.

It should also be clear that if the members of staff have concerns about co-workers, they have an obligation and a duty to report this. The organisation should have a whistle blowing policy that facilitates an independent and confidential means of reporting such concerns to ensure clarity, transparency and fairness when dealing with incidences of staff fraud.

Common techniques employed by dishonest staff

The cash register

- Serve the drinks and/or food and collect the money while the register is being closed out at the end of a shift.
- Phony walk outs: keep the cash and claim that the customer left without paying.
- Short register: charge the customer the actual price, under-register the sale on the cash register.
- No sale: charges the customer the actual price but did not ring up the sale.
- Voided sales: the cashier voids the check or some of the items on the check and keeps the proceeds.
- Over-rings: the cashier records an "over-ring" to reverse an actual sale.
- Fictitious pay outs.
- Alter the breakdown of tip and check amounts on credit card receipts to overstate the tips and understate the sales.
- Charge the customer full price, but register the sale at the discounted price.
- Jam the cash drawer during critical trading hours so that it must be left open.

The customer

- Short-change the customer (for example, by giving change for a €10 instead a €20).

- Have the customer sign their credit card slip in advance and overcharge for food or drinks.

- Short-pour, where bartender pours less than a standard measure to cover up drinks given away or sold on the side. Be alert for measures which are not the official standards in use in your bar.

- Omit most of the spirit or liqueur from cocktails or mixed drinks (especially if several drinks have been served to the customer).

- Pour a lesser quality spirit or liquor after the first few drinks and charge for the more expensive premium brand.

- Overcharge the customer for more drinks or food than actually served.

- Resell returned beverages. If a customer leaves an expensive spirit or liqueur the bartender may resell it to the next customer.

- Steal the customer's change left on the bar. Some employees wet the bottom of their drink trays and set them down on top of the customer's change. The cash sticks to the bottom of the tray.

Bar/restaurant

- Returned drinks: bartender claims that a drink was returned when it was sold.

- Give-aways: if no detailed internal controls exist, the bartender might give away free drinks to friends from the trade or sometimes in anticipation of receiving larger tips from customers.

- Phantom bottle: bartender brings his or her own bottle of liquor and pockets the cash earned from its sale. This scheme is much more devastating than merely stealing a bottle of spirits because even though the cost of the bottle is nominal, the lost margin on sales from the bottle is significant

- Collusion between the bartender and waiter or lounge staff to overcome a dual inventory control system.

- Barter, where the bartender trades the chef or cook free drinks for free dinners.

- After-shift drinks provided to, but not consumed by, employees are sold to customers.

- Cook requests a beverage (such as brandy, wine, vermouth, sherry, or other cooking spirits) for use in the kitchen, but drinks it instead.

- Steal bottles of liquor or food. Easy access to the food and beverage stores can encourage this activity

- Keep funds from the vending machine

- Steal bar supplies, e.g. measures, detergents, and cocktail equipment, or silverware, glassware, napkins, table cloths, etc.

8

- Give away or sell artefacts from the bar or restaurant (such as pictures or statuary).
- Revisit the bar or restaurant during closed hours and steal whatever is available.
- When obtaining change from another cash register, don't reimburse it fully and pocket the difference.
- Misuse of the manager's cash register keys (for example voiding actual sales).

Conclusion

There are various methods of payment used today in the bar, from mobile transfer, cheques, cash, use of cards to electronic transfers, even vouchers in some circumstances. Each of these methods has individual risks associated with their regular use which bar owners must carefully consider. The responsibilities allocated to bar staff and management to supervise and manage bars with autonomous control in recent years have created the fertile conditions, scope and the opportunity for dishonest actions by some staff members. The real challenge to bars going forward in this area will be to ensure that the best practices procedures, controls and policies they have adopted for handling cash and payments in the bar are consistently followed, rather than being compromised for convenience or expediency.

9 Sales and Marketing

Aims and learning outcomes

This chapter introduces the areas central to the marketing and sales of products and services offered in bars. On completion of this chapter the learner should be able to:

- Describe the external and internal factors influencing the success of a bar operation.
- Apply management tools and marketing strategies to influence consumer behaviour.
- Demonstrate the formulas and pricing policies used in bars to control costs and to generate profits.
- Adopt sales skills and personnel projection techniques to increase sales in the bar.
- Use the appropriate techniques and diagnostic methods for monitoring customer satisfaction in bars.

9.1 Introduction

Marketing and sales are critical components of running a bar business. The majority of bars use marketing and sales strategies but unfortunately a lot of them do it in an ineffective and inefficient manner. Successful marketing and sales programmes grow organically and evolve with your customers' demands. Marketing strategies are commonly associated with endeavors such as branding, selling, advertising and many other functions.

9.2 The changing marketplace for bars

Changes are constantly occurring in the community, and a bar must also deal with the growth of competition not only with other local bars but also with supermarkets, clubs and pop-up premises. Successful marketing will only occur when your customers have satisfied their needs and wants through exchange of your bar's products and services. Beyond creating these short-term exchanges, bar owners need to build long-term relationships with their customers and their suppliers. There are numerous benefits to marketing a bar, but the most crucial element is of course to create additional revenue streams.

External changes which can affect a bar's operation include:

- Political: government legislation, change in taxation structures, specific government taxes (VAT, local charges)
- Economic: rising costs of labour, fuel, rates and insurance, sales instability, disposable income changes, credit facilities, high interest rates, access to finance
- Demographic, social: changes in population distribution, socio-economic groupings, and growth in ethnic minorities, food fashions, family composition, and mobility of the market
- Technical: mechanization for food service and production, product developments and innovations, advances in technology.

Internal changes which can affect a bar's operation include:

1 **Products**: wastage and bad portioning control, low standard yields, perish ability of food, recipes and portion sizes to be reviewed, pilferage problems.

2 **Staff**: employees shortages, absenteeism, illness, use of part-time staff, poor supervision, lack of job descriptions and proper on the job training.

3 **Financial controls**: correct pricing systems, stores and cash control and collection, high frequency of low average spend transactions.

Dramatic changes in the marketplace are creating many marketing opportunities and challenges for bars. Major marketing developments can be summed up in single theme – connections. The huge growth in connecting technologies (social networks, IPhones, laptop computers, telecommunications and information technologies) has created exciting new ways for bars to learn about and serve consumers in large groups or one-to-one. Bar owners are redefining how they connect with their customers, locally and internationally.

9.3   Marketing opportunities and strategies

Marketing research, mapping a market

Marketing research involves systematically collecting, storing and analysing information, both internally and externally for the bar. The use of marketing research is a problem solving approach following a number of logical stages:

1 What information does the bar need, in terms of market size, segments, consumer behaviour, market feasibility for new product launches?

2 Where will the information be collected? Primary research, secondary research, inside and/or outside the organization.

3 How will the information be collected? Sampling and interviewing techniques, consumer panels, interview methods.

4   How will the information be analysed? This depends on how the information is collected.

5   How will the information be utilized? It should be used creatively to target offering products, eliminate poor selling products and focus on more effective promotion for your market.

6   Mapping the market: you should try to complete a full picture, isolating the main elements of where people live, where they work or shop and where they eat or drink, marking in all the competition to your bar.

SWOT analysis

SWOT (strengths, weaknesses, opportunities and threats) analysis may be used by bars as part of their market planning. Strengths and weaknesses are often referred to as internal, opportunities and threats as external. SWOT analysis can be used as a management tool to help provide a comprehensive analysis of all aspects of a bar business. It should also include a detailed review of all marketing functions especially in the formulation of the marketing mix (see below). SWOT analysis helps bars to innovate rather than react; for example, an analysis might identify:

- **Strengths**: pub features distinguishing it from others, for example the building (size, style, location, and facilities), and the personnel (the licensee or staff). When assessing strengths, be critical, viewing it as a customer might.

- **Weaknesses**: For example, lack of car parking, poor toilets, bad visibility from the road, late bars. Be sure that these are really seen as weaknesses by customers. Find out by asking them.

- **Opportunities** to develop: Awareness of environment, for example new housing areas, factories. Seek out those openings.

- **Threats**: Identify changes, for example closing of factories, increased competition. The whole activity of promoting the pub could in fact be disastrous.

9

Figure 9.1: SWOT analysis, to summarize basic market research, adapted from Kotler & Armstrong (2001)

Strengths	Weaknesses
Good reputation	Poor reputation
Popular products	Poor products
Quality products	Low value, high price
Unique selling points	Slow service
Value for money	Unskilled staff
Opportunities	**Threats**
Gowth potential	Very competitive market
Niche markets	Limited growth possibilities
Competitive pricing	Limited finance
Increase product range	Lncreasing costs
Efficiency update	Construction & road work problems

9.4 Positioning for competitive advantage

Bars cannot appeal to all purchasers in their markets, or at least not to all consumers in the same way. Bar owner must carefully design their marketing plans to ensure that they complement their bar capacity, capabilities and financial constraints. They must also allow for constant adaptation to consumer changes and economic conditions. By carefully selecting and attracting specific groups of customers, a bar can attain the necessary profit margins which will allow it to continue to compete in the industry.

Market segmentation

Market segmentation is the act of dividing a market into distinct groups of buyers with different needs, characteristics, or behaviour, who might require separate products or marketing mixes. It is an important aspect of market planning. Your bar cannot be all things to all people. Segmentation of the market may be viewed from two different standpoints.

- One is to study customers' characteristics using demographic and geographic criteria: age, sex, religion, occupation, income, etc.

- The other is to study customers' behaviour. Why do they buy our bar's products? What attributes of our product are important to our customers? Why do they buy our products instead of other bars, or indeed vice versa?

In the bar industry, some of these criteria may be used to identify market segments: geography, age group, socio-economic classification, income and family life cycle.

The target concept

Once the segmented groups have been identified for a bar, market targeting evaluates each segment's attractiveness and suggests one or more to enter.

- Evaluating market segments: to target the best market segments, a bar should first evaluate each segment's size and growth characteristics, structural attractiveness, and compatibility with company objectives and resources.

- Selecting market segments: it then chooses one of three market-coverage strategies. The seller can ignore segment differences (undifferentiated marketing), develop different market offers for several segments (differentiated marketing), or go after one or a few market segments (concentrated marketing).

Much depends on company resources, products and its competitive marketing strategies.

Market positioning

Once a company has decided which segment to enter, it must decide on its market positioning strategy, i.e. which positions to occupy in its chosen segments. The positioning task consists of four steps:

1 Identifying a set of possible competitive advantages upon which to build a position: if positioning begins with differentiating the bar's marketing offer so that it will give consumers more value than competitor's offers along the lines of product, services, people, or image.

2 Choosing the right competitive advantages: (single differentiating factor) a bar should develop a unique selling proposition (USP) for its number one attribute.

3 Selecting an overall positioning strategy: the bar and its brand's full positioning is called its value proposition – position your products either, more for more, more for the same, the same for less, less for much less, or more for less.

4 Effectively communicating and delivering the chosen position to the market: deliver the position and the tactical positioning strategy to support this position.

Objective for the bar's marketing message, using AIDA

The majority of marketing messages are used to promote a new service, product or the bar itself. Your marketing messages will have various objectives; for example, you could be trying to make people aware that you have started providing Sunday carvery lunch or weekend party nights each Friday and Saturday. Remember with the target audience, image is important, so segment your markets and sell the benefits of your particular products. To carry out this activity effectively you should use the AIDA form of advertising.

■ **Attention**: size and colour give impact, a bold design, stirring attention and creating awareness.

■ **Interest**: After obtaining readers' momentary attention, create an interest by different or new expressions.

■ **Desire**: Having obtained the interest, create a desire to the reader which they can easily understand, for example a free glass of wine with meal, or theme nights.

■ **Action**: Finally it should be clear what they have to do to obtain this benefit.

Large food and beverage companies spend a lot of money on advertising. Make sure that you encourage these companies to advise you when programmes are in your area that can benefit your bar and your customers.

9.5 The mix for your marketing strategy

The different elements of your marketing strategy can be divided into seven basic decision areas that bar owners may use to devise an overall marketing strategy for a single product or the complete bar. This is often referred to as the, seven Ps: product (concept and attributes), place (distribution), promotion, price, process physical evidence and participants and these seven decision areas are applied to bars the following way.

Product

Products are tangible (i.e. quality of the draught beer or food) and intangible features (i.e. the atmosphere, image or attitude of staff). Many marketing offers consist of combinations of both, ranging from pure tangible goods at one extreme to pure services at the other.

Price

This is the only element of the marketing mix that produces revenue. All the other elements represent costs, so price is the most flexible element of the mix. Pricing problems often arise in the bar industry because prices are too cost-oriented, not revised frequently enough to reflect market changes or not consistent with the rest of the marketing mix, or not varied enough for differing products, market segments, and purchase occasions. In bars it can be the balance between the need for profit and what customers are willing to pay (for example service charges on meals, corkage charges on wines, cocktails made with only fresh ingredients).

Coordinating prices for your drinks

Most pricing in bars is whimsical, inconsistent and illogical. A good coordinated policy should consistently deliver profits over all food and drink products (beer, wine, liquor, meals, and snacks). For example a good policy for pricing drinks should be built around a three-tiered pricing: House, Up-sell, Premium.

Why do we need coordinated prices? It can increase transaction speed, simplify decision making for guests and it is ideal for promoting and positioning brands.

How does it work? You designate specific brands of, for example, vodka as either house (the default) , up-sell or premium brands, adjust the pricing so the house brand is the cheapest. Always establish the house brand as the default pour.

Making money with three tiered pricing

- **House brand**: represents high margin for the establishment through generic drinks orders (i.e. vodka and red bull). Say one measure of house spirit has a cost (at the bar)of €0.48, and retails to the guest for €1.95, giving a pouring cost of 25% and a gross margin of €1.47.

- **Up-sell brand**: represents high margin for the establishment through specific drinks orders (i.e. Black Bush and Coke). If one measure of Black Bush whiskey costs €0.64, retails to the guest at €2.20, giving pouring cost of 29% and gross margin of €1.56, this is 6% higher than the house brand.

- **Premium brand**: represents a high margin for the establishment through brand specific ordering, adding massive value to the guest experience. Say one measure Havana Club 7 year old, costs €0.82, retails to the guest for €3.25, giving a pouring cost of 25% and a gross margin of €2.43, which is 121% more than for the house brand and 56% more than for the up sell brand.

Be careful when you choose to use tiered pricing. Two or four tiers is plenty. Pricing is part of a total marketing and sales package and doesn't work in isolation.

Three-tier brand-oriented pricing leads to better margins across all products, and helps to create higher contribution rates and increased profits. For a further explanation on pricing policies and prices methods which can be used in bars, see Chapter 10 under 'Policies for pricing'.

Promotion

Bars have to inform consumers about product benefits and carefully position their products in consumer's minds. To do this, they must skilfully employ three mass-promotion tools these include advertising, merchandising and public relations.

Advertising: Advertisers should set clear objectives as to whether the advertising is supposed to inform, persuade, or remind buyers. The aims and objectives of a bar advertising policy should be contained within the marketing plan, properly organized and effective managed (see Web resources – McMullen Brewers).

Merchandising techniques: at the bar level, merchandising refers to the variety of products available for sale and the display of those products in such a way that it stimulates interest and entices customers to make a purchase. Listed below are some of the merchandising techniques which you may adopt for your bar.

- *Fields of vision*: normal field of vision is about six feet, customers will therefore focus on the centre, in a short display the customers can easily see all the products in one glance, the majority of customers look left to right.

- *Arrival point*: you should maximise your merchandising here.

- *Hot spots*: the prime selling spaces, used to sell the products that the bar really wants to sell (i.e. top bottle shelf, around the cash register).

- *Mass facing*: mass facings create impact and increase sales.

- *Leading edge:* products brought to the front of a shelf have good impact.

Figure 9.2: Leading edge.

9

- *Special displays*: the back bar is a prime selling space. Create displays which help to stimulate sales.

- *Vertical stacking*: if space is at a premium save vertical stacking for impulse purchases and high profit earners.

- *Impulse and demand products*: these products will sell better if they are highly visible. Demand products are those which people will ask for even though they cannot see them, use the best space to merchandise impulse products.

- *Food merchandising:* The merchandising of food operations in the bar involves the point of sale promotion. The major forms of catering merchandising include the following:

  - ❑ *Floor stands and A boards:* free standing floor stands, bulletin boards in the waiting, reception or outside areas to advertise special events and selected specials.

  - ❑ *Posters*: Wider circulation can be used in many areas, careful of display heights.

  - ❑ *Wall displays*: illuminated wall displays, blackboards and banners.

  - ❑ *Tent cards:* placed on dining tables, useful to advertise other attractions.

  - ❑ *Menu clip-ons:* good for featuring higher profit earning food and beverage items.

  - ❑ *Children's menus:* reduced prices for children's portions, games puzzles.

  - ❑ *Visual food and beverage display:* displays-aid impulse buying, trolleys or carts – hors d'oeuvres, desserts, liqueurs, hot and cold meat joints, guerdon cookery – used for finishing off or flambé desserts encourages sales, display cookery, beverage display – wine racks, cooled fruit juices.

- *Audio*: need captive audience to promote goods.

- *Other sales tools*: place mats, napkins.

Figure 9.3: Bar back display.

When you have selected the types, techniques and processes which you will use for your bar, it is crucial that you or a nominated person evaluate their effectiveness and impact on a regular basis. You should ideally carry out this activity through a mystery visit to your premises using a diagnostic audit similar to the one listed below. Obviously no two bars will adopt the same merchandising techniques and will offer different products and services so this template can be altered to suit your individual requirements.

Figure 9.4: Diagnostic audit tool for merchandising for bars (Murphy, 2009)

	Meet	Below	N/A
Category: *This is the area covered i.e. (Pub Service) (Restaurant Service)*			
Premises: *Enter here the bar location*			
Date and time: *Enter here the date and time of arrival*			
Standards evaluated	**Meet**	**Below**	**N/A**
Standards: External premises			
1. Could you clearly identify the opening times of the premises?			
2. Was the customer's initial impressions of the premises encouraging?			
3. Did you or prospective customers have a clear view into the premises?			
4. Was the external and immediate entrance warm and welcoming?			
5. Did the entrance lobby offer helpful advice?			
6. Were all the entry doors, excluding the main entrance, warm and welcoming?			
7. Was the outside clean, tidy and presentable?			
9. Were the surrounding areas (car parks, small lawns and gardens) clean and tidy?			
9. Was it clearly evident that the premises were actually open?			
10. Were the external lighting systems working and correctly used? (early evening, afternoon, morning)			
Standards: Arrival			
11. Was the customer acknowledged and greeted appropriately (good morning/evening sir/madam)?			
Standards: Internal premises			
12. Was the bar/lounge/restaurant furniture properly cleaned, including under the edges of the tables and the bar surfaces?			
13. Were the internal lights working properly?			
14. Were the internal lighting systems appropriate for the time of day?			
15. Was the customer flow carefully controlled or pre-planned?			
16. Was the signage for (toilets and other amenities) clearly signed?			
17. Were the toilets clean, fresh smelling and stocked with soaps, papers, etc?			
19. Was there background music playing?			
19. Did the music type suit the (time of day, clientele) for the premises?			
20. Was the music playing at an acceptable volume?			
21. Was the furniture in good working condition?			
22. Was the furniture strategically placed to maximise customer volumes and comfort?			

9

Standards: Back bar			
23. Had the stock facings been carefully planned behind the bar?			
24. Was the leading edge full?			
25. Had hot spots been capitalised on?			
26. Were the bottled products properly chilled?			
27. Were the bottle shelves vertically stacked (shelves/fridge areas)?			
29. Was the wine selection properly displayed?			
29. Were the spirit/liqueur bottles clean and presentable?			
30. Had the back bar shelves been stocked from the rear (FIFO stock rotation)?			
31. Did the merchandising displays clearly recommend products to customers?			
32. Was the eye level space compatible with the sales mix for these premises?			
33. Were the spirit optic displays grouped effectively?			
34. Were the price lists correct and easily visible to customers?			
35. Was the back bar clear of debris?			
Standards: Point of sale material			
36. Was the point of sale material consistent for any one product?			
37. Were inappropriate/out of date/negative notices all removed?			
39. Does the point of sale material tie in with current media advertising?			
39. Were the chalkboards of good quality, and good working order?			
40. Did the displayed point of sale enhance the product appeal?			
41. Were the advertising posters clear, well written and relevant?			
42. Was the point of sale material clean and in date?			
Standards: Food merchandising			
43. Was it apparent from your external evaluation that the premises sold food?			
44. Was it clear that multiple payments methods were in place (credit cards, laser, and cheque)?			
45. Were the food service periods clearly displayed and conveyed to customers?			
46. Was it clear how to purchase food?			
47. Were the food menu boards well written?			
49. Suggestive selling: Were the food extras such as desserts, cheese boards and coffees offered?			
Total number of standards:	**Meet**	**Below**	**N/A**
48 - to be evaluated			
(Enter your total percentage score here out of 100%) This score is based on the total number of standards to meet. Disallow the not applicable ones for the premises under audit.			

LEAP - Merchandising code

- **Large, medium or small**? (for example, coffee offered per cup, mug or pot) Are key items being promoted and offered at optimum size? Are all items being offered at a size which produces optimum profits and satisfaction?

- **Extra items need offering**: Tempt customer's purchases by offering all the related items to the product selected, for example a pint of Guinness, brown bread and smoked salmon.

- **Added value is what customers want**: The benefits of the product help to sell it, so are your products described to the best advantage? For example tasty, special names, well known brands.

- **Presentation is the key**: Covers every aspect that the eye can see. Cleanliness is crucial. Are displays relevant, attractive, clean, helping to sell?

Public relations

PR is a communication and information process. It is crucial that PR is prioritised as a method to promote your bar. Its two main functions are:

- Problem solving or troubleshooting: where there are negative publicity or detrimental reports which could directly affect a bar's image and sales, a good PR campaign can restore this image.

- To create positive publicity for your bar: involvement in local festivals, hosting a charity event, announcing awards won by your bar.

THE LONDON SKY BAR PICKS UP MAJOR PRIZE

London. 6th June 2011.

Just months after opening, THE LONDON SKY BAR, part of the groundbreaking Altitude London riverside complex, was tonight voted Best New London Bar at the prestigious London Club & Bar Awards 2011.

Club and bar owners, promoters, DJs, event organisers, venue managers and showbiz impresarios all gathered at The Intercontinental Hotel in Park Lane to honour the very best of the capital's nightlife. Pick of the crop was undoubtedly the sexy and spacious THE LONDON SKY BAR, whose innovative and exciting offering so impressed voters and judges alike.

Perched at the top of the iconic Millbank Tower, THE LONDON SKY BAR combines the best views of the capital with elegant and minimalist surroundings. Here guests can listen to the worlds best DJs and artists whilst sipping on a range of innovative and delicious cocktails.

Little wonder that so many people have found the overall result so intoxicating!

Commented Altitude London's global brand owner Justin Etzin: "The London Club & Bar Awards is the first, largest and definitely most important nightlife industry ceremony in the world and we are incredibly honoured that it has

bestowed such an honour on THE LONDON SKY BAR. "Right from the outset we were confident that we had given the capital an original and dynamic new nightlife option - and it's brilliant that so many others agree!"

THE LONDON SKY BAR is open 7 days a week from 6.30pm until late.

THE LONDON SKY BAR, Millbank Tower, 21-24 Millbank, London, SW1P 4QP.

www.londonskybar.com

For further information please contact: ....

Figure 9.5: Sample press release (www.londonskybar.com, 2012)

Writing an effective PR Web press release is the best way to get seen on the Web and win more customers for your bar business.

Tips to get you started: Avoid jargon – use plain language that everyone can understand. Be concise – some search engines or editors won't read long messages. Don't be an advert – you're sharing a story.

Advertising does not sell. It is there to stimulate interest, and to influence a customer towards buying an operation's product above those of its competitors. The customer's action is translated into a purchase at the point of sale, further stimulated by effective merchandising, and possibly sales promotion techniques, all working together in a favourable environment created by good public relations.

Place

Place means the location where your bar is or will be established. Important questions to ask, particularly for bars include:

- What will the customer see and experience when they visit the bar?
- How easy is it to find the bar?
- What does the surrounding area look like?
- What draws customers to your bar?
- Do you provide a location map for your customers?
- Why did you choose this location for the bar?

Consider also the issues highlighted in Chapter 1 under 'modern bar design, layout and location' .

Process

Internal and external procedures, mechanisms and flow of activities by which the service is delivered. Although many bars are independently owned, an increasing number are now branding together under some form of corporate or contractual organization.

Physical evidence

This is the interior/exterior appearance, restaurant floor plan, lighting, table layout, staff uniforms, menus, tent cards, etc.

Participants

These are the individual staff (bartenders, waiter, bar & restaurant manager) and other customers with whom the customer interacts (see Chapter 2 under organization of beverage service personnel)..

Remember different marketing mixes are required for different market segments.

9.6   Sales in the bar

Macleod (1994) contends that pleasing the customer, is a tall order, as all customers are different with varying interests, ideas and demands. Selling is a natural part of customer service. In fact, you are already selling, without realizing it, as everything the bartender does on behalf of the bar for the customer is an act of selling whether it's selling the services, products or the pub's reputation. Knowing everything about a bar's products or services is not enough; the bartender must be able to apply this knowledge to the solution of the customer's request. Customers do not buy from salespeople who fail to understand their needs.

To find out the customer's needs and expectations, the bartender needs to listen, ask questions and look at things from the customer's point of view. Croner (1998) contends that selling is verbal, face to face recommendations and suggestions. You must remember that telling is not selling. Communicate with the customer to ascertain their needs, and personalize the sales pitch to take their expectations into account and demonstrate the benefits of the product or service to them.

Selling techniques

Conversation selling: Open conversations with your customers and their upcoming events or birthdays, etc. can highlight opportunities for functions, parties for your premises.

Over-selling: Crowding or dominating the guest does not work, and could completely turn off the guest from returning (so be careful not to be too pushy).

Related selling: When a customer asks for a product there is often another item, which naturally accompanies it. In addition to selling this requested item, the related product should also be offered (see LEAP above).

Suggestion selling: The undecided customer gives us opportunities to take the initiative and suggest food and drinks (for example the empty pint glass, the coffee after dinner.

Selling up: These are opportunities to sell something of greater quantity, higher quality, and higher price.

Silent selling: It is vitally important that the bar owner spends time behaving as a customer and a useful exercise is to do just that. For example, check the outside. Is name clear to drivers? Are the entrances to different bars and food areas, clearly indicated? Are the outside adverts, menus and pathways clean? The bar's untidiness caused by dirty ashtrays and cluttered counters are rarely accepted. These silent irritants turn people away. The back of the bar/off license counter can be the most important silent selling area. Remember, 'good selling is aided if the customer knows what is on offer'.

9

Personal selling (preparation, sales play, the follow-up)

The emphasis today is on flexibility, adaptability and responsiveness to customer needs. This will involve the staff members who are in contact with customers being aware of sales opportunities. Consumers want staff members who listen to their concerns, understand their needs, and respond with the right products and services. Selling consists of several steps that staff members must master.

- Prospect and qualify: staff identify qualified potential customers
- Pre-approach: staff learn as much as possible about a prospective customer
- Approach: staff meet and greet the buyer to get the relationship off to a good start
- Presentation: staff tells the product story to the buyer
- Handling objections: staff seek out, clarify, and overcome customer objections to buying
- Closing: staff ask the customer for an order
- Follow-up: the last step in the selling process in which the staff member follows up after the sale to ensure customer satisfaction and repeat business.

Remember your staff members are one of the most important assets of the bar. Too frequently waiters, bar staff, counter assistants, are seen only as 'order takers' and not as sales people.

What motivates customers to buy?

Customers buy for many different reasons, for instance:

- Price: suits the customer's pocket
- Value for money: customers like getting a good deal
- Competition: there are no bars offering the same products locally
- Staff attitude: helpful and friendly staff
- Peer pressure: a desire to be seen doing the right things by friends and colleagues.

Bar managers must evaluate these points and ask themselves, why do their customers come to their bar in the first place?

Staff communication, rules of selling, nature of persuasion

You must operate an effective communication system with your staff, and to do this you must be willing to empathize and listen to them, make and be happy to receive suggestions from them and to offer them some of your own. Try to anticipate their needs, desires and aspirations in the same way as they will do for your customers, and always set to consistently exceed their requests (within reason).

Rules of selling

If bartenders are to sell effectively, they must take control, have more knowledge, believe in the products and in themselves, having confidence in their skills. Most importantly staff members must to be able to read their guests and use every opportunity to up sell.

Reading guests, with their different personalities and backgrounds, takes a little experience, but you could use the following five control points to influence their decisions:

- **The nodding dog**: nod your head slowly three times when suggesting an option on the drinks or food list, this technique uses the psychological phenomenon of mirroring, but remember this can also work in reverse.

- **Bookending**: mention the preferred brand twice – once at the start of the list and again at the end, this technique uses the psychological phenomenon – we remember first and last the most, it combines lethally with the nodding dog.

- **Which? questions**: encourage the guest to make a choice from the selection you control, use the word 'which'. Try and be honest, read your guest.

- **Petrol tank theory**: offer another drink before the first one is completely empty, take control of the flow of ordering, drinking and re-ordering.

- **Shoot ducks while they're flying**: use all the techniques when it's busy, better service for guests, easier life for bartenders and kitchen staff, higher sales and better margins for establishment.

The nature of persuasion

The problem in the licensed industry is that too many people try to persuade in a way that alienates customers instead of in a way that involves them. You stand a better chance of influencing someone, if you:

- Use open questions to involve the other person, and search for areas where your offering will benefit your customer

- Probe so that you and your customer understand the full benefits they will receive from your offering

- Present what it is you have to offer in terms of those benefits.

9.7 Food costings

Trying to control your food costs is very challenging because of the perishability of the product, the unpredictability of the business and customers' selections, and the varying yields obtained from food products, your staff and your equipment.

Nonetheless we must start by understanding our gross profit margins on our food offerings. When you begin to cost your food for the menu, all of the factors mentioned previously under menu (Chapter 5, *Serving food*) must be taken into account. The most important issue to consider is how much money you need monthly to pay for all the operating and capital expenses and the profit. This means that 30 cent of every euro or dollar obtained from the menu price is needed to pay for the cost of materials Most bars would run their food operations on an industry average of 30 percent food cost. In some locations this figure could be lower but if this figure was higher then you must reduce your food costs. .

Portion cost and plate cost

The cost to serve the guest a portion or plate is a basic ingredient in the search to properly price the menu. Portion costs and plate costs come from the price we pay for our products, the yield on the product, the recipe cost, and the portion size and cost. In addition, when we actually plate the food, any garnish or decorating of the plate is an additional cost that needs to be factored into the menu price. If the garnish is a piece of parsley, then the cost is insignificant, but if the garnish is a sauce, such as a coulis, that is skillfully used to decorate the plate, then the cost of food and labour must be considered.

Dopson & Hayes (2011) add that the items which you elect to serve on your food menu will also have a profound effect on your employees ability to produce these items quickly and efficiently. So the real question here could be 'how menu choices do you offer ?'. They suggest that this answer depends on the operation, the skill level of employees, and the level of menu variety management feels is necessary to properly service the guests' (p. 296).

Food cost percentage

The food cost percentage compares the cost of the food with its selling price. A food cost percentage can be determined for each item on the menu, or an aggregate food cost percentage can be determined for total food cost and food sales by day, week, month, or year. The formulae used are shown below.

Food cost percentage for individual menu items or the overall food sales:

Food cost % of a menu item = cost of food / menu price × 100

e.g. Irish stew: Cost €3.75, menu price €12.50

Food cost % = 3.75/12.5 × 100 = 30%

Overall food cost % = total cost of food / total food sales × 100

e.g. Single day totals: costs €275, sales €980

Overall food cost % = 275/980 × 100 = 28%

Now that you have established the relationship between cost and price, you have a formula to work with. Every bar will determine its own cost percentage for producing the profit required to sustain the business. You can project the selling prices by dividing the total cost of the food item by the cost percentage you require.

Using the cost percentage to project a food sales price:

Sales price = cost of food / cost %

e.g. Irish stew: cost €3.75, cost% = 30%

€3.75 / 30% = €12.50

Projecting food selling prices using a multiplier

Another common method for projecting every food item's sales price (inclusive of VAT) on a menu, when its cost is known, is to use the multiplier which corresponds with the required gross profit percentage (see Table 9.1 below). For example, a food item costs €3.75 to fully prepare, and you want to achieve a gross profit of 70%. First look up the relevant multiplier in the table – for 70% it is 3.917. Multiply the cost (€3.75) by this, and you get a VAT inclusive sales price of €5.69.

Table 9.1: Projecting food sales prices (including VAT at 23%) using multipliers. (Elliott, 2007)

projected gross profit (%)	relevant multiplier	projected gross profit (%)	relevant multiplier
30%	1.679	60%	2.938
35%	1.808	65%	3.357
40%	1.958	70%	3.917
45%	2.136	75%	4.700
50%	2.350	80%	5.875
55%	2.611		

9.8 Control and calculation of costs to achieve profit margins

The pricing of the food and beverages is perhaps one of the most important mathematical functions we perform in the bar. Most bars have a high proportion of fixed costs, and this applies particularly to bars, hotels and restaurants. The crucial factors which you must consider include the need to make a sustainable level of profit. You must also consider the customers' perception of value for the prices you set, the location of your bar, the quality of the food and beverages offered, and the expertise of the employees.

The first area you must consider is the cost of your stocks and beverages – what you are actually paying for these products. Are you obtaining the best possible cost prices?. You must formulate a proper costing structure, which includes the cost prices you are paying for incoming stock. You must initially consider:

■ Your bar company's formation and the owner's philosophy. The differences between a small bar and a large pub group will be their ability to drive the best deals through their purchasing power, and in some circumstances the value and beliefs of the company founder or bar owner in supporting certain local or national food and drinks companies.

- Scale selling prices to different areas of the bar premises to achieve performance yields, e.g. late bars, restaurant, night clubs, and private bars.

- Low yields from recommended retail price items such as cigarettes, cigars, and snacks. Although these sundry items of stock generate low yields, they are usually a necessary evil as their purchase initiates further purchases from your business.

- VAT levels on drink, food, and cigarettes.

- Price discounts from companies given to major key account holders.

- Free goods, deals for bulk buying or new goods.

Generating costs and sales prices to calculate profits

It is crucial to update regularly the cost of the goods which your bar sells, to achieve profit margins acceptable to the business. The formulas listed below with examples of their use will help you towards planning your profit levels for the bar. These formulas are based on the gross profit method, which is the most common standard system for pricing food and beverages.

You should check your local and national taxes for food and beverages. The examples here are based on Value Added Tax (VAT), the sales tax used in Europe, which is currently at 23%.

Cost price =

total price divided by the number of units divided by amount per serving

Sales price, excluding VAT =

sales price inc VAT × 100 / (100 + VAT%)

Gross profit (GP) =

Sales price – cost price

Gross profit % =

gross profit / sales total

Calculating your gross profit percentage is useful for working out the acceptable profit margin which you would require for individual bar products.

Sales price to meet a gross profit percentage =

(100 – GP target) = cost%

Cost price × 100 / cost% = sale price ex. VAT

Sale price ex. VAT × (100 + VAT percentage) = sales price inc. VAT

You start by finding what percentage of the sales price will be made up of cost, then find the cost of this percentage. Finally add VAT to get the price to the customer.

Example one: calculating the gross profit on individual products per measure. A measure of whiskey (3.5cl) at €1.50

1. Remove the VAT content (23%): €1.50 / 1.23 = €1.22 (sales price)
2. Calculate the cost price per measure: €200 case / 12 (70cl) bottles = €16.67 per (70cl) bottle. A 70cl bottle / 20 (3.5cl) measures = €0.85 per measure
3. Gross profit = sales price €1.23 – cost price €0.85 = €0.38
4. Gross profit % = €0.38 / €1.23 = 30.8%

Example two: calculating the sales price when a gross profit percentage target is required. A measure of whiskey (3.5cl) costing price of €0.85 and a 60% GP required by management

1. Sales price before VAT: 100 - 60% (GP% target/margin set) = 40 (cost%) then
€0.85 × 100 / 40 = 2.13 (sales price ex. VAT)
2. add the relevant VAT level to the sales price:
2.13 (sales price ex. VAT) × 1.23 (23% VAT level) = 2.62

Example three: calculate the gross profit and gross profit percent

1. Gross profit = sales price (1.24) – cost price (€0.85) = €0.39
2. Gross profit % = gross profit (€0.39) / sales price (€1.24) = 31%

Example four: calculate the sales price excluding VAT

• Sales price (€1.50) / 1.23 (100+23% VAT) = €1.22

Example five: calculating the individual cost price on a pint of draught beer with a keg price of €150

• Total unit price (keg of beer €150) / 90 (90 pints in a 11 gallon keg) = €1.67

Figure 9.6: Calculating costs and sales price and profit margins – some examples

9.9   The mystery shopper

Mystery shoppers pose as normal customers and perform specific tasks, such as purchasing a pint and a sandwich, asking questions about the general bar facilities, registering complaints about the service offered or the produce ordered or behaving in a certain way to create real life scenarios and problems to be solved. They then provide detailed reports or feedback about their unique experiences within your bar for the owner and or management team.

Some of the areas which the mystery shopping team will explore include:

■ Date and time of the pre-visit phone call
■ Name of the bar visited
■ Number of employees in the premises on entering
■ How long it takes before the mystery shopper is greeted

- Name of the employee and whether or not the greeting is friendly
- The questions asked by the shopper to find a suitable product
- Types of products shown and if or how the employee tried to close the sale
- Whether the employee invited the shopper to come back to the bar
- Cleanliness of the bar and the other service staff
- Speed of service and compliance with the agreed company standards relating to service, bar appearance, and grooming/presentation.

Shoppers are often given instructions or procedures to make the transaction atypical, to make the test of the knowledge and service skills of the employees more stringent or specific to a particular service issue. For instance, mystery shoppers at a restaurant may pretend they are lactose-intolerant, celiac or unreasonably disruptive. Not all mystery shoppers include a purchase. From there, the shopper (or the owner's professional colleague) will submit the data collected to the bar owner directly or to the nominated mystery shopping audit company in question. The details captured from using this mystery shopper audit tool helps to assist in the preparation of a detailed report. The tool can be altered to suit specific bars and to target specific areas requiring improvements (see Appendix III).

Some companies invite their customers to become a mystery shoppers who can give comments instantly via their smart phone app. They give their customers loyalty points (see loyalty schemes) for their feedback (Global News, 2011).

9.10 Loyalty schemes

Your greatest resource as a bar owner are your returning customers – the people who love your bar and come back regularly. However getting new customers to come to your bar and become regulars is challenging and generally you have to give them something in order to entice them and retain their business. Both of these challenges can be accomplished with a good loyalty program, but not all loyalty programs are the same. Sharp & Sharp (1997) contend that "loyalty programs are structured marketing efforts that reward, and therefore encourage, loyal buying behaviour – behaviour which is potentially beneficial to the firm". Loyalty schemes and cards are a system of the loyalty business model. In the United Kingdom it is typically called a loyalty card, in Canada a rewards card or a points card, and in the United States either a discount card, a club card or a rewards card. Cards typically have a barcode or magstripe that can be easily scanned, and some are even chip cards. Small key ring cards (also known as keytags) which serve as key fobs are often used for convenience in carrying and ease of access. This section reviews five different kinds of loyalty schemes. You must consider which scheme will best suit your bar's individual requirements. Keep in mind that your loyalty program should be generous, easy to use and easy to join (Inside Hospitality, 2012).

Rewards

Award points for purchases. Points can be exchanged for rewards, unrelated to the brand. Use this type of program when you want your program to also serve as a new customer acquisition program and to differentiate your brand from the competition. This is especially useful if you have a limited product line. Administration can be complex – it needs special equipment, cards and database systems to optimize the benefits of a program. Members will also expect to be able to track and redeem their points online. Example: the Chicago-based Lettuce Entertain You restaurant group offers a wide range of travel, wine and spa packages as rewards for members of their Frequent Diner program.

Rebate

Awards a gift certificate redeemable for the next purchase, when the guest reaches a certain spending level. When you have a wide selection of products, this reward program can be used to motivate new incremental purchases. It can also be used to increased store traffic. Department stores use this method to build additional sales from existing guests. Example: the popular Coffee Cards (i.e. Costa, Starbucks, McDonalds) — your card is stamped every time you buy a daily coffee: once you have 5, 7 or 10 or stamps, you receive one free. Very simple to administer. Clubs and casinos use this method where members and card-holders have a swipe card, and can accumulate points from their gambling expenditure and apply them to food and beverage purchases.

Appreciation

The goal with this scheme is to increase your customer's LTV (lifetime value), not to acquire new guests. It can also be used as a device to get good customers to sample more of your other products and services. Airlines, hotels, phone companies use this to accumulate points for additional services within their own brand. Seat upgrades, free tickets, hotel stays at different locations, etc. Examples: Bars and restaurants use a frequent diner's club which offers a free dinner for two to four people voucher once a certain level of spending is reached. This encourages customers to spend up, and it keeps the rewards in-house – crucially they should be offered only redeemable on mid-week days, Monday to Thursday, to help business in this period. These regular customers are also likely to bring customers who had not visited your bar before.

Partnership

Rewards a guest's accumulated purchases with a partner's products or services. Your primary goal is to acquire new guests where you have a partnership arrangement to use the partner's extensive guest database. Airlines use this frequently when they give you points for renting cars and sleeping in hotels. Examples: your bar could offer rewards to the clients of other local businesses, in return for that business promoting you to their customer list. This scheme also works very well in small rural areas with businesses (shop local concept, local loyalty rewards)

9

who are trying to keep the money in their immediate area to protect local businesses, employment and the local economy.

Affinity

Once a customer climbs the loyalty ladder and reaches 'advocate' status, your brand is firmly planted in their minds. An affinity program offers special communications, value added benefits and bonuses and recognition as a valued guest. This is used where rewards are no longer needed to cultivate a long term relationship, just as a reminder to learn more about your other products and services. Examples: airline frequent flyers earn Silver or Gold status once they have earned a certain number of air miles. Upmarket, trendy bars and Night clubs have access to special rooms and benefits for members who have reached a special level of spending or are regarded as VIP customers.

(Inside Hospitality, 2012)

Loyalty coupons

Coupons are offered as a component of an overall loyalty reward scheme where the customer is rewarded for dining and drinking in your bar or local establishments. This loyalty scheme also encourages customers to become a VIP member to get valuable coupons, offers and event information delivered straight into their computer or mobile phone inbox. Customers are requested to either print a hard copy of their coupons for presentation upon their arrival at your bar or to present their loyalty card or mobile with their coupons (digital copy, or code) to take up the special offers or loyalty rewards.

Although loyalty schemes, cards and coupons offer bar businesses so many opportunities to increase their business, Livingston as cited in Anderson (2012) contends that some businesses use them as a distraction from the fact they are not price competitive.

Top trends in loyalty schemes

Loyalty schemes are changing and the pace of change is faster than ever. When putting together a loyalty program, if you're looking to keep pace with innovation, pay close attention to these trends that will make your loyalty scheme more effective and attractive. Remember you are in very crowded space with thousands of loyalty schemes are already in operation. Highlighted below are some of top trends which you should consider.

- *Uniqueness is expected:* technologies are enabling any bar to look and perform like it's operating a mature million-dollar program. The storytelling, loyalty rules (tiers, thresholds, award types) and functionality are increasingly available out of the box. Your bar can't just have a loyalty program; you need one that gives your customers an ongoing loyalty experience (e.g. www.starwood-hotels.com/preferredguest)

- *APIs and easy connections are required.* Integrating with user authentication and larger rewards programs will benefit your bar in the end (e.g. Facebook, Twitter, Paypal, Janrain, Shopkick and Apple Passbook). Your success is as much about what you are connected to as it is about your brand and your loyalty program.

- *Develop your brand's signature insight*: what is your bar's unique point of view? You need a point of differentiation to really capture the power and reward of a modern loyalty program. Focus on the audience you are targeting and build your program from there.

- *Game mechanics fuel today's loyalty programs:* Gamification is the next required ingredient for today's loyalty marketer to generate the engagement your bar needs. You want more LTV and revs? You can't ignore the power of game mechanics. Social is yesterday's story and it's now an assumed ingredient of your loyalty programs

- *Payments is the new PLCC (private label credit card):* don't be seduced into tying your program to a PLCC unless your target customer is in their late 50s. Instead, focus on mobile payments and keep your loyalty program separate from any credit cards. (e.g.: Starbucks' mobile apps, SquareWallet, LevelUp, PayPal wallet, Google Wallet and increasingly, features inside Apple's Passbook)

- *Invisible payments are replacing POS*: Cloud computing is taking over point of sale (POS) cash registers so you need to design your loyalty program to run across all your consumer touchpoints, not just the cash register.

- *Traffic is everywhere.*: don't think you need to just go to Facebook or Twitter to find it. Find the consumer Internet play that most closely aligns to your business. The band Green Day found make-your-own music powerhouse Soundcloud. Soundcloud's million of registered uniques powered Green Day's NumeroUnoFan program to incredible heights. Green Day has hundreds of thousands of loyal fans thanks to SoundCloud.

- *Real-time is the real deal*: there is an event-based transformation going on in loyalty. Members expect to be rewarded in real time — anytime, anywhere, you need to reward and provide real-time surprise, real-time magic. Harrah's does it with their Total Rewards program — in Las Vegas and around the world. You get points and awards in literally anything you might do once you arrive at one of their properties — and even before you get there.

adapted from (Goldstein, 2012).

9

Loyalty coupons – types and usage

- *Buy One Get One Free*: this coupon is straight forward – when you purchase one item you get another of the same type item free of charge.

- *Catalinas* - these coupons are typically generated at the cash register for specific items, or to be used as cash on your next purchase.

- *Coupon insert* – these are the coupons relating to your bar which you have placed in your newspaper, magazines, local newsletters.

- *Double (or triple) coupons* – this is a policy used in some establishments which matches the face value of manufacturer's coupons, effectively doubling (or tripling) their value. Policies vary from bar to bar – some bars will double on certain days of the week, and others double every day. Printed Internet coupons are usually not accepted for doubling.

- *Extra Care Bucks (ECBs)* – this is a CVS program that requires you to apply for an Extra Care card. When you have your card, you can earn ECBs through the purchase of specific products. These can be used like cash on almost anything in the store. ECBs print at the end of your receipt, so be careful to not lose them or throw them out by accident! CVS has both monthly ECB offers, which are detailed in a circular that comes out on the first of the month, and weekly ECB offers, which can be found in their weekly sale flyers.

- *Loss leader*- these are deeply discounted items offered to attract customers. The price is usually lower than the bar's cost for the item. You can usually find loss leaders on the front (and sometimes back) page of weekly sale flyers.

- *Manufacturer's coupon (MFC)*: these are coupons issued by food and beverage manufacturers. The majority are found in the Sunday newspaper coupon circulars.

- *Peelie:* these are coupons in the form of stickers on product packaging.

- *Store coupons* – these are coupons which you issue in your own bar.

- *Your Mileage May Vary (YMMV)* – this means that coupon deals, such as those promoted on the Internet for a pub group, may not apply at your specific bar, due to geographical price variances or simply because your bar doesn't participate.

(coupondivas.com, 2013)

9.11 Social media

Social media refers to a group of Internet-based applications that build on the ideological and technological foundations of Web 2.0, and that allow the creation and exchange of user-generated content (Kaplan & Haenlein, 2010). Social media depend on mobile and web-based technologies to create highly interactive platforms via which individuals and communities share, co-create, discuss, and modify user-generated content. It introduces substantial and pervasive changes to communication between organizations, communities and individuals (Kietzmann & Hermkens, 2011). Agichtein et al (2008) and Morgan et al (2012) contend that social media differentiates from traditional/industrial media in many aspects such as quality, reach, frequency, usability, immediacy and permanence. Savvy bar and restaurant owners know that social media is one of the hottest marketing tools today. In this section we highlight how social media can help you attract and retain customers for your bar.

Geolocation platforms

Geolocation lets customers use the GPS feature in their smartphones to 'check in' at your bar or restaurant. Customers can check in on Facebook or Foursquare, a geolocation app that links with their Twitter and Facebook accounts. When their friends see that they're at your bar or restaurant, they'll be motivated to come by as well. Try to encourage your customers to check in by offering promotions and discounts such as a free drink, a discount off their meal, or some other reward. Get creative; look for check-in rewards that are likely to get shared. Visit Facebook and Foursquare for more on marketing your bar or restaurant with check-ins.

Review sites

Once you've claimed and optimized your bar's listing on local search, ratings and review sites, you need to monitor your reviews. Check the sites daily, since even setting up a Google alert on your bar name won't show you all the reviews. Try to respond quickly to negative reviews, but don't get defensive. Thank the reviewer for their feedback and try to remedy the situation. If necessary, ask to contact the person privately via email or telephone to discuss the issue. Ensure that you thank individuals for good reviews as well remember the point of social media is to engage with your customers. And personalize your comments whenever possible. If someone comments on how good your cocktails or wines are, don't reply with a simple thanks, but add a longer more personal message. Ask your customers and reviewers if you can feature their reviews on your website or marketing materials as testimonials.

Remember that all reviews are a (free) opportunity to learn what your bar's services and products need to improve.

9

Social media sites

Facebook and Twitter are the best-known social media sites, but up-and-comer Pinterest, where users 'pin' photos to virtual 'pinboards', is attracting attention with its visually oriented focus. All three can work well for your bar. Twitter is a great way to share timely information — for instance, you can tweet about today's lunch special at 11:00am, when people are starting to think about lunch, or send a 3:30pm tweet with a code good for a free happy hour appetizer. Pinterest is more branding-focused; use mouthwatering photos of food and drink (cocktails, cold beer), or create theme boards ('beers of the world' or 'super Saturday'). Facebook is a happy medium of both — you can use it for timely posts and deals, while also featuring drool-worthy visuals. Listed below are just some considerations to assist you when adopting and using social media sites;

- *Be visual*: even on Facebook and Twitter, photos often get more response than text-only posts. Try posting photos of the daily lunch special at your bar, or a special wine or craft beer you have on draught. Post photographs of events at your bar, like the 'Friday madness' with reduced priced food, drinks promotions or special evening menu.

■ *Engage:* social media isn't a one-way street, engage with customers by asking questions 'what's your favourite item on our appetizer menu?', conducting surveys 'what cocktail would you like our mixologists to create for you?', or getting quick feedback 'what should we name this dish?'

■ *Have fun:* social media isn't supposed to be corporate, so make sure your pins, posts and tweets reflect your and your business's personality.

■ *Track results:* Facebook and Twitter offer free analytics tools you can use to measure the results of your social media activity; use them. Note what types of posts and what times of day or night get the most responses. More important, note which social media promotions actually drive traffic into your bar or restaurant.

■ *Cross-promote:* include links to your social media accounts on your bar website, and put signage in your windows, at your hostess station or on your menus encouraging users to follow you on Facebook, Pinterest or Twitter.

(Lesonsky, 2012)

Managing social media / Pros and Cons of usage

Managing social media can get overwhelming, but you do have some third party apps and tools to simplify things.

■ *NutshellMail* will monitor your bar's Facebook and Twitter activity related to your business and email you a summary of events and activities.

■ *Mediafeedia,* for Facebook, lets you schedule posts, manage multiple Facebook pages, get email notifications about activity on your pages and more.

■ *Tweetdeck* (owned by Twitter) helps you sort all your incoming Twitter data, schedule tweets and manage multiple Twitter accounts.

Finally there are some overall pros and cons involved in adopting social media. The pros are that these marketing and sales tools are free, and they uniquely tap into the social nature of the bar experience. The only major drawback is even though you won't have to invest any money in social media tools, they do require an investment of time and effort to succeed. You might have to hire (part-time) somebody with information technology skills if you are struggling with the technology involved in operating social media. Younger (technology savvy) members of your family can be most helpful in this regard.

9.12 QR codes for marketing

QR codes are similar to the standard bar codes that currently appear on all types of consumer products, except QR codes can contain much more information than traditional barcodes. QR codes in advertising and promotions provide paper-based hyperlinks that connect the physical world with the online world. A QR code works by simply scanning the code with a mobile device that is equipped with a camera and QR code reader application. These applications can be downloaded for free on popular smartphone platforms such as iPhone and Android.

Once the QR code is scanned using the device's camera it is translated into actionable information, such as a text message or mobile web page. There are a number of practical ways QR codes can be used for marketing and promotions in a variety of settings. QR codes can be integrated into just about any type of printed materials, including conference/event displays, print advertisements, business cards, brochures, posters and flyers, postcards and mailers. If a high proportion of your customers in the bar use smartphones then a QR Code can be a great way to differentiate your bar and reach people in new ways.

There are numerous ways that QR Codes can be used to strategically bridge offline and online media. Here are a few examples which your bar can adopt:

- QR code with a link to the bar's Google Places page with customer reviews and coupons.

- QR code next to the bar main products to view product demonstrations and reviews.

- QR code on a food, beverage, cocktail takeout menu, which links to a mobile bar and restaurant website for online reservations, orders and interactive directions.

(Human Service Solutions, 2012)

Conclusion

The first rule of marketing is to know your consumers. The location of the bar and its crowd is a crucial factor in determining where consumers feel comfortable to eat, drink, socialise and stay for longer periods. Identify what you sell best – food, drink, music or the atmosphere, and then find out about the market place. Consider your bar's overall location. Consider what are you customers needs when they come to your bar. And what is the local competition for their disposable income? Decide which products and services your bar can promote better than others to give your business a competitive advantage. Ensure that people know about you through advertising, publicity and sales promotions. If you also want to generate more money from existing guests, train your management and staff to use selling skills and techniques.

9

10 Beverage Control Systems

Aims and learning outcomes

This chapter aims to provide the knowledge and skills to understand and adopt stock and beverage control systems for their bar. On completion the learner should be able to:

- Identify the major planning areas involved to manage costs, pricing and revenue for achieving profits
- Apply the controls, techniques and documentation for receiving, storing and issuing products
- Outline the rationale and procedures for stock control in bars
- Explain the point of sale systems used for stock and beverage control in bars

10.1 Introduction

This chapter introduces the learner to the areas of stock and beverage control. There are many benefits for having specific procedures for the control and recording of stock and beverages in bar premises. Operating a regular and rigorous system of stock taking and beverage control within a bar will help to control costs, achieve profit margins acceptable for the success of the business and identify problem areas in relation to the products, stocks, beverages, etc. of the bar business.

10.2 Managing costs and revenue to make profits

In Chapter 9, under the sub headings 'Food costing' and 'Control and calculation of costs to achieve profit margins' we highlighted the relationship between cost of the food and beverages and the prices needed to achieve profit margins acceptable to the business. It would be a little simplistic to believe that excellent cost to sales relationships automatically results in profit for the bar. A large numbers of bars operate with higher than normal cost percentages and continue to achieve acceptable profits. Dittmer & Keefe (2006) contend that it is possible to obtain a higher food cost percent by lowering menu prices to increase customer volumes, but the effect on profit must by judged by management. Katsigis & Thomas (2007) argue that profit is the primary goal of a beverage enterprise, but by itself profit does not indicate the degree of business efficiency, moreover profit figures are not significant until they are expressed in relation to other elements. Lillicrap and Cousins (2010) refer to these elements as "the relationship between the costs of running the operation, the revenue that is received and the profit that is made". Dittmer & Keefe (2006) agree and add that an understanding of these relationships is the key to fully comprehending cost control in food and beverage operations.

A plan for profit generation and financial sustainability

The money your bar receives is revenue, and this income incurs expenses (over-heads and the cost of products and services required to maintain the business). As a bar owner, you or your shareholders will not continue to invest in a bar which does generate profit. A good financial plan which includes a monthly or annual budget with projections for expenditure and income is an excellent starting point. This approach will provide you with a roadmap or basis to evaluate the bar's performance compared to the objectives of your financial plan. Try to be detailed, objective and realistic when formulating your projections of costs and revenue in relation to the desired profit. Katsigris & Thomas (2007) suggest that you should gather as much data as possible and be flexible with adjustments before applying it to a future that might change before it arrives. The ideal method used to monitor your projections is a Sales Projection sheet (digital or hard copy – see Table 10.1).

Table 10.1: Sales Projection sheet

Sales Projection Sheet								
Sales period date from: _____ to: _____								
Date	**Mon**	**Tues**	**Wed**	**Thurs**	**Fri**	**Sat**	**Sun**	**Totals**
Shift period 11am-6pm								
Week ending:								
Week ending:								
Week ending:								
Week ending:								
Month totals								
Shift 6pm - closing								
Week ending								
Week ending								
Week ending								
Week ending								
Week ending								
Month totals								

10

A large selection of templates for sales projections are available on line for free. If you bar is already trading, simply extract your past sales information to project your future sales, and try to be as detailed as possible (e.g. previous different trading periods, days of the week, impact of promotions, entertainment, special events, others bars). This information will be used to plan for the month/year ahead, (e.g. do you need more or less staff members, add new products and services or maybe carry out renovations because of local competition).

You now need to project the **bar expenses** (see Table 10.2 - provisional projected budget) for the same period as your sales projections above (month/year). Again, if you are currently trading you could use past figures for expenses (see Table 10.3) and add these to any upcoming ones which you have identified (try to be as forensic as possible).

Table 10.2: Provisional projected budget

Provisional Projected Budget		
	Allocated amount.	**Percent of revenue (sales)**
Projected Revenue (Sales)	**Enter in this column: total amount from sales projection sheet above.**	**Percentage: 100%**
Variable costs	Enter in this column the projected amount for each expense.	Enter in this column the percentage of each expense in relation to projected revenue (sales).
Wage costs (variable i.e part-time employees)		
Costs of beverages		
Administration		
China, glassware, flatware, linens		
Operations and maintenance (repairs)		
Marketing and advertising		
General expenses		
Utilities		
Fixed costs		
Rent		
Insurance		
Interest		
Taxes (local and national)		
Wages costs (fixed – full-time employees)		
Depreciation		
Projected profit		
TOTAL	Total amount from sales projection sheet above.	100%

adapted from (Katsigris & Thomas, 2007)

Your major expenses are classified as *fixed* and *variable*. Fixed costs (i.e rent, insurance and taxes, etc) usually remain the same irrespective of your sales volumes whereas variable costs (i.e. advertising, supplies, beverage costs, etc) can change depending on your bar sales volumes. Total the bar's expenses and express them as a percentage of your projected sales for the bar for the month/year. Dopson & Hayes (2011) explain that to find the percent of your revenue (sales) which you pay for your expenses, divide the individual expense or total expense into the revenue (sales) figure. If you calculate these expenses as a percentage of your projected sales for month/year you will obtain precise figures which express the relationship between a given expense to the sales it will produce – "a measure of the performance versus the plan" (Katsigris & Thomas, 2007). The final task is to find your projected profit, as a percentage of sales. Add all your expenses together and compare the total to your projected revenue (sales) figure. If these figures match then you should meet your plan; if not you must consider reducing costs and increasing sales. In some circumstances you might consider reducing your projected or predicted profit (this figure might have been unrealistic). Using these tools and techniques can help you to formulate a profit generating budget and to work towards creating a sustainable financial position for your bar.

Refining your budget

Understanding your bar's financial situation allows you to plan for the upcoming months and year and to base your projections on previous annual or monthly profit and loss income statements, as highlighted in Table 10.3, and incorporating the changes and costs you envisage for the upcoming year, as highlighted in Table 10.2. Katsigris and Thomas (2007) contend that you also have two other kinds of forecasts available to you for your projections which are particularly useful if you are opening a new bar. They highlight the break even point and the cash flow forecast (both discussed below). These financial tools allow owners and managers to refine, track and analyze their bar's progress and overall performance based on their projections.

10

Projecting profit levels

This area can be difficult and you must be realistic in your expectations, but how can you assemble the information to base your profit projections for your bar, Elliott (2007) highlights some options for your considerations. You should remember however that some of these options might not be available to you in your specific situation so try to be creative and use all your contacts, friends and specialists in the industry when sourcing the information:

Table 10.3: Profit and Loss Statement (monthly income statement). Adapted from (Davies et al, 2012)

Sullivan's Bar & Restaurant
Profit and Loss Statement (Monthly Income Statement) - June 2012

	Amount	Percentage
Sales Revenue		
Food	40,000	80%
Beverage	10,000	20%
Total Revenue	50,000	100%
Cost of Sales		
Cost of Food	14,000	35% of 40,000 (food cost)
Cost of Beverage	2,000	20% of 10,0000 (beverage cost)
Total Cost of Sales	16,000	

Gross Profit (total revenue – total cost of sales)

50,000 – 16,000   = **34,000** (profit before variable and fixed costs are deducted)

Operating Expenses (variable costs)		
Salaries and Wages	12,000	24 % of 50,000 (direct labour cost)
Employee Benefits	3,000	6 % of 50,000 (benefit cost)
China, Glassware, Flatware, Linens	50	
Cleaning Supplies	295	
Uniforms	525	
Menus	0	nil amount in this month
Paper Products	400	
Administrative and General expenses	255	
Marketing and Advertising	50	
Operations and Maintenance	325	
Utilities	1,200	2.4% of 50,000 (utilities)
Total Operating Expenses (variable costs)	**18,100**	36.2 % of 50,000 (total variable costs)

Income Before Capital Expenses
(gross profit – total operating expenses)

34,000 – 18,100   =   **15,900**

Capital Expenses (fixed costs)		
Insurance	750	
Rent	4,000	
Real Estate Taxes	800	
Interest Expense	1,450	
Depreciation	2,900	
Total Capital Expenses	9,900	19.8% (fixed cost of total revenue)

Profit Before Income Taxes
(income before capital expenses – capital expenses)

15,900 – 9,900 =   **6,000**

- *Business rates*: government websites normally contain rateable value for most bars.

- *Overheads / costs*: sometimes outgoing bar owners or tenants will furnish you the main expenses (i.e. rates, wages costs, energy costs, council taxes).

- *Sales information*: the brewery or pub company might provide you with this information in relation to the types of products sold at this establishment in the last year.

- *Rent costs*: normally provided by the brewery or real estate agent.

- *Profit and Loss (income statement)* estimates: these are traditionally calculated by the brewery or pub company and normally this information will be made available for you.

- *Private eye:* ask local questions and carry out local observations. You might be able to change the business.

- *Trade patterns and values:* observing trade patterns over a whole week (e.g. Wednesday – closed in the morning, quiet in the afternoon and steady in the evening, counting averages for meals, beverages and multiplying them by the prices charged will give you a estimated idea of turnover. Be careful to make allowances for increases in trade (special events ,etc).

Variable rate, contribution rate and break even point

Achieving acceptable profit returns for all your products and overall business also involves understanding additional rates and break even points which play a pivotal role in the relationship between cost, revenue and profit in the performance of your bar operation. These rates are referred to as the variable rate, the contribution rate and the break even point.

Variable rate

Dittmer & Desmond (2006) maintain that the variable rate is the ratio of variable cost to dollar (or local currency) sales and it is determined by diving variable cost by sales and is expressed in decimal form, similar to a cost percent. Let's use this formula based on the above income statement (Table 10.3)

$$\text{variable rate} = \frac{\text{variable cost}}{\text{sales}} \quad \frac{(18,100)}{(50,000)} = 0.362 \quad \text{or } 36.2\%$$

This formula means that 36.2% of every sale is needed to cover the variable costs. Your bar sales and the variable costs required to cover these sales will rise simultaneously, linked by this percentage rate.

Variable cost

This reverses the variable rate calculation. If you know the variable rate, you can find the variable cost, by multiplying the total sales by the variable rate.

$$50,000 \times 0.362 = 18,100 \text{ (variable cost)}$$

10

Contribution rate

If 36.2% of every dollar (or local currency) is required to cover the bar's variable costs, then the remaining amount (63.8%), commonly referred to as the **contribution rate**, is left to cover other costs (i.e. fixed costs and to provide an acceptable profit level). When your bar sales rise you will have more money to cover your fixed costs and to increase your profits expectations. Let's use this formula based on the above income statement (Table 10.3)

100 − 36.2% (variable rate) = 63.8% (contribution rate)

Contribution margin

The contribution rate can also be calculated from the contribution margin, using the following formulas. The examples are from the above income statement.

Contribution margin = total revenue − total variable costs

50,000 − 18,100 = 31,900

Contribution rate = contribution margin / total revenue

31,900 / 50,000 = 63.8%

Break even point

A break even point is the level of operation at which total costs equal total sales which means that there is no profit or loss (Katssigris & Thomas (2007). Significantly they add that this is the level that a new bar must reach fairly quickly it is to survive, because no bar can be termed profitable until all the fixed costs have been paid (Dittmer & Keefe, 2006). A good point to start when generating a break even point for your bar is to calculate your fixed costs, add wages, product costs (beverages & food) and divide this figure by the number of days you intend to open your bar. The figure generated will give you the amount you need in the register each day to break even. You could break this formula down further to calculate the daily break even point which is useful when planning your staffing arrangements, or even days when you should close early. Let's use the formula based on the above income statement (Table 10.3)

Break even point = total fix costs / contribution rate

9,900 / 0 .638 = 15,517

This means that the *Sullivan's Bar & Restaurant* above needs to make 15,517 each month just to break even. If you add in 5,000 profit which has been budgeted by the owner and re-set the break even formula, you will extract the required sales figure needed to generate the extra 5,000 monthly.

9,900 + 5,000 = 14,900

14,900 / 0.638 =23,354   (required sales figure for this establishment).

To calculate the daily break even point for your bar (using the figures from the income statement above), divide your monthly break even sales by the number of trading days you wish to have (i.e 30 days).

15,517 / 30 = 517.23 (amount required daily to break even).

Now accepting that the owner wants a 5,000 profit each month (we need to revise our formula to incorporate the planned profit).

23,354 / 30 = 778.46 (amount required daily).

Cash flow projections

If your bar cannot meet its weekly or monthly cash obligations to settle the bills, salaries and general overheads as they fall due, your creditors – suppliers, staff members and ultimately your bank – will stop supplying products and services to your business. Cash does not enter and exit your bar business at the same rate; sometimes you may tie up some money in supplies or new equipment. A cash flow forecast is a short term forecast of cash flowing into your bank and cash flowing out weekly or monthly (Katsigris & Thomas, 2007). To create the forecast:

1 **Predict your total income** which includes capital introduced, drink and beverage sales, food sales and any other forms of income coming in for example if you have rooms above the bar – accommodation income or income from machines around the bar – pool tables, etc.

2 **Predict your total expenditure – fixed and variable costs** which includes loan payments, VAT and tax payments, fixtures, fittings and equipment, beverages and food purchases, wages and salaries, rent, business rates, energy costs – heat, light, repairs & decoration, marketing, accountants & stocktaker fees, motor expenses, water rates training costs, bank charges, equipment rentals, glassware & crockery, cleaning materials, waste fees, uniforms, entertainment, TV pay channels, general costs, owner's drawings.

3 **Subtract your total income from your total expenditure to obtain the income less expenditure (costs) figure** .

4 Enter separately below all these totals the **figure for the Cash at the start of the month** and the **Cash at the end of the month**.

5 Complete this task each month for the next 12 months and you will obtain a Cash flow statement for your bar which includes all your projections and allows you to meet your financial obligations as they fall due.

Managing your cash flow is about having the right amount of money available in the right place at the right time (Sargent & Lyle, 2003). Some of the areas which causes bar owners most problems are the separation of their own (personal) and the bar's expenses (costs), unpaid or inappropriately prepared tax returns. The services of a **good accountant** are crucial here in providing you with comprehensive financial statements and expert advice in relation to the strengths, weaknesses and opportunities of your business. For a further discussion on Cash flow projections see *Marstons Pub Company – Planning your Business* and *Santander – Business Guide Industry Sector Public House* under Website resources.

10

10.3 Policies for pricing

Policies for pricing food and beverages can differ from bar to bar. These policies and their corresponding methods and techniques for calculating profits can sometimes be used inconsistently or set to rigid policies and formulas agreed by the local management team. Lillicrap & Cousins (2010) maintain irrespective of the method adopted, you should have a clear pricing policy or objective in mind. They propose the following pricing objectives for your consideration:

- Sales volume maximisation: used to achieve the highest sales possible
- Market share gain: used to increase the number of customers relative to the total possible market and competition
- Profit maximisation: used to achieve the highest profit possible
- Market penetration: to move from a position of a zero or low market share to a significant market share

(pp. 378-379)

When you have decided on the policy, you will need to adopt the most suitable pricing methods, which could include a mix of the methods highlighted below.

Pricing methods

The major considerations for bar owners when setting prices are to stay consistent (using a standard pricing system) and to set the prices to maximise the bar's gross profit or contribution margins. Every food and beverage product in the bar needs to be priced to meet these two factors. Listed below we highlight the major pricing methods:

Method 1. Gross profit

This method for pricing drinks and cocktails is the most popular. It is used to express the amount of gross profit realised on the sale of one drink or cocktail and is determined by dividing the gross profit by the sales price. Here's how it works: First subtract the cost of the drink from its selling price to get the gross profit, then divide this by the selling price. This gives you the gross profit margin as a percent.

Gross Profit = Selling Price – Cost of the Drink

11.40 – 3.99 = 7.41

Gross Profit margin = Gross Profit / Selling Price

7.41 / 11.40 = 0.65, or 65%

You can **reverse** this method to set the sales prices of drinks and cocktails. But first you must use the gross margin percent to get a reciprocal figure, then divide this into the cost of the drink. Let's look more closely at how it works:

To projecting the sales price from a cost price of 3.99 when the desired gross margin is 65%. Find the reciprocal of the gross margin – this gives you the proportion of the sales price that covers the cost.

$$1.00 - 0.65 = 0.35, \text{ or } 35\%$$

Divide the cost of the drink by the reciprocal amount:

$$3.99 / 0.35 \quad = 11.40 \text{ (sales price)}$$

Method 2: The demand/price relationship

It is impossible to estimate the real effect of price on demand as sometimes prices and margins can rise and the amount of drinks can fall, which affects sales volumes. Conversely, when prices and margins go down sales can increase. The clever bar owner will usually set their prices based on their individual customers, the market place and of course the local competition, to stimulate demand. The challenge is to create a balance across all your food and beverage offerings which helps to drive the best margin for each product, so you must be careful when setting your individual prices. Introduce them incrementally and observe the changes carefully to gauge their effect.

Method 3: The cost/price relationship

Start by calculating a percentage relationship between cost and price, which will give you a simple pricing formula to work with. The cost percentage of the price paid for the ingredients in the drink, and the remaining percentage of the price (gross margin) goes to pay that drink's share of all of your other costs and your profit. The cost percentage will be about the same as the beverage-cost percentage of your budget. Every bar must determine its own cost percentage to produce the profit needed. To find the selling prices, divide the total cost of the ingredients by the cost percentage (you require). e.g. for a White Lady Cocktail.

Sales Price = Total Cost of Ingredients / Cost percentage

$$3.99 / \ 0.35 \ = \ 11.40$$

10

You can turn this formula around and convert the cost percentage into a multiplier by dividing it into 100, which represents the sales price. Using multipliers is also discussed under food costing in Chapter 9.

100% (Sales price) / 35% (Cost percentage) = 2.857 (Multiplier)

2.857 x €3.99 (Cost) = €11.40 (Sales Price)

For a further discussion on strategies to coordinate your prices and control costs to achieve profit margins see Sections 9.5 'Price' and 9.8 'Control and calculation of costs to achieve profit margins'. Remember to check your price structure regularly and ensure that your prices compare well with your competitors and are reasonable, logical, in line with your local market and most importantly they create profit levels which are line with your budget and profit expectations.

10.4 Stock control

Why do we count stock? To calculate the profits on sales from the bar, we also count the stock and beverages to calculate the cost of these sales and to determine the gross margins achieved on them. This information can help you in relation to decisions regarding the selection, purchasing, receiving, storing, issuing and accounting for the numerous products which are sold in the bar. It can also highlight problem areas such as short stocks, overstocking, fraudulent or dishonest activity, which can include theft.

When we should count the stock? Preferably at the start or the end of the day's trading, ideally when the bar is closed. The frequency of these counts really depends on the size of the bar. In small bars, stock accounting may be carried out once a month, whereas in medium to large bar operations, stock accounting may be carried out sometimes daily.

Why stock control is needed

You should always remember that, stock is money. Stock control is needed in every bar for the following reasons:

- It helps to eliminate over-stocking, tying up the bar's financial capital unnecessarily. Research studies indicate that purchased goods in bars can represent as much as 60 percent of their turnover.

- It helps to eliminate under-stocking, which affects the quality of service that the bar provides. For example if a customer orders their favourite quarter bottle of wine or bottle of beer, it's crucial that you have the type and brand which they require.

- It helps with accounting for all items of stock and beverages, highlighting possible problem areas, for example pilferage by customers or staff, product or stock wastage, the types of breakages, their amounts and frequency.

- It provides information which can be used to ascertain current stock levels and their relevant prices, highlighting slow-selling lines within the stock offering. It also assists with decisions in relation to storage space requirements.

- It provides an ongoing reference of prices (which should be updated regularly) paid for your stock and beverages ordered and received previously. This information is useful in making decisions in relation to setting out the purchasing policy to achieve the best margins and deals for the bar.

- It assists with internal inventory management techniques. For example (a) the regular and active rotation of all stocks in various departments of the premises using the FIFO system, (b) to track the movement of stock between different areas of the bar premises, highlighting current stock requisition procedures and identifying slow moving and fast selling stock items

- It provides information on the value of stock throughout the trading year for insurance purposes, for example the valuation of expensive stock at certain trading periods, e.g. festivals weekends, major sporting and cultural events, and Christmas.

- The ultimate reason for stock taking is to provide the business with a stock control system, and not just a stock record. This information is vital to high-lighting poor controls, which can lead to the abuse of stock by customers and staff, overbuying, under buying, paying over the necessary amounts for your stock and the other relevant information listed above in points (1) to (5)

Types of stock accounting

Annual stocktaking: the traditional end of year stock take, which for taxation purposes usually takes place on or before the year end. This stock take can include all the stock and assets of the business, for example fixtures and fittings, machinery and equipment, cutlery, glassware plus the actual stock. These figures will primarily be used to draw up the full accounts of the business (i.e. trading account, profit and loss and the balance sheet) to provide a complete picture of the bar business assets and liabilities

Perpetual inventory: this type of stock accounting is used to check stock and fixtures and fittings on a continuous basis. It's amazing what can go missing within businesses, e.g. expensive fittings, paintings, special or unique items or valuable memorabilia belong to the bar. The perpetual inventory focuses on all the small, medium and large items of the business, cookers, tables, chairs, glasses, electronic equipment, etc., some of these items will depreciate in value over time or go missing

Periodic stocktaking: in this type of stock accounting, the period could be every week, every fortnight, each month or every three months. The frequency of the stock accounting always depends on the size, financial turnover or varied product offering of the premises in question.

Stock accounting procedures, best practices

10

- Always provide at least two responsible and experienced staff (e.g. stock controller, bar manager or owner) to work together during stock accounting. One of them will need to call out the items of physical stock, its description and quantity and the other person should then record the items accurately in the stock accounting control sheets or stock book. This person can also act as a second pair eyes during the stock count. The physical counting of stock can be a mentally challenging operation, especially if one of these people is constantly interrupted during the stock accounting period, for example by mobile phone calls.

- Recheck sections for mistakes - compare sample delivery docket against the physical stock.

- A system of spot checks can be made to ensure the initial accuracy of the stock counted.

■ If there are any mistakes, a re-checking of some sections may be necessary. Some of the most common causes of mistakes include fixtures genuinely missed during the stock count, mistaken stock item sizes calculated, for example 1 litre bottles recorded instead of the actual bottle size 700 millilitres, and faulty electronic accounting devices, such as calculators, weight scales, scanners.

Duties of the stock controller

1   Take cash register's reading. The printout gives the takings since the last stock take, with the takings analyzed over the various products sold. The readings and takings are compared with the takings or cash sheet.

2   Count the physical stock. Two people should work together, one counting measures while the other records. If there is a cellar, its closing stocks should be reconciled with opening stocks, deliveries and transfers to the bar.

3   Calculate theoretical sales units. To do this, start with the opening stock from previous stock take, add deliveries in units, and subtract the closing stock in the cellar and bar. If the cellar is separately controlled start with the opening stock in the bar, add requisitions from the cellar, and subtract the closing stock in the bar.

4   Calculate theoretical sales at cost. Take the sales units from step (3) and cost them at cost price, for example: Lager sales are 5 full kegs and four tenths at 145 a keg, so $5.4 \times 145.00 = 783.00$ at cost.

5   Calculate theoretical sales at selling price. Take the sales units calculated in step (3) and cost at selling price including VAT to the customer. For example: lager kegs sales are 5 full (11 gallon) kegs and four tenths. Convert to pints = $5.4 \times 11 \times 8 = 475$. $475 \times$ selling price $4.00 = 1,900$ at selling price.

6   Value the closing stock. Take the units counted in step (2) and value at purchase price (cost price excluding vat). For example: closing stock is 5 kegs of lager @ 150 net of vat = 750 closing stock value.

7   Surplus and deficiency calculations. Compare theoretical sales units at selling price with the cash register readings (actual takings). For example, sales at selling price from step (5) is 1,900 but sales as per register is 2,000 = a surplus of 100.

8   Establish actual gross profit margin and gross profit % margin. This is calculated as follows: the bar takings at selling price excluding vat less the theoretical sales at cost price. For example, bar takings less vat = 944, less sales @ cost price = 780, gross profit margin = 164, gross profit % = 164/944 = 17%

9   Do the financial report. Prepare a suitable report showing the surplus, deficiency and the basic margin calculation and percentage.

Stock control methods – management tools

Minimum stock levels

This is one of the simplest methods and often used in bars. It relies on the bar owner or manager visually checking stock levels. Once a stock item reaches a predetermined minimum stock level you re-order. Some bars will use this system with the more effective, card system that provide reminders of low stock. These cards are placed behind each item of stock in the cellar or main stores areas. A more comprehensive system, which is far more efficient than the card system, is a software stock control program that updates stock levels in real time as stock is received and sold. This is done by scanning the product's bar codes to ensure accuracy and low stock levels are flagged according to predetermined settings.

Just in time (JIT)

This stock control system was popularised in Japan as an effective way to reduce money tied up in stock. It relies on a close and trusting relationship with suppliers. The advantages are that it transfers stock holding costs back to the food and beverage suppliers who act as the warehouse.

Stock forecasts

This useful management tool functions like cash flow forecasts, showing an opening stock balance, expected sales for the month and a closing stock balance. The expected sales can be based on historical sales, and figures can be adjusted for growth and seasonality.

Good supplier relationships

Whatever stock control method you adopt, good relationships with your key suppliers are important in gaining their trust, getting reliable supplies of quality stock and negotiating better payment terms for your bar.

10.5 Receiving, checking, storing and issuing controls

Receiving stock and beverages

This is first step in your control system. All stock and equipment of the bar is expensive and if mistakes go unnoticed at the point and time of delivery, and a supplier is paid for items that the bar has not received, this will result in reduced profits. There is also a risk that poor stock control receiving systems actually encourage dishonesty, which leads to suspicion amongst employees and the eventual deterioration of workplace relationships. A comprehensive system which includes establishing standards for receiving stock and beverages can counteract these threats and should be adopted and actively operated at the point of delivery for the bar. Access to the main storage areas should be restricted to authorized staff members and not staffed by people with little or no specialized knowledge. All goods received have a monetary value and it is essential to ensure that this value in goods is properly accounted for and received.

Checking the stock and beverages and signing for deliveries

Most bars make crucial mistakes here by taking short cuts.

- Take the necessary time to inspect the delivery dockets
- Check the items on the docket correspond with the items in the order book
- Any inaccuracies with the delivery, must be communicated to the manager in charge for a quick decision
- Examine the stock for best before dates, breakages or missing seals
- Note any discrepancies for re-checking purposes, and never sign any delivery dockets until you are fully sure that the order for delivery is intact and correct.
- Carry out 'spot checks' during and after the stocks are received to ensure that staff members and delivery personnel are operating in a professional and ethical manner (i.e. look out for collusion, theft or missing free goods due to the bar).

Storing of beverages

Food and beverage supplies must be stored until needed, secure against theft and deterioration. Dopson & Hayes (2011) contend that the storage process in most foodservice establishments consists of four main parts which include placing the products in storage, maintaining their quality, safety and security and determining the stock's value. Storage areas must be kept clean, tidy and clear of any litter in the passage ways. You should adopt a F.I.F.O (first in first out) system for rotating your stocks, especially perishable foods or beverages with a short shelf life. This means that the oldest stock is always used first and new stocks are stored (placed) beneath the old stocks. Remember that stock is money, so ensure that your stock is given the attention and respect it deserves.

Storage of beverages is ideally separated into five areas:

- Main storage area for spirits and red wine (13-16°C).
- A refrigerated area of (10°C) for storage of white and sparkling wines.
- A cold room for kegs (3-16°C), with the temperature depending upon the beers stored. Never store foods in this room (see also Chapter 7 on 'Cellar safety techniques').
- An area at a temperature of 13°C for storage of bottled beers and soft drinks. A small amount of bottled beverages (beers, soft drinks) is sometimes stored in the cold room. This practice ensures that the beverages are cold and ready for immediate service when transferred to the bar service area.

■ A totally separate area for empties.

Cellar records: If the value of a bar's cellar stocks is high, it is usual to maintain a system of books to control all cellar records (see below).

Storage of foods

Food products will require additional storage areas within your establishment:

■ *Frozen (freezer) storage areas*: keep these units between (-18°C and - 23°C), and freeze storage foods quickly when received. Check the food's overall condition. Keep these units clean and maintained and ensure that the thermometer which monitors them can be easily read and is in good working order.

■ *Dry storage areas*: keep these between (18°C and 24°C). Keep a good amount of dry, clean shelving at least 12 inches (300mm) off the ground for hygiene and ventilation (never store dry foods directly on the floor). Keep bulk items like flour in wheeled bins for easy transportation. Keep it neat and well organised for stock checking and rotation purposes.

■ *Refrigerated storage area*: keep this area between (0°C and 2°C). Never allow warm foods to be placed in the refrigerator and ensure that they are kept at least 6 to 10 inches (150 to 250mm) off the ground. Clean them regularly, and insist that items placed in the refrigerator are properly stored (e.g. in see-through plastic boxes) labelled, wrapped and rotated.

Issuing food stocks and beverages

Assign the responsibility for storing and issuing stock and beverages to one or two senior persons. Dittmer & Keefe (2006) suggest that you should keep the beverage storage area locked and to issue a single key to one person, but make a second key available in the safe or a secure location to be signed out when the nominated person is away from the bar. In some bars the owner might also decide to install electronic code entry locks, which control the times at which the doors to the storage areas were unlocked and or relocked, or a CCTV (closed circuit television cameras) in and around the storage areas for additional security and monitoring.

Par stock

This technique coupled with a good requisition system will help you to establish good standard procedures for issuing stock in your bar. Par stock is the quantity, stated in numbers of bottles or other containers that the bar needs on hand at all times for each product. Par stocks vary from one bar to another. They should be checked regularly and changed according to customer demand. Be careful however not to overstock your bar, as this ties up your capital and space in the bar.

The issue of any stock should be recorded on a requisition form (see below) , usually from an authorized member of staff, for example, head chef, restaurant manager or from the storekeeper, informing the purchasing manager of low levels of items (Bamunuge et al, 2010). In big bars you might have an individual 'control' office which will process all requisitions and orders. In small bars it can be the same staff member who draws up the requisition and receives the order (see also 'requistion book' below).

Location: Burlington Hotel (Irl) Ltd - Food storeroom requisition

Area: Kitchen (1)   Date: 12/7/2011

Quantity required	Items	Quantity issued	Unit cost price	Total cost (€)
3 bottles	Vanilla essence	2 bottle	2.00	4.00
2 kilo	Granulated sugar	2 kilo	.85	1.70
3 kilo	Cake flour (1.5 k)	3 kilo	.50	1.00
			Total	6.70

Requisitioned by: James Murphy

Figure 10.1: Food storeroom requisition (sample form) adapted from (Bamunuge et al, 2010).

Location: Burlington Hotel (Irl) Ltd - Beverage requisition form

Bar: Diplomat cocktail bar   Date: 12/6/2012

				Cost price		Selling price	
Bin, bottle code number	Quantity	Unit, bottle size	Item/s	Unit value	Total value	Unit value	Total value
400	2	700ml	Jameson whiskey	25.00	50.00	66.50	133.00
402	2	700ml	C.D.C Gin	23.00	46.00	72.20	144.00
621	2	700ml	Absolut Vodka	26.00	52.00	66.50	133.00
106	2	2 cases (24 x 185ml)	Chardonnay, Domaine AC 2003	40.00	80.00	108.00	216.00
	Cost and Sales Price			114.00	228.00	313.20	626.40
	Add: other requisition/s Less: Credit				25.00		52.00 175.00
	Total				253.00		503.40

Received by: James Murphy   Requisitioned by: Joe Leavy

Figure 10.2: beverage requisition (sample form) adapted from (Bamunuge et al, 2010).

10.6 System of bar books

The importance of keeping a good system of bar books is often underestimated by bar owners. The titles and format of the bar books can vary between bars but the general content and intention are usually similar. Medium to large bar businesses will operate a wider set of internal bar books (usually in electronic format backed up by a comprehensive software package).

Delivery book

Traditionally two of these are required for your business – one for drinks and one for foods. You should ensure that these books are of a duplicate or triplicate format. It is important to have the ability to create multiple or electronic copies of the information contained in these books because you will need to issue the contents within these books to different departments or external accountants. A sample layout of entries used in this book is given below.

Delivery notes, or delivery dockets, which are the wholesaler's copy of your order (fully itemized with no prices) are usually kept in a folder close to the delivery book. These notes also contain details of any free goods and credit items, and have an area for your staff member to sign when the goods are received and checked in full.

Delivery book, sample listing of sample deliveries

Company name:	United Beverages Ltd
Docket number: 23	**Date of delivery:** 20th March 2012
Quantity of stock	**Description of Stock**
10 cases	Fanta orange (18cl: returnable bottles)
20 cases	Budweiser (33cl: returnable bottles)
5 cases	Heineken (33cl: non-returnable bottles)
10 cases	Carlsberg (50cl: non-returnable cans)
Empties returned:	20 cases of (18cl: split size) returnable bottles
	10 cases of (33cl: longneck size) returnable bottles

Breakages, short deliveries: record all relevant breakages and short deliveries here.

....

....

....

10

Purchase order book

To centralise all your ordering processes and procedures, this book could contain companies' contact details, the bar's individual account numbers, the stock required, closing stock figures to help gauge sales and drive deals, agreements and billing periods. In some bars it is common practice to use an official purchase order form. Instead of using a purchase book, these forms could be stored in electronic format and e-mailed to the company when placing an order. A sample layout of the headings traditionally used in this book is listed below. Some bars could use instead an order form with the drinks and foods to be ordered, all orders are then sent via email or telephone to a telesales operator.

Purchase order book, listing of sample entries

Date ordered: 24/03/11	Company: Diageo Ltd	
Stock to be ordered	**Description**	**Closing stock figure**
20 kegs	Guinness regular	15 kegs.
15 kegs	Budweiser	20 kegs.
13 kegs	Carlberg	10 kegs.

To be delivered: Monday (AM – before noon), delivery only by mat, lift.

Notes, comments: *need some drip mats, extra collection of keg empties, any special beer deals, promotions, RB (returnable keg) labels.*

Returnable bottle (R.B kegs) book

It is important that you have a proper account of your kegs of draught product needed to return for credit. This information is required for stock accounting (control) purposes. A sample layout of the headings, which can be used in this book, are listed below.

RB book, listing of sample entries

Product	Keg weight	Tag/ keg number	Date returned
Guinness	10 gallons	083/1245789	23/03/12
Smithwicks	Full keg	021/14678932	19/04/12

Spillages, discounts, ullage book

The purpose of this (or these) book/s is to centralise allowances for items of stock and beverages that have been discounted for customers, spilled by customers or staff, and stock waste incurred on draught product, staff drinks or just daily waste.

Spillages, discounts, ullage books, listing of sample entries

Date	Stock	Event	Staff name
21/03/07	6 cans of lager (Heineken)	discount €1 per can	James Murphy
19/02/07	2 pints cider (Bulmer's)	customer spillage	Joe Brown
07/05/07	5 pints Guinness	staff drinks	Harry Murray
14/03/07	3 pints lager (Carlsberg)	clean beer lines	Liam (tech rep)
04/03/07	2 bottles Evian	cellar breakage	Lisa Armstrong

Other areas which may be notes in this book include: waste from draught beer drip trays, promotional drinks, donations and festive giveaways of food or drinks

Cash and safe control book

The information contained in this will assist you in finding solutions to cash problems, for example when you have cash register shortages. Shortages in this area can derive from various elements, which include human error, cash or cheques, over- or under-charging for food and drinks, payouts not recorded or incorrectly distributed, cash register and safe float checks, or staff theft.

Requisition book

Using the requisition book depends on the size of the company. It is usually best suited to medium or large bars, or locations with multiple bars on the same site where large amounts of different and expensive stock are transferred daily around the premises. Dittmer & Keefe (2006) maintain that a requisition system is a highly structured method for controlling issues and in beverage control a key element in the system is the the bar requisition form (see above).

This system tracks stock into the different bars and helps management to identify exactly what stock is being used and sold in individual bars for the stock control process. To gain stock for your bar you must fill out exactly what you require into the duplicate book and send the order or requisition down to the main store area. A supervisor or manager would usually also sign this order. The stock is assembled and sent to your bar. Similarly any inter-bar stock movements (between internal bars), for example the main bar transferring stock to the night-club or restaurant bar, is duly recorded and signed

Other forms and books used in bars

Invoice

This document will be issued to your bar after you receive a delivery and have signed the delivery note for your suppliers. This form will set out the cost of the food and beverages you have received. You should check all invoices carefully to ensure that you are charged only for the stocks which you actually received. For small bars the delivery note, credit note and invoice could be all included on the same form (Banuage et al, 2010).

Statement

This form will be sent to bar owners periodically from their suppliers (usually at the end of each month) detailing the total amount of moneys which you bar owes each supplier. Always check in detail all your invoices against these statements to ensure their accuracy and correctness.

10

10.7 Cellar management

The cellar plays an important part in the day-to-day operations of any licensed premises (Banuage et al, 2010). Its main role is provide an area where beverages and stocks can be stored in a secure, safe, hygienic fashion. This area must also be easily accessible and have a good lighting system (not direct sunlight).

Layout and configuration

To ensure this access you must configure your cellar in an orderly and structured layout. This should ideally keep all the major categories of drinks together (i.e. section for beers, section for soft drinks, section for distilled spirits or wines). Dittmer & Keefe (2006) suggest that your bar should keep your floor plan of the cellar affixed to the door of the cellar so that authorized personnel can easily locate items and keep the cellar in the ideal order for efficiency.

Some of the other conditions and techniques which you need to consider include:

- *Ventilation:* a healthy supple of fresh air or a forced ventilation system is crucial because cellars contain dangerous gases and equipment which can occasionally leak. Proper ventilation will also prevent build up of stale air, bacterial growths and mould (Banuage et al, 2010).

- *Humidity:* cellars need to contain a regular humidity level of between 45 to 65%. If the level rises above 85% this can cause dampness and spoil expensive products.

- *Temperature:* ensure that the air temperature and the ambient temperature is kept constant at between 12 to 16°C to maintain the quality and integrity of the products. High temperatures can cause bacterial contamination.

- *Beverage crates*: poorly stacked crates can cause accidents and expense due to broken products, so ensure that creates of different shapes are never stacked together. Don't stack on uneven surfaces, and watch the height levels – don't over stack. Keep empty crates and full crates in their own individual piles.

- *Kegs:* be careful of faulty kegs and never tap one. Move kegs with a trolley or lift – don't lift them on your own – and remember kegs are always pressurised, empty or full, so be extra cautious.

- *Cellar flap doors and handrails:* keep them in good working order with safety signs regarding their use.

- *General safety notices*: check that all your equipment and safety notices are in good order and visible.

- *Chains and wall attachments*: ensure that all chains for anchoring gas cylinders and regulators are in good working order

- *Lighting*: proper illumination, switches and wiring in good working order and plenty of spare bulbs etc.

■ *Cleaning agents and chemicals*: keep records of the chemicals and cleaning agents used and ensure that they are stored properly with the correct labels for instructions and only used for their intended purpose.

Healthy wine storage and cellar organisation

1   Provide a good cellar – a concrete floor is a necessity, concrete walls and floor ceiling if possible. Make sure that your storage is generous.

2   Maintain a constant cellar temperature – around 50 to 55°F (10 to 13° C), an air conditioner is very useful here. The absence of central heating is an obvious condition. No wine will stand alternate boiling and freezing. In high temperatures the wine will age quicker, and there is the danger of it seeping around the cork.

3   Maintain the humidity at about 70 to75%. Wine breathes through the cork and if the atmosphere is too dry air will be sucked into the bottle, oxidation will occur and the quality of the wine will be destroyed.

4   If wine is to be kept for some time, to improve with age (vins de garde), the bottles should always be kept lying down to prevent the cork from drying and shrinking and letting in air. Properly constructed racks so that bottles can easily be taken from the top to the bottom are a good addition.

5   Control lighting. Light should be restricted, especially neon lighting, as it has a browning effect on white wine and causes ageing and loss of colour particularly in red wine.

6   Sources of vibration (e.g. boiler or other machinery) should be avoided at all costs.

7   Unwanted smells and odours. Only wine and spirits should be stored in the wine cellar as wine absorbs smells and pungent odours very easily.

8   Systems of books (detailed wine biography). The efficient running of the wine cellar involves keeping an up to date cellar book where quantities can be recorded, as well as the delay between ordering and supplying required by each supplier. If the wines are really expensive it should also record details about the vintage, vineyard, merchant, price and maybe an estimation of when a vintage will peak.

9   Bars, restaurants and hotels with a good wine consumption will discover that a properly structured and professionally organised wine cellar may prove a good economical investment. This will serve to improve the quality of the wine, as well as being practical for tutored tastings, for example.

10   Remember the primary objective here is to help your wines achieve their full potential.

11   Corks should be inspected regularly to ensure that no leaks have occurred and that the packaging surrounding the cork is in tact.

From Murphy (2006)

Bin cards / product labelling

These cards can be fixed to the shelves similar to shelf labels. Usually you would have one bin card to each item. The card can also contain information in relation the product, its size, special storage information, the brand name and the movements of stock (i.e. new delivered stock or requistions). In some bars a code will be assigned to these cards (bin number) which can also be used to indicate the exact location of the wine or spirit in the cellar, this technique is really useful in large cellars. Some bars will also stamp their expensive wines and spirits with their own company stamp for security reasons to make it impossible for staff members to claim that a bottle was their personal property.

Health and safety in the cellar

The cellar area contains numerous dangers especially gases, machinery and chemicals. Only trained or senior staff members should be allowed to work in this area and staff should ideally inform their fellow colleagues when they intend to work there and the estimated time period which they intend to spend in the cellar in case of an accident (see also Section 7.12 'Cellar safety management' and *The Drinks Handbook*, Sections 1.13-1.16).

10.8 Control of possible losses in the bar

Highlighted below are some of the most common areas which can lead to stock losses in the bar premises. Consider these carefully with your management team.

- Pilferage, by staff or customers, shoplifting, sometimes even during the delivery period when receiving your actual stock for the bar.

- Stock waste control, continued overflowing of beer, spirits or wine due to poor in-house practices, poor storage conditions leading to poor product (high beer), lack of waste reduction techniques in use.

- Bar owner's requisitions recording. Owners can move stock out of the bar for their personal use or to transfer the stock for use in another location.

- Cash register control, understatements by staff or management, for example use or misuse of the error correct or void buttons on the register, too many open sale buttons, cash register buttons constantly sticking or broken, cash register not properly programmed with the most recent information required (updated prices) to produce accurate detailed reports.

- All free drinks, discounts or allowances for goods need to be properly recorded.

- Accounting errors or missing delivery dockets, (free goods, purchase prices, returns, credit notes not accounted).

- Bar and food accounts and sales are mixed, incorrectly or deliberately.

- Credit losses, when food and alcohol has been allowed on credit to customers.

- Department requisition mistakes, between bars, lounges, restaurants, nightclub bars.

- Overbuying – the structure of the order book is crucial to assist in the proper estimation and forecast of future stock orders to reduce overbuying.

- Mixed drink pricing problems. These can arise from the actual quantities used within mixed drink specials, cocktails or when you have inconsistent prices for your overall mixed drinks offering.

- Stock taking by inexperienced personnel, sometimes these individuals might have entered the accountancy field through other forms of business and are not familiar with the unique terminology, the product sizes used or served and the culture of the bar industry.

- Staff employment – it is crucial that staff references are thoroughly checked.

- Security and safety of the stock: the layout and arrangement of the stock is also crucial in relation to proper cellar management. Under no circumstances should any unauthorized personnel gain access to stock areas for any reasons.

10.9 Controls for beverage production

In the bar industry it's crucial to adopt control systems and techniques which help to establish standard procedures for the preparation, size and production method for all your food and beverages. If your bar can keep control in this area you will have a significant opportunity to maximise your profits on all your products. Highlighted below are some of the systems and techniques which will assist you in creating controls in this area:

- *Setting a standard drink size for beers, spirits and wines:* agree a size, but this decision could be set by your local government rules.

- *Adopting standard food and cocktail recipes*: containing defined, specifically measured ingredients and strict methods of production agreed by management. (see also Chapter 5, Section 5.4 'Standardised recipes for food').

- *Standard glassware, crockery*: choosing a standard glass size for your wines, beers, cocktails, coffee and food items.

- *Free pour*: in a lot of countries this highly entertaining technique for pouring alcohol is illegal. If however your bar allows this practice for pouring alcohol, you must ensure that your staff members are highly skilled and test their accuracy regularly because you can lose a lot of money this way.

- *Hand held measures, jiggers and optics (or metered bottle dispensers):* these dispense devices and equipment help to control the exact measurement of alcohol according to your bar or government requirements. Ensure this equipment is not damaged and or been compromised and crucially that the equipment dispenses the correct intended amount.

For further information and a comprehensive set of food and beverage conversion tables used for controlling portion sizes (see Appendix IV, Conversion tables for food and beverage control).

10

10.10 Point-of-sale systems for stock and beverage control

Computerized systems – for example Micros and Geller MP systems with integrated microcomputer links – are quite common in the bar industry. The primary function of most POS systems is to track sales (Katsigris & Thomas, 2007). A good system will be able to record the following information in hourly, daily, and month-to-date increments as needed: product sales mix, revenue (per shift, sales period, or server), an open check report, server-tips report (which is also used for tax purposes in the USA), and total revenue (Katsigris & Thomas, 2007).

More sophisticated POS systems interface with inventory and purchasing programs to follow beverages and other bar items from initial purchase, to use, to the eventual collection of revenue.

Figure 10.3, 10.4: Hand held stock control system. Micros system for the bar.

POS systems – additional capabilities

Few contemporary bar businesses can run successfully without an electronic point of sale (POS) system. Busy nights with lots of people require these systems to help organize orders and account for transactions. A POS system is ideal for keeping track of transactions as well as analyzing sales as it acts as a cash register as well as a computer. In fact, is has the ability to perform a multitude of functions, which includes the following;

- Calculate cash due for every order entered
- Record the method of payment
- Keep track of the cash in the cash drawer
- Create hourly and daily sales reports
- Allow hourly employees to clock in and out
- Calculate labour and payroll data

- Record daily check averages for each worker
- Keep track of menu items sold
- Record information on repeat customers

POS systems can consist of multiple stations, including credit card terminals, receipt printers, display screens, hostess stations and server stations. Having a POS system in place in your bar can add convenience, accuracy and save time in busy situations.

Conclusion

Effective stock and beverage control can make a significant difference to the efficiency and the profitability of a bar business. Stock control is about having the right amount of stock on hand when it is needed. Efficient stock control will ensure that a bar's financial capital is not tied up unnecessarily and ensures that adequate levels of products are maintained to satisfy customer demand.

Stock and beverage control can be useful in limiting losses to the bar through theft, fraud or poor working methods, which can result in high levels of waste especially in perishable goods or breakages. It can also identify fast and slow moving stock. It is crucial that a bar adopts a comprehensive system for receiving, checking, storing and issuing stocks. This should be supported by an internal system of bar books to control all the products, services and functions of the bar. No control system can genuinely claim to be 100 percent safe and secure, and it is crucial that the bar manager continues to identify problematic areas to control possible losses.

Finally the sustainability of any bar is based on its ability to generate profits. Bar managers must formulate a proper costing structure (updated regularly) for the bar, which focuses in detail on the individual and collective cost and sales prices, plus the gross profit margins achieved.

10

Appendices

Appendix I: I am your customer

Every bar should have this, or something like it, pinned where owners, managers and staff will see it, so no-one forgets why they are there.

I am your customer, satisfy my wants, add personal attention and friendly touch, and I will become a walking advertisement for your pub and services. Ignore my wants, show carelessness, inattention and poor manners, and I will simply cease to exist – as far as you are concerned. I am sophisticated. Much more so than I was a few years ago. My needs are more complex. I have grown accustomed to better things. I have money to spend. I am an egotist. I am sensitive. I am proud. My ego needs the nourishment of a friendly, personal greeting from you. It is important to me that you appreciate my business. After all, when I buy your products and services, my money is feeding you.

I am a perfectionist. I want the best I can get for the money I spend. When I criticize your pub or service – and I will, to anyone who will listen, when I am dissatisfied – then take heed. The source of my discontent lies in something that you or the products you sell have failed to do. Find that source and eliminate it or you will lose my business and that of my friends as well. I am fickle. Other pubs continually beckon to me with offers of 'more' for my money. To keep my business, you must offer something better than they. I am your customer now, but you must prove to me again and again that I have made a wise choice in selecting you, your pub and services above all others.

Our aim is 100% customer satisfaction

Appendix II: Food safety training – supervision and instruction

The bar owner must ensure that food handlers are supervised and or trained in hygiene matters commensurate with their activities. In bigger companies there may be job demarcation, in which case different types and levels of supervision and training may be required. However, in most small bars everybody plays an active part in the food safety training. If you are a bar owner or manager, I would suggest that you could include some of the areas addressed below in your employees' handbook, as bullet points under the general heading of food safety and hygiene.

■ Food safety training - induction stage one

This stage is ideally carried out before food handlers and non-food handlers who can affect food safety are allowed to commence work. The training should be carried out in close supervision. The emphasis is on the employee demonstrating the skill and knowledge required. The list below covers the skills, which the employee must be able to demonstrate at this stage.

Date of Training _____

Name of employees	Department

Where a skill has been covered during the training session place a ✓ in the appropriate skills covered box otherwise, place an X in the appropriate box.

Signed by Employees

Training in food safety skills	Skills covered ✓ or X
Wear and maintain uniform/protective clothing hygienically	
Maintain a high standard of hand-washing	
Maintain a high standard of personal hygiene	
Demonstrate correct hygienic practice if suffering from ailments and illnesses that may affect food safety	
Refrain from unhygienic practices in a food operation	
Demonstrate safe handling practice	
Maintain staff facilities in a hygienic condition	
Obey food safety signs	
Keep work areas clean	

Signed by employees

_____   _____

Signed by manager/supervisor _____ Date: _____

Figure A.1: Induction stage one (source: FSAI, 2013)

A

Food safety training – induction stage two

This stage is ideally carried out within the first month of employment. Note: for employees involved in low-risk activities, this stage of training may be delivered within 3-6 months of employment. The level of supervision may be reduced following the satisfactory completion of stage two. The emphasis again is on the employee demonstrating the skill and knowledge required. The list below covers the skills, which the employee must be able to demonstrate at this stage.

Date _____

Name of employees	Department

Where a skill has been covered during the training session place a ✓ in the appropriate skills covered box otherwise, place an X in the appropriate box.

Training in food safety skills	Skills covered ✓ or X
Know their legal responsibility in ensuring safe food for the consumer.	
Recognise how food can be put at risk by chemical, physical and biological hazards.	
Demonstrate an understanding of cross contamination and the hygiene practice necessary to prevent it.	
Explain the difference between high and low risk activities.	
Avoid unnecessary handling of food, food utensils and surfaces.	
Where applicable to the job, record the temperature of foods as required.	
Keep appropriate food safety records.	
Keep pests out of the food operation and operate a satisfactory waste disposal system.	
Take action when aware of unhygienic practices that may put the safety of food at risk.	
Co-operate with authorized enforcement officers.	
Where applicable to the job, check deliveries appropriately.	

Signed by employees

_____   _____

Signed by manager/supervisor _____ Date: _____

Figure A.2: Induction stage two (source: FSAI, 2013)

Table A.1: Bacteria and associated illnesses

	Salmonella	C.P (welchii)	Staphylococcus Aureus
Incubation period	12 – 24 hours	8 -22 hours	2 – 6 hours
Duration of illness	1 – 2 days	12 – 24 hours	6 – 24 hours
Diarrhoea	common	common	common
Vomiting	uncommon	rare	extremely common
Abdominal pain	+	+	+
Pyrexia (fever)	+	-	-
Prostration	rare in early stages	common	common
Foods most frequently implicated	poorly cooked meats and sausages, unpasteurized frozen, whole egg	re-heated meat poultry, large rolled joints of meat	ham, tongue, beef, cold meat, pies and dairy products

Table A.2: Basic causes of food poisoning

	Explanation	Examples of food poisoning	Time from eating to illness	Usual source
Bacterial toxins	toxic chemicals produced by bacteria	botulism staphylococcal	2 hrs to 8 days usually within 24 hrs. 1–6 hrs usually 2–4 hrs	soil, water, animals, man.
Bacteria	these bacteria cause illness	salmonella streptococcal typhoid	6–72 hrs, usually 18 hrs. 2–18 hrs, usually 12 hrs. 3–38 days, usually 7 to 14 days	man, animals, poultry, man, man.
Parasites	harmful worms living in man and animals	trichinosis tapeworm	24 hrs to 7 days, usually 6 days 1– 3 months, usually 18 days	pork beef, pork, fish
Contaminants	strong chemical poisons	pesticides, cleaners, disinfectants	very short to very long	

A

Appendix III: The mystery shopper diagnostic auditing tool for bars

This tool evaluates 46 standards within a typical licensed premises and grades them individually as meeting or being below standard, or in some circumstances as not applicable (for example a bar not serving food cannot be evaluated on its food offering).

Figure A.3: Diagnostic auditing tool for bars

	Bar Service			
	Category: *Enter the area covered (i.e. the main bar, the restaurant)*			
	Premises: *Enter the bar's location*			
	Date and time: *Enter arrival details*			
	Standards evaluated	Meet	Below	N/A
	Standards: service			
1	Was the guest greeted or acknowledged within 1 minute of arrival?			
2	Did the employee greet the guest in a pleasant and friendly manner?			
3	When the guest placed their order at the bar, did the employee demonstrate good product knowledge?			
4	Did the employee ask if the guest would like ice in their drink (if applicable)?			
5	Did the employee maintain eye contact during order taking?			
6	Were the drinks served within 2 minutes of placing the order?			
7	Did the employee handle glass from stem or base at all times?			
8	Did the employee supply and place drinks on coaster?			
9	Was the drinks order correct?			
10	Did the employee offer to pour the drink in the case of canned, bottled or mixed drinks?			
11	Were the drinks served in the correct glassware?			
12	Were glasses clean, polished and free of any cracks or chips?			
13	Were garnishes fresh and appropriate?			
14	Was the drink appropriately chilled (if applicable)?			
15	In the case of a mixed drink, was a stir stick provided?			
16	Were vacated tables promptly cleared?			
17	Were all drinks cleared using a tray?			
18	Was a bartender or employee visible at all times?			
19	Were ashtrays cleared regularly – exterior, beer gardens (if applicable)?			
20	Upon leaving the bar was the guest thanked/ acknowledged?			

	Standards: accounting – bill presentation			
21	Was the bill, till receipt provided within three minutes of request?			
22	Was the bill, till receipt clearly itemized and correct?			
23	Did employee collect payment promptly?			
	Standards: the employee			
24	Did employee appear organized and work as a team?			
25	Was the employee dressed in a clean, pressed and complete uniform?			
26	Were employee's shoes of a company (Health and Safety) standard?			
27	Did the employee wear a name badge (if applicable)?			
28	Was the employee well groomed?			
29	Did the employee maintain eye contact with the guest?			
30	Did the employee smile and exhibit a friendly manner?			
31	Did the employee have a good working knowledge of English or the local language?			
32	Did employee respect guest's presence when interacting with other colleagues?			
33	Was the employee attentive to the guest's needs at all times?			
	Standards: Product – physical condition of bar / lounge			
34	Were the carpets/tiles free and clean of any stains or debris?			
35	Were all light fixtures fully illuminated?			
36	Were all walls clean and free of any chips, scuffs or marks?			
37	Were all mirrors polished and free of any smudges?			
38	Were all windows clean and free of any streaks or spots?			
39	Were all plant and floral decorations fresh (if applicable)?			
40	Were ample ashtrays available (exterior if applicable)?			
41	Was the table steady?			
42	Were the table /chair legs free of any scuffs/ scratches and matching in colour?			
43	Was the chair's upholstery clean, matching and in good repair?			
44	Was the bar counter clean, dry and free of any debris?			
45	Were all brand bottles prominently displayed, free of any dust with the labels facing forward?			
46	Was appropriate music played at a pleasant level?			
	Total number of standards:	Meet	Below	N/A
	46 - to be evaluated			
	(Enter your total percentage score here out of 100%) This score is based total number of standards to meet. Disallow the ones not applicable to your premises			

A

Appendix IV: Conversion tables for food and beverage control

The following tables can assist you in understanding the weights, measures and amounts of distilled spirits or draught beers, which are available in various packing sizes for the bar. You must remember that standard portion sizes for beers and spirits will differ in each country or state, so you should initially check to see the standard service sizes for your own area, before you use these tables to project costing and profit margins for your bar.

Table A.3: Distilled spirits bottle sizes and number of measures (based on a selection of national measures) (Murphy, 2012)

Distilled Spirit Products							
Bottle Size	20ml Measure	25ml Measure	30ml Measure	35.5ml Measure	40ml Measure	50ml Measure	70ml Measure
500 ml	25	20	16.67	14.08	12.5	10	7.14
680 ml	34	27.2	22.67	19.15	17	13.6	9.71
700 ml	35	28	23.33	19.71	17.5	14	10
710 ml	35.5	28.4	23.67	20.00	17.75	14.2	10.14
750 ml	37.5	30	25	21.12	18.75	15	10.71
1,000 ml	50	40	33.33	28.17	25	20	14.29
1,125 ml	56.25	45	37.5	31.69	28.12	22.5	16.07
1,130 ml	56.50	45.2	37.66	31.83	28.25	22.60	16.14
1,500 ml	75	60	50	42.25	37.50	30	21.42
2,250 ml	112.50	90	75	63.38	56.25	45	32.14
3,000 ml	150	120	100	84.50	75	60	42.85
4,500 ml	225	180	150	126.76	112.50	90	64.29
5,000 ml	250	200	166.66	140.84	125	100	71.42

Table A.4: Draught brewed products – Keg sizes and number of measures (based on a small selection of national measures). (Murphy, 2010)

Product Keg Type	Keg Weight Full / Empty	No. per keg (568ml)	No. per keg (500ml)	No. per keg (400ml)	No. per keg (250ml)	No. per keg (200ml)
Beamish Stout, Beamish Red	60.1 kg (F) 10.5 (E)	50 litres 88 pints	100	125	200	250
Beamish Stout	39.6 kg (F) 9.9 (E)	30 litres 52.8 pints	60	175	120	150
Carling, Fosters, Miller, Scrumpy Jack	63.2 kg (F) 13.6 (E)	50 litres 88 pints	100	125	200	200
Kronenberg 1664	44.7 kg (F) 14.7 (E)	30 litres 52.8 pints	60	175	120	150
Bulmers Cider	63 kg (F) 12.5 kg (E)	50 litres 88 pints	100	125	120	250
Budweiser, Carlsberg, Harp, Smithwicks, Kilkenny, Guinness	61.7 kg (F) 11.8 (E)	50 litres 88 pints	100	125	200	250

Heineken Murphy	61.8 kg (F) 11.8 (E)	50 litres 88 pints	100	125	200	250
Murphy	39.5 (F) 9.5 (E)	30 litres 52.8 pints	60	175	120	150
Coors light	42-43 kg (F) 12 kg (E)	30 litres 52 pints	60	175	120	150
Tennents, S.Artois, Bass	60.3 kg (F) 9.5 kg (E)	50 litres 88 pints	100	125	200	250
Blacktorn Cider	62.9 kg (F) 12.2 kg (E)	50 litres 88 pints	100	125	200	250

The following food and beverage tables lists the appropriate metric weights and volumes and their US equivalents

Table A.5: Metric volume units of measure and U.S. equivalents. Adapted from Jones (2003)

Litre (L)	Millilitre (ml)	Fluid ounce	
3.8	3800	128	1 gallon
1	1000	33.8	
.95	946	32	1 quart
	750	25.4	
	500	16.9	
.47	474	16	1pint
.24	237	8	1cup
	30	1	
	15		1 Tbs
	5		1 tsp

Table A.6: Metric weight units of measure and U.S. equivalents. Adapted from Jones (2003)

Weight	Metric	Pound (lb)	Ounce (oz)
1 Ton	1.0161 tonnes	2,240	16,258
1 Hundredweight	50.802 kilograms	112	1,792
1 Stone	6.3503 kilograms	14	224
1 Kilogram	1000 grams	2.2	35.2
	454 grams	1	16
	28.35 grams		1
	1 gram		.035

A

Conversion between traditional US units of measure and the Metric system

The world is becoming more globalised and as part of this international community, most countries are leaning towards adopting the metric system. In culinary publications it is common to see recipes whose ingredients are listed in both the traditional U.S quantities and their metric equivalent. The relationship between the units of measure is constant, so a multiplier can be developed to express these relationships. The easiest way to convert a recipe from the traditional U.S units of measure to the metric system units of measure, or vice versa, is to use a multiplier, provided in Table A.8.

Table A.7: U.S / Metric Conversion Multipliers. Adapted from Jones (2003)

Multiply	By	To Find
Volume		
Gallons	3.7853	Litres
Litres	1.0567	Quarts
Quarts	.946	Litres
Pints	.474	Litres
Cups	.237	Litres
Weight Units		
Kilograms	2.2046	Pounds
Pounds	.4536	Kilograms
Grams	.0022	Pounds
Pounds	453.5924	Grams
Grams	.0353	Ounces
Ounces	28.3495	Grams

B Bibliography and Web resources

Agar Hotel Shop. (2012) available at agarwalhotelshopee.com/crockery.html#crockery [accessed 12/3/12].

Agichtein, E, Castillo, C, Donato, D, Gionis, A, Mishne, G (2008) Finding high-quality content in social media. WSDM'08 - Proceedings of the 2008 International Conference on Web Search and Data Mining: 183–193.

Allen, G, T. (1936) Egyptian stelae in *Field Museum of Natural History* - Volume 24.

Anderson, G. (2012) Publix to Test Digital Coupons Sans Loyalty Card, available at www.retailwire.com/discussion/15978/publix-to-test-digital-coupons-sans-loyalty-card, [retrieved 2/3/13].

Austin, G, A. (1985) *Alcohol in Western Society from Antiquity to 1800: A Chronological History*, Santa Barbara, CA: ABC Clio.

Babor, T. (1986) *Alcohol: Customs and Rituals*, New York : Chelsea House.

Bamunuge, H, Edwards, G, Nutley, J. (2010) *Food & Beverage Service*, 2nd ed, City & Guilds, Essex : Heinemann.

Banks, S.E.; Binns, J. W. (2002). *Gervase of Tilbury/Otia Imperialia: Recreation for an Emperor*. Oxford University Press: UK.

Barkeeper.ie (2012) Bar Manager – responsibilities and duties, available at http://www.barkeeper.ie [accessed 10/3/12]

Barna, L, M. (1994) 'Stumbling blocks in intercultural communication.' In L.A Samovar & R. E. Porter (Eds), *Inter cultural communication: A reader*, 7th edn, Belmont, CA: Wadsworth.

Bates, P, M. and Phillips, P, S. (1999)'Sustainable waste management in the food and drink industry, *British Food Journal* 101 (8) 580-589, England : MCB University Press.

BOC Gases. (2010) Sure Serve Programme, Ireland: BOC.

Bowie D. and Buttle F. (2004) *Hospitality Marketing, an introduction*, Oxford: Butterworth Heinemann,

Brandwood, G.K, Davison, A. and Slaughter M. (2004). *Licensed to sell: the history and heritage of the public house*. English Heritage.

Braudel, F. (1974) *Capitalism and Material Life, 1400-1800*, NY: Harper & Row.

Brislin, R. W and Yoshida, T. (1994a) *Improving intercultural interactions: Modules for cross-cultural training programs*, Thousand Oaks, CA: Sage.

Brown, J. and Miller, A. (2009) *Spirituous Journey: A History of Drink, Book Two*. USA : Mixellany Limited.

Brown. G, Hepner. K and Deegan, A. (1994) *Introduction to Food and Beverage Service*, England: Pearson Education Ltd.

Bryson, B. (1994) *Made in America*, USA: Black Swan Publishers.

BSA. (2012) Cafelicious, Swindon - BSA 2012 Award Winner, available at http://www. beveragestandardsassociation.co.uk/Cafelicious,-Swindon---BSA-2012-Award-Winner [accessed 10/03/13]

Business4Sales.co.uk. (2012) Pub Tenancies Explained, available at www. business4sale.co.uk/Related_Guides/Pub_tenancies_explained_27 [retrieved 07/052012].

Cavan, S. (1966) *Liquor License: An Ethnography of Bar Behavior*, Chicago: Aldine Publishing Co,

Cherrington, E. H. (1925) *Standard Encyclopaedia of the Alcohol Problem*, Westerville, OH: American Issue Publishing Co.

ciwmb.co.gov. (2012) available at http://www.ciwmb.co.gov [accessed 1/5/12]

Clarke. J, Hanley, V. (2006) Eight of nine top restaurants and pubs in the capital reveal evidence of contamination, 18th June, Dublin: Ireland on Sunday.

Cole, S. (2007) *West from Paddington*. UK: Etica Press Ltd.

Cronin, M, O'Connor, B. (2003). *Irish Tourism: image, culture, and identity*. Channel View Publications. p. 83. ISBN 978-1-873150-53-5.

Cousins, J. and Lillicrap, D. (2010) *Essential Food and Beverage Service*, London: Hodder Education

Coupondivas.com (2013) available at http://www.coupondivas.com [accessed 14/3/13]

Craddock, D. (2013) Why hot cocoa is healthier than hot chocolate, available at http://www.statssheet.com/articles/article61849.html [accessed 20/03/13].

Croner. (1998) *Croner's Management of Public Houses*, Surrey: Croner CCH Group Ltd.

Davies, B., Lockwood, A, Alcott, P., Pantelidis,I. (2012) *Food and Beverage Management*, 5th ed, Oxford: Routledge.

Davis. B,. Lockwood. A., and Stone, S. (2002) Food and Beverage Management, *The Cornell Hotel and Restaurant Administration Quarterly*, USA: Butterworth-Heinemann.

Dittmer. R.P and Keefe. D, J. (2006) *Food, Beverage and Labor Cost Controls*, 8th ed, New York: John Wiley & Sons Inc.

Dopson, L. R., Hayes, D. K. (2011) *Food and Beverage Cost Control*, 5th ed, New Jersey: John Wiley & Sons.

Doxat, J. (1972) *The World of Drinks and Drinking*, N: Drake Publishers.

Drink Aware (2013) at www.drinkaware.co.uk (accessed 2/3/13)

Driver, G. R. & Miles, J. C. (1952) *The Babylonian Laws*, Oxford: Clarendon Press.

Drucker, P. F. (1954) *The Practice of Management*, New York: Harper & Brothers.

Edwards, G. (2002) *Alcohol: The World's Favourite Drink*, England: Thomas Dum Books.

Elliott, M. S. (2006) *How to Run a Successful Pub*, Oxford: How to Books

Escoffier, G, A. (1921) *Le Guide culinaire, 4th edn*, France: Flammarion.

European Communities. (2000) *Hygiene of Foodstuffs Regulations*, (S.I No. 165 of 2000), Dublin: Government Publications.

European Foundation for Quality Management (2013) at www.efqm.org (accessed 2/3/13)

FSAI. (2013) Food Safety Authority of Ireland, available at http://www.fsai.ie [accessed   10/2/13]

Global News. (2011) Loyalty schemes across the globe, March issue, available at www.foodtravelexperts.com [accessed 6/3/13].

Goldstein, M. (2012) The top ten trends in loyalty today, available at blog.badgeville.com/2012/10/23/the-10-top-trends-in-loyalty-today/ [retrieved 3/1/13].

Granet, M. (1957) *Chinese Civilization*. London: Barnes and Noble.

Grivetti, L, E.; Shapiro, H. (2009). *Chocolate: History, Culture and Heritage*, USA: John Wiley and Sons.

Haigh, T. (2007) *Vintage Spirits and Forgotten Cocktails*, USA: Quarry Books, Quayside Publishing Group

Hall, E.T. (1952) *The Silent Language*, :Greenwich, CT: Fawcett.

Hall, E.T. and Hall, M.R. (1990) *Understanding Cultural Differences*, Yarmouth: Intercultural Press.

Hospitality. (2009) Designer Hospitality – smart bars and restaurants, Jan, Vol. 45 Issue 1, pp.19-22, NZ: TPL Media.

Hospitality Assured (2013) at www.hospitalityassured.com (accessed 3/3/13)

Hudson, W, H. (1920). Dead Man's Plack and an Old Thorn, London: J. M. Dent & Sons Ltd.

Human Service Solutions. (2012) QR Codes for Marketing: A Unique Way to Bridge Offline and Online Media, accessed at www.hswsolutions.com/services/mobile-web-development/qr-code-marketing/ [retrieved 6/2/13]

IBA. (2008) *A Guide to Social Responsibility*, The Netherlands: International Bartenders Association.

Inside Hospitality. (2012) Restaurant Loyalty Programmes, restaurantfunds.com [retrieved 7/4/12].

Irish National Alcohol Awareness Campaign (2001-03) Phases and Booklets, Dublin: Irish Health Board.

Jandt, E. F. (1995) *Intercultural Communication – An Introduction*, Sage Publications: UK.

Johnson, G., Scholes, K. and Whittington, R. (2008) *Exploring Corporate Strategy, Text and Cases*, 8th edition, Harlow: Prentice Hall.

B

Johnston, R. and Clark, G. (2008) *Service operations management* 3rd edition: Essex: Prentice Hall.

Jones, T. (2003) *Culinary calculations – simplified math for culinary professionals,* New York: Wiley Publishing Ltd.

Justice, A. (1707) *A General Discourse of the Weights and Measures,* London.

Kaplan. A , Haenlein. M, (2010), Users of the world, unite! The challenges and opportunities of social media, *Business Horizons,* Vol. 53, Issue 1.

Kasavana, M. and Smith, D. (1982) *Menu engineering: a practical guide to menu analysis,* Lansing, Michigan: Hospitality Publications

Katsigis, C. Thomas, C. (2007)*The Bar & Beverage Book,* 4th ed, New Jersey: John Wiley & Sons Inc.

Kietzmann, H.J, Hermkens. K., (2011) Social media? Get serious! Understanding the functional building blocks of social media. *Business Horizons* 54: 241–251.

Keynote Market Research Reports (2013) at www.keynote.co.uk (accessed 5/3/13)

Kotler, P. and Armstrong, G. (2001) *Principles of Marketing,* 9th edn, USA: Prentice Hall International Edition.

Kotler, P., Bowen, J., and Makens, J. (2010) *Marketing for Hospitality and Tourism,* Harlow: Pearson Education.

Kotler, P., Keller, K., Brady M., Goodman M. and Hanser T. (2009) *Marketing Management,* Harlow: Pearson Education.

Larousse encyclopaedia of wine (2001), C. Foulkes (Ed), London: Hamlin.

Lesonsky, R. (2012) Bar and Restaurant going social, accessed at www.score.org/resources/bar-and-restaurant-going-social [retrieved 10/1/12].

Lillicarp, D. and Cousins, J. (2010), *Food and Beverage Service,* 8th edition, London: Hodder Education.

Lipinski, B. Lipinski, K. (1996). *Professional Beverage Management,* New York: John Wiley & Sons

Liquid Gold. (2010) Serving Hot Chocolate, available at http://www.beveragestandardsassociation.co.uk/Serving-Hot-Chocolate---Liquid-Gold [accessed 12/03/13].

Londonskybar.com. (2011) available at http://www.lonsdonskybar.com [accessed 15/11/11]

Lucia, S, P. (1963a) *A History of Wine as Therapy,* Philadelphia, PA: J. B. Lippincott.

Macleod, S. (1994) *Food & Drink Service in the Restaurant,* Edinburgh's Telford College, UK: Hodder and Stoughton.

Mahon, A, M (2006) Fixed-Point retail location in the major towns of Roman Britain, UK: *Oxford Journal of Archaeology.*

Marstons Pub Company (2013) *Planning your business,* available at www.marstonspubcompany.co.uk/RunYourOwnPub/Finance/PlanningYourBusiness.aspx [accessed 10/2/13]

Mastercard. (2012) DataCash launches contactless payments system for bars, available at www.finextra.com/news/announcement.aspx?pressreleaseid=47212 [retrieved 9/3/13].

MCM. (1990) *Conflict and violence in pubs*, MCM Research Ltd., Oxford: England.

Mintel Global Consumer, Product and Market Research at www.mintel.com (accessed 5/3/13)

Mok, M. (1932) Stone age had booze and Prohibition, May, Bonnier Corporation: *Popular Science Monthly*.

Molloy, C. (2002) *The Story of the Irish Pub*, Vintners Federation of Ireland, Dublin: Liffey Press.

Morgan. N, Jones, G, Hodges, A. (2012) Social Media, The Complete Guide to Social Media From The Social Media Guys, [retrieved 12/12/12]

Murphy. J. (2005) Dress to impress, *Licensing World*, August, Dublin: Jemma Publications Ltd.

Murphy,J. (2005) A problem shared – disorderly conduct, *Licensing World*, October, Dublin: Jemma Publications Ltd.

Murphy,J (2006) Customer care, *Licensing World*, November, Dublin: Jemma Publications Ltd

Murphy,J. (2006) Storing your wines, *Licensing World*, October, Dublin: Jemma Publications Ltd.

Murphy,J. (2008) Importance of good planning in the design and planning of licensed premises, *Licensing World*, April, Dublin: Jemma Publications Ltd.

Murphy,J. (2008) Prevention of conflict and violence in licensed premises, *Licensing World*, June, Dublin: Jemma Publications Ltd.

Murphy,J. (2008) Insurance for the publican, *Licensing World*, February, Dublin: Jemma Publications Ltd.

Murphy,J (2008) Improving your customers overall meal experience, *Licensing World*, November, Dublin: Jemma Publications Ltd.

Murphy,J. (2009) Bar design – converging form and function, *Licensing World*, April, Dublin: Jemma Publications Ltd.

Murphy,J (2009) The importance of cellar safety, *Licensing World*, October, Dublin: Jemma Publications Ltd.

Murphy, J (2009) The personality factor, *Licensing World*, Dublin: Jemma Publications Ltd.

Murphy, J. (2005) Dealing with intoxication, *Licensing World*, November, Dublin: Jemma Publications Ltd.

Murphy, J. (2005) Hazards of poor hygiene, *Licensing World*, Dublin: Jemma Publications Ltd.

Murphy, J. (2006) Glassware management, *Licensing World*, June, Dublin: Jemma Publications Ltd.

B

Murphy, J. (2006) Sourcing and retaining Irish bar staff, *Licensing World*, Dublin: Jemma Publications Ltd.

Murphy, J. (2007) Bartending as a career – the lifestyle choice, *Licensing World*, Dublin: Jemma Publications Ltd.

Murphy, J. (2007) Stock management vital to maintaining profits, April Issue, *Licensing World*, Dublin: Jemma Publications Ltd.

Murphy, J. (2008) Overcoming fraud and dishonesty, December Issue, *Licensing World*, Dublin: Jemma Publications Ltd.

Murphy, J. (2009) Customer Relationship Management (CRM) in the licensed trade industry, *Licensing World*, March Issue, Dublin: Jemma Publications Ltd.

Murphy, J. (2009) Promoting bar sales, November Issue, *Licensing World*, Dublin: Jemma Publications Ltd.

Murphy, J. (2009) Strong merchandising can drive sales, July Issue, *Licensing World*, Dublin: Jemma Publications Ltd.

Murphy, J. (2010) Improving customer service through mystery shopping, *Licensing World*, Dublin: Jemma Publications Ltd.

Murphy, J. (2012) Cash handling requires constant control, January Issue, *Licensing World*, Dublin: Jemma Publications Ltd.

Murphy, R. (2002) *Developing an Alcohol and Drug Policy for your Workplace*, Western Health Board: Ireland.

Mutton, T & Sampson J .(2012) Fres Home Design & Architecture, at freshome. com/2012/07/30/how-to-design-restaurants-bars-that-enhance-the-customer-experience/#sthash.gsR888Hf.dpuf [accessed 2/2/12]

Newall, M. (1965) *Mood and Atmosphere in Restaurants*, London: Barrie & Rockliff.

Norrington-Davies, T. (2005) Is the gastro pub making a meal of it? 24th November, London: *The Daily Telegraph*. Retrieved [1/6/08]

O'Gorman, K. D (2010) *The Origins of Hospitality and Tourism*, Oxford: Goodfellows Publishers Ltd.

Patrick, C, H. (1952) *Alcohol, Culture, and Society*, Durham, NC: Duke University Press.

Paul, M. (2004) 'Green Yourself – How to become an eco-pub', *Licensing World*, May Issue, Dublin: Jemma Publications Ltd.

Payment News (2012) First Fully Integrated Contactless Payment System in UK, available at www.paymentnews.com [retrieved 26/8/12].

Payment Sense. (2013) Contactless payments: The pros and cons, available at www.paymentsense.co.uk/blog/contactless-payments-the-pros-and-cons/#ixzz2NLVQSxH2 [accessed 10/3/13].

Porter, R. (1990) Introduction. In: Sournia, Jean-Charles. *A History of Alcoholism*. Trans by Hindley and Stanton, Oxford: Basil Blackwell.

Portio Research (2008) Payment Systems, available at www.portionresearch.com [accessed 9/3/12].

Portman Group (2012) Marketing Alcohol Responsibly, www.portmangroup.org.uk/assets/documents/Guide%20to%20the%20fifth%20edition%20of%20the%20Code%20of%20Practice.pdf [accessed 9/1/13]

Pubshop (2012) Freehold, Leasehold or Tenancy, www.pubshop.co.uk/tenure.php#Tenancy [retrieved 10/2/13].

Quinn, F. (2006). *Crowning the Customer: How to Become Customer-Driven*, Dublin: O'Brien Press Ltd.

Raymond, I, W. (1927) *The Teaching of the Early Church on the Use of Wine and Strong Drink*, New York: Columbia University Press.

Regan, G. (1993) *The Bartender's Bible*, US: Harper Torch.

Regan, G. (2003) *The Joy of Mixology*, New York: Clarkson Potter.

Roberts, R. (2008) Drinks Focus Bar Design, September, *Hospitality Ireland*, Dublin; Madison Publishing Ltd.

Robinsons Pubs. (2012) Tenancy explained, at myrobinsonspub.com/support/tenancyexplained, [retrieved 20/3/12].

Roger, T. (2003) *Conferences and Conventions: a global industry*, Oxford: Butterworth-Heinemann

Santander (2013) Business Guide-Industry Sector Public Houses, available at https://www.alliance-leicestercommercialbank.co.uk/bizguides/full/pubs/index.asp.

Sargent.M, Lyle,T. (2003) *Successful Pubs and Inns*, Oxford: Butterworth-Heinemann .

Science News. (2013) Hot Cocoa Tops Red Wine And Tea In Antioxidants; May Be Healthier Choice, available http://www.sciencedaily.com/releases/2003/11/031106051159.htm [accessed 24/03/13].

Security Industry Authority. (2010) Specifications for Learning and Qualifications for Door Supervisors, accessed at [www.the-sia.org.uk].

Sharp..B, Sharp, A.(1997) Loyalty Programs and Their Impact on Repeat-Purchase Loyalty Patterns, *International Journal of Research in Marketing*, **14** (5), 473-86.

Snarr, J. and Pezza, K. (2000) *Recycling Guidebook for the Hospitality and Restaurant Industry*, Information Centre Metropolitan Washington Council of Governments.

Stone, M. and Young, L. (1993) *Competitive Customer Care*, Croner: London.

The Loyalty Guide 4. (2012) at www.theloyaltyguide.com/executive-summary.asp (accessed 29/2/13)

The Nibble. (2013) Some like it hot: best hot chocolate mix, http://www.thenibble.com/reviews/main/beverages/cocoas/hot-chocolate-overview.asp [accessed 22/04/13]

Times (1928) *The New York Times*, January 7th Issue: USA.

Toptable (2013) at www.toptable.com (accessed 30/2/13)

Treavor, P .(2012) Tied House Laws Revisited - Middle Ground May Be the Way to Go, VanEast Beer Blog, eastsidebeer.blogspot.ca/2012/05/tied-house-laws-revisited-middle-ground.html [retrieved 29/5/12].

B

Turback, M. (2005) *Hot Chocolate*, USA: Ten Speed Press.

US Legal .(2012) Tied House Law and Legal Definition, definitions.uslegal.com/t/tied-house/ [retrieved 15/4/12]

Verifone. (2012) Improve the Customer Experience with Mobile Payment, at www.verifone.co.uk/industries/hospitality [retrieved 2/3/13].

Valvera. (2010) National Supervisory Authority for Welfare and Health – Alcohol issues in Licensed Premises, Helsinki, Finland, at skirjaamo@valvira.fi [accessed 1/12/12].

Waste Reduction in Hotels and Motels and Food Service Waste Reduction (2010), available at www.ciwmb.ca.gov/mrt/wpw/wpiz/fshotelz.html [accessed 10/5/10]

WCU. (2008) Catering Safety, at www.wcu@hsa.ie [accessed 19/5/11 .

Wilson, T, M. (2005) *Drinking Cultures: Alcohol and Identity*, Oxford: Berg.

Wondrich, D (2007) *Imbibe: From Absinthe Cocktail to Whiskey Smash, a Salute in Stories and Drinks to 'Professor' Jerry Thomas Pioneer of the American Bar*, USA: Perigee Trade.

Woods, B. (2006) 'Get out of the red by going green', *Licensing World*, March Issue, Dublin: Jemma Publishing Ltd.

Augmented Bibliography

ACORN Classification at www.caci.co.uk/acorn-classification.aspx (accessed 3/2/13)

Acton. J, Adams.T, and Packer. M (2006). *Origin of Everyday Things. Happy Hour*, NY: Sterling Publishing Co.

Armstrong G, Kotler P, Harker M and Brennan R (2009) *Marketing an Introduction*, Harlow: Pearson

ASI. (1998). *Sommelier, Profession of the Future*, Italy: Bertani.

Barth, S.C., (2008) *Hospitality Law: Managing Legal Issues in the Hospitality Industry*, 3rd Edition, Oxford: John Wiley and Sons

Betz, B. (2012). PayPal Moves Toward Mobile Payments in Bars, Restaurants, available http://www.investorplace.com/2012/03/paypal-moves-toward-mobile-payments-in-bars-restaurants-ebay/ , accessed [22/06,12].

Bowie D and Buttle F (2011) *Hospitality Marketing, Principles and Practice*, 2nd edition, Oxford: Butterworth Heinemann

Burgoon, J.K., Boller, D.B., Woodall, W.G. (1996). *Non-verbal communication: The Unspoken Dialogue*, pp.83, 352, 2nd Ed: Harper & Row.

BNIC (2012) Bureau National Interprofessionnel du Cognac, www.cognac.fr [accessed 4/02/12].

Canadian Laws (2010). 'Canadian Food and Drug Regulations '(C.R.C., c. 870), Canadian Whisky, Canada: Canadian Rye Whisky or Rye Whisky (B.02.020.).

DeGroff, D. (2002). *The Craft of the Cocktail*, NY: Clarkson Potter.

Foskett, D., Paskins, P., Rippington, N. and Ceserani, V. (2011) *The Theory of Hospitality and Catering*, 12th ed, London: Hodder Education

Ghaliounqui, P. (1979) 'Fermented Beverages in Antiquity', in: Gastineau, Clifford F., Darby, William J., and Turner, Thomas B. (Eds.) *Fermented Food Beverages in Nutrition*, NY: Academic Press.

Katsigris, C, Thomas, C. (2009) *Design and Equipment for Restaurants and Foodservice: a Management View*, Institute of Hospitality ebook held in the Institute's Online Catalogue (accessed 3/3/13)

Murphy, J. (2004) *Intercultural Communications in the Irish Hospitality Industry*, Unpublished MSc Thesis, Dublin: Dublin Institute of Technology.

NCCRI (2004). Managing Diversity in the Workplace available at http://www.nccri.ie [accessed 10/05/12].

Neuliep, J.W. (2000) *Intercultural Communication: A Contextual Approach*, Boston, MA: Houghton Mifflin.

New Larousse Gastronomique (2009) London: Hamlin

Kosmos, J & Zaric, D. (2010) *Speakeasy: The Employees Only Guide to Classic Cocktails Re-imagined*, US: Ten Speed Press.

Kummer, C (2003). *The Joy of Coffee: The Essential Guide to Buying, Brewing and Enjoying*. Boston: Houghton Mifflin.

Heawood, J. (2003). 'London, city of sin and gin', London 1753 Exhibition British Museum, London WC 1, London:*The Observer Review*.

Highfield, R. (2004). "Archaeologists reveal Chinese first Tipplers 9,000 years ago, 7/12/04, Dublin: Irish Independent

Pratten, J.D. (2007): Responsible Alcohol Service: Ethics and the Licensee, *The Service Industries Journal*, **27** (5), 605-616 .

Qualman, E. (2011) *Socialnomics: How social media transforms the way we live and do business*, New Jersey: Wiley and Sons Ltd

Robinson, J. (2006) *The oxford companion to wine*, Oxford: Oxford University Press

Robinson, J, Johnson, H. (2007) *The World Atlas of Wine* 6th ed, UK: Mitchell Beazley.

Spence, G. (2003) *Teach Yourself Wine Tasting*, UK: Wine & Spirit Education Trust.

Schneider, D. (2008). Gregg Smith - Beer: A Different glass for every brew can add to the drinking experience, US: The San Francisco Chronicle.

Sequin, G. (1986) 'Terroirs' and pedology of vine growing". *Experientia* 42:861-873

Sinclair, A. (1962) *Prohibition: The Era of Excess*, Little, Boston: Brown & Co.

Tarling, W. J. (1937) *Café Royal Cocktail Book*, London: Pall Mall Ltd.

Taylor, S. (1983) *Ireland's Pubs*, NY: Penguin Books.

Thomas, J. (1862). *Bar-Tender's Guide & Bon-Vivants Companion*, NY: Dick and Fitzgerald.

USA Regulations (2006). 'Standards of Identity for Distilled Spirits', Title 27 Code of Federal Regulations, Pt. 5.22., pp. 48-49, USA.

Visakay, S. (1997) *Vintage Bar Ware*, Paducah, KY: Collector Books.

B

Web resources

History

History of alcohol and drinking around the World: www2.potsdam.edu/hansondj/controversies/1114796842.html.

USA bar history: www.smithsonianmag.com/history-archaeology/The-Spirited-History-of-the-American-Bar.html .

History of British pubs: www.historic-uk.com/CultureUK/The-Great-British-Pub/

Bartending

BarMedia, USA mixologist newsletter: www.barmedia.com

Bartenders' magazine: www.bartender.com

Bartending resources: www.webtender.com

50 signs of poor bartending: www.artofdrink.com/2007/03/50-signs-you-are-a-bad-bartender.php

DexRef, refrigeration company: www.aDexref.com

Bar equipment and portable bars (Cantilever): www.ipbartenders.com

Automatic cocktail bar: www.kiscocktailbar.com

Speciality Coffee Association of Europe (SCEA): www.scea.com

Glassware and cocktails: www.artofdrink.com/2007/02/is-glassware-a-barrier-to-cocktail-accep.php

Analysis of body movements in the hospitality industry: www.safework.sa.gov.au/uploaded_files/hospJobDict2Restaurants.pdf

Responsible sale of alcohol

Serve-safe USA: www.servsafe.com

International Centre for Alcohol Policies: www.icap.org/Publication/ICAPBlueBook/tabid/148/Default.aspx

APSAD Australia: www.apsad.org.au

European Forum for Responsible Drinking: www.efrd.org

National Restaurant Association, how to serve alcohol responsibly: www.restaurant.org/legal/law_alcohol.cfm#incident

Institute of Alcohol Studies, alcohol and accidents factsheet: www.ias.org.uk/resources/factsheets/accidents.pdf

Institute of Alcohol Studies, binge drinking factsheet: Available at: www.ias.org.uk/resources/factsheets/binge_drinking.pdf

Food service

Calculating food costs: www.kendallhunt.com/uploadedFiles/Kendall_Hunt/Content/Higher_Education/Uploads/McVety_Ch7_4e.pdf

Food production records: www.kn-eat.org/SNP/SNP_Docs/SNP_Guidance/
Menu_Planning_Guidance/Menu_Plan_FB_Ch6.pdf

Selling safe food: www.wellington.govt.nz/services/foodsafety/pdfs/safe-food.pdf

Waste management

Focal Water Free Technologies, Waterless Company: www.falconwaterfree.com/

Sustainable hotel: www.sustainablehotel.co.uk/Improve_waste.html

Environmental protection: www.ibec.ie/IBEC/IBEC.nsf/
Search?OpenForm&Query=waste%20management

University of Liverpool Waste Management: www.liv.ac.uk/sustainability/Waste%20
Management/main%20page.htm

Marketing and management

NCR Corporation, US computer hardware and electronics company: www.ncr.com/

European Central Bank (notes and coins security features): www.ecb.int/home

McMullen Brewers, business and marketing plan for tenancy: www.mcmullens.co.uk/
businessplan.pdf

Goats Head pub marketing plan: m.wpi.edu/Pubs/E-project/Available/E-
project-121909-212418/unrestricted/GoatsHead IQP.pdf

Case study: www.morningadvertiser.co.uk/Opinion/The-Guv-nor/A-marketing-plan
-can-really-help-your-pub

Customer care articles and advice: ezinearticles.com/?Customer-Care-Strategy&id=
317986

Liquor controls for the hospitality industry: www.bergliquorcontrols.com

Bar stock control systems: www.bar-stock.com

Bar stock control systems: www.smartbar.eu

Food and beverage studies

Bar Zone: www.barzone.co.uk

Beverage Net: www.beveragenet.net

International Bartenders Association: www.iba-world.com

Napkin Folding: www.napkinfoldingguide.com

United Kingdom Bartenders Guild: www.ukbg.co.uk

Trade magazines

Caterer and Hotelkeeper Magazine: www.caterersearch.com

Decanter Magazine: www.decanter.com

Imbibe Magazine: imbibemagazine.com/

B

Government and regulatory

Drink Aware (UK): www.drinkaware.co.uk

European Food Safety Authority: www.efsa.eu.int

Food Safety Authority of Ireland: www.fsai.ie

Food Standards Agency: www.foodstandards.gov.uk

Health and Safety Executive: www.hse.gov.uk

International Standards Organisation: www.iso.ch

 UK Home Office: www.homeoffice.gov.uk/drugs/alcohol/

World Health Organisation: www.who.int/en/

Education, training and careers

City & Guilds of London Institute: www.city-and-guilds.co.uk

Council for Hospitality Management Education (CHME): www.chme.co.uk

Ecole Hoteliere de Lausanne (EHL): www.ehl.edu/eng/

Edexcel Foundation: www.edexcel.org.uk

Hospitality Skills Academy: www.hospitalityskillsacademy.co.uk

Le Cordon Bleu: www.cordonbleu.edu/

UK Education providers: www.uksp.co.uk/Find-Training/Training-Providers?page=1

USA Education providers: www.uscollegesearch.org/hospitality-colleges.html

Wine and Spirit Education Trust (WSET): www.wset.co.uk

Trade and professional bodies

Academy of Food and Wine Service: www.acfws.org

Association of Catering Excellence: www.acegb.org

British Beer and Pub Association: www.beerandpub.com

British Hospitality Association: www.bha-online.org.uk

British Institute of Innkeeping: www.bii.org.uk

Court of Masters Sommeliers: www.courtofmastersommeliers.org

Craft Guild of Chefs: www.craftguildofchefs.org

Institute of Hospitality: www.instituteofhospitality.org

Institute of Masters of Wine: www.masters-of-wine.org

International Guild of Hospitality & Restaurant Managers (bartending courses) :
   www.hospitalityguild.com/Bartending.htm .

International Hotel and Restaurant Association: www.ih-ra.com

National Association of Licensed House Managers: ww.pubunion.org.uk

Security Industry Authority (SIA): www.the-sia.org.uk.

Speciality Coffee Association of Europe UK Chapter: www.scaeuk.com

Tea Council Ltd: www.teacouncil.co.uk

Visual resources

Video sharing websites like YouTube also offer short movie clips, training advice and a wide variety of user generated video content which can enhance your understanding of bar and beverage management. Simply type in the topics that interest you. You will be surprised how much material is available.Please be mindful of copyright infringement if you are thinking of using them for public presentations.

B

I Index

accountability 151–152
affinity programs 184
alcohol
  and body chemistry 65
  and social activities 63
  calculating units 64
  in ancient times 2–4
  laws relating to its provision 62–63
  responsible service of 62–63
    staff training 67
  safe levels of consumption 64–65
alehouses 2
ales, origins 4

barback, role 30
bar books 207
bar counter 10
bar design, modern 13
barista 31
bar layout, and food safety 106
bar manager 29
bars 1–21
  alehouse 4
  bierkellers 2
  brewpubs 2
  design, location & layout 13–14
  development of 10–13
  franchised 18–20
  gastro pub 9–10
  impact of stagecoach 7
  kabaks 8
  location, effect of 15
  Middle Ages 5
  origin of the word "bar" 7
  ownership types 17–19
  public houses 6
  social behaviour in 16–17
  super pubs 9
  taverns 4
  types 11–13
bar spoons 39

bartender
  best practice procedures 25–26
  job description 27–28
  necessary attributes 23
  personal appearance 24
  personality 24
  role 22–32
beverage control 190–215
beverage service personnel 29
bierkellers 2
Blind Pigs (speakeasies) 20
blood alcohol concentration (BAC) 65–67
break even point 195–196
brewpubs 2
budgets 192–193

cabinet coolers 36
cash
  cashing up 156
  counterfeit money 158
  counting 155
  procedures for handling 154
  sorting and counting machines 156–157
cash floats 155
cash flow projections 197
cashier's checkout sheet 157
cash register 146
cellar
  health and safety 212
  layout and organisation 210
  safety regulations 133–134
cellar management 210–212
  safety 131–135
cellar safety 131–135
  gas leaks 134
Champagne
  origins 7
  service 57–58
cheques, cashing 159
cocktail
  first recorded use, 1798 8
  service 58

Code of Hummurabi 2
coffee and liqueurs service 59
coffee machines 37
    cleaning and training 38
competitive advantage, gaining 166
complaints, dealing with 82
contactless payment systems 149
contribution rate 195–196
conversion tables 222–224
costs
    and profit margins 179–181
    food 177–181
    portion or plate 178
    prices and profits 180–182
    revenue and profits 190–192
counterfeit money detection 158
countries
    China 3
    Greece 3
    Iran 2
    Iraq 2
    Turkey 2
crowd control 126
cultural diversity 96
    action plan 99
    and food 101–102
culture models 97
customer care 91–103
    importance of 91
    need for commitment 92
    scenarios 94–95
customer satisfaction
    and food service 80–84
    food service, checklist 83
cutlery 50–51

decanting 56–57
deliveries, checking 204
designated driver program 67
distillation, discovery of 6
Drink Aware 69

Egyptians 3
electronic cash register (ECR) 147
electronic point of sale (EPOS) 148
energy efficiency, refrigerators 36
energy saving schemes 144
environmental health officers (EHOs) 105
equipment 33–53
    bar condiment units 39
    bar spoons 39
    blender and liquidizers 41

canelle knife 40
chopping boards 40
cocktail shaker 40, 43
dash bottles 41
hawthorn strainer 40
juice extractors 42
mixing glass 42
muddlers 43
spirit measures 44
spirit optic 45
spirit pourer 44
storage containers 43
wine knife 45
ergonomics in bar design 14

Facebook 187
financial planning 191–192
fire 120–122
    extinguishers 122
    insurance premiums 131–132
    triangle 122
first impressions 93
flambé 61
floor supervisor 31
floor waiter 31
food
    costings 177–181
    cost percentage 178–179
    influence of religions 101–102
food and beverage manager, role 29
food menus 75–77
food poisoning bacteria 109
food safety 105–115
    and bar layout 106
    and hygiene 107
    and ice 114–115
    cleaning 110
    labelling of foods 115–117
    temperature control 109
    training 217
food service 73–90
    best practices 87
    customer satisfaction 80–84
    equipment 49–50
    in bars 74–75
    procedures 85
    standardized recipes 79
    types of operations 78
fraud 158–160
    by staff 159–161
free house 18–20

gas leaks 134
gastro pub, origins 9–10
geneva. *See* gin
geolocation platforms 187
gin
    Acts of 1736 and 1751 8
    origins 7
glassware 46–49
    cleaning 48–49
    handling 47–48
glass washing machine 33
Greece ,ancient 3

Hall, E.T., culture model 97
Hammurabi, Code 2
hangover symptoms 71
happy hour 16
hazard analysis critical control point 107
hazards, identifying 118–120
head waiter 31
health and safety 116–122
    cellar management 131–135
    employees' obligations 117–118
    employers' responsibilities 117–123
    young workers 118–124
Highballs 61
Hofstede, culture model 97
hops, first use 4
hot chocolate, service 60
hygiene 107, 112–114

ice 34–36
    and food safety 114–115
    commercial production begins 8
    crushers 42
    food safety 35
    tongs and shuffles 41
    types 34
ice making machines 34
insurance 128–131
    business 128–129
    fire 131–132
    personal 130–131
intercultural awareness training 100
intercultural communication, barriers 98
intoxication, preventing 68

junever. *See* gin

ladies' nights 21
layered shooters 61

legislation
    adulteration of beer or wine iin Scotland 7
    earliest recorded 2
    Gin Acts of 1736 8
    innkeepers' licences introduced 6
    Licensing Act 2003 19
    prohibition in USA 8–9
    UK Home Office 19
liqueurs, service 59
location, effect on bar 15
lock-in 16
loyalty coupons 185–186
loyalty programs 182–183

marketing 163–189
    challenges 163–164
    merchandising techniques 169–171
    message 167
    mix 167
    promotion 169
    QR codes 188
    research 164
    segmentation 166
market segmentation 166
mead 3
menus 75–79
    engineering 75
    presentation 78
merchandising
    diagnostic tool 171
    LEAP code 172
merchandising techniques 169–171
mobile payment systems 150
mystery shopper 181–182
    diagnostic auditing tool 220–221

Neolithic period 2
non-nationals, induction training 99

Paracelsus 63
par stock 205–206
payments 146–162
    accountability 151–152
    best practice for handling 152–153
    controls for receiving 151
    touch and go systems 149
    vouchers 159
payment systems
    contactless 149
    mobile phones 150
persuasion, for sales 176–177

pest control programmes 114–116
Pinterest 187
place settings 85
pousse café 61
pricing
    cost/price relationship 199
    methods 198
    policies 198–199
    three tiered 168
Profit and Loss statement 194–195
prohibition 8
promotion 169
public houses 2, 6
public relations (PR) 173
pubs, Middle Ages 5
pub signs 10–11

QR codes 188

reduce and reuse 139
refrigerators 36–37
refusal of service technique 70
restaurant (food service) manager 29
review sites 187
Romans 3
rum, first distilleries 7

sales 163–189
    in the bar 175–176
    selling techniques 175–176
security
    areas to protect 126–127
    door supervisors 127
selling techniques 175–176
service tray, best practice procedures 89
shots 62
snug 8, 11
social media 186–189
    managing 188
social media sites 187–188
sommelier 31
speakeasies 20
spirits and liqueurs, service styles 61–62
stagecoach, impact on bars 7
stereotypes 98
stock accounting
    best practice 201

stock control 190–215
    bar books 207–209
    beverage production 213
    control of losses 212–213
    duties of controller 202
    methods 203
    par stock 205–206
    point-of-sale systems 214
    purpose 200
    receiving stock 203–204
stocktaking 201
storage
    foods 205
    of beverages 204
    wine 211
suspending service 69
SWOT analysis 165

taberna (taverns) 3
tableware 53
tea
    service 59
    speciality teas 60
temperature control and food safety 109
tenancy 17–19
Thomas, Jerry 8
tied house 17
touch and go systems 149
Twitter 187

ullage 208–210

violence
    calming strategies 124
    prevention of 122–123
vouchers, for payment 159

waiter 31
waste audit 138
waste management 136–144
    developing a plan 136–138
    equipment 141
    hierarchy 137
    programs 142
wine
    service 55–56
wine waiter 31